Creative Compartments

A Design for Future Organisation

Creative Compartments

A Design for Future Organisation

Gerard Fairtlough CBE

ADAMANTINE PRESS LIMITED

First published in the United Kingdom in 1994
by Adamantine Press Limited
3 Henrietta Street
Covent Garden
London WC2E 8LU
England

Composed in Linotron Plantin
by Saxon Graphics Ltd, Derby

British Cataloguing in Publication Data

A full catalogue record for this book is available from the British Library.
(Adamantine Classics for the 21st Century; v. no. 14)

ISBN 0-7449-0103-0 cased
      0-7449-0104-9 paper

Printed and bound in the United Kingdom by
Redwood Books, Trowbridge, Wiltshire

A volume in the series
Adamantine Studies on the 21st Century

Business strand editor: Sheila Moorcroft

Contents

**To everyone who taught me
and helped my learning**

Foreword

This book is needed. It is the right book at the right time by the right author. *Creative Compartments* is the right book for small companies getting larger and large companies getting smaller – which covers most companies in today's troubled marketplace.

The times are proving tough for large companies. They are finding themselves losing market share to smaller, nimbler companies that are quicker and closer to their customers. *Creative Compartments* will help these larger companies behave like smaller companies by showing the way to break up into working units of a couple of hundred people.

The times are favoring smaller companies, many of which are suffering the curse of their own success, and falling into old patterns of bureaucracy as they grow. *Creative Compartments* will show these smaller companies how to retain the energy and intimacy of their origins without sacrificing the advantages of scale.

Gerard Fairtlough is the right author to meet the challenges of these times. His experience includes a stint at Royal Dutch/Shell – one of the largest of the multinationals. More recently he's proven his mastery as an entrepreneur head of Celltech, a successful biotechnology startup. So his messages to companies both large and small are messages forged in the kiln of real experience.

Fairtlough's messages – and they are too many to summarize here – almost invariably reflect a maturity of judgement, a balance, a quality of soundness rare in business writing. Too many authors of business books try to rise above the clutter by pushing some simple cure – excellence, one-minute management, re-engineering. Fairtlough has a focus – the creative compartment – but the focus is surrounded by a sense of the whole, *a balancing of extremes, a sensitivity to both sides of most dilemmas*.

While he respects Schumacher's famous dictum that small is beautiful, for example, he recognizes that puny may be ineffective. So the creative compartment is not the cadre of twelve, but the compartment of a couple of hundred, which may be linked or bridged to other compartments of hundreds. And Fairtlough tells us just how to build the bridges. He sees that in high-tech, capital intensive industries, a certain level of scale is inevitable. So he helps us balance the need for market scale with the need for human scale.

A second balance in this book – both in its form and its content – is the balance between simplicity and complexity. If I may take a bird's-eye view of the unique contribution this book makes (and do so in a way that excuses my inability to summarize its contents), Fairtlough replaces a simplistic, mechanical view of business with a biological perspective that honors complexity. The metaphor for the creative compartment is the living cell. And as founder of Celltech, Fairtlough knows quite a bit about cells. This biologically inspired, organic perspective encourages insights into the true complexity confronted in any business involving human beings. Fairtlough understands the importance of boundaries that act like porous membranes, blocking the unwanted while allowing passage of important nutrients. For all of this respect of complexity, however, Fairtlough's text unfolds with a clarity and simplicity that belies the complexity of its subject matter.

Back in the late seventies, in a book on decentralization, I borrowed from the biologist, Warren McCulloch, an ungainly word – heterarchy – and introduced it into the discourse on the governance of large corporations. McCulloch developed the concept in an essay on the architecture of nervous nets where neuron A stimulates B and inhibits C; neuron B stimulates C and inhibits A; neuron C stimulates A and inhibits B. An example of heterarchy is the game of paper, rock and scissors. Paper covers rock; rock crushes scissors; scissors cut paper. Other examples include the system of checks and balances among executive, legislative and judicial branches of government. Despite the ungainliness of the term, heterarchy, I liked the way the concept cut through the Gordian knots tied in too many arguments over the conflicts between hierarchy and anarchy. Heterarchy represents a balance between the need for some hierarchy, combined with the need for the lateral, horizontal links in a network of relationships. Rather than glibly claiming a transition from hierarchies to networks, Fairtlough picks up the concept of heterarchy as a closer approximation of the structure of relationships in complex organizations.

Third, Fairtlough achieves balance in his handling of the complex human issues that arise so frequently in post-industrial environments where the management of minds replaces the management of hands. On the one hand he emphasizes the importance of openness and trust; on the other he recognizes the role of critique.

A fourth balance struck in this remarkable book is the balance between scholarship and experience. For a busy executive, Fairtlough's bibliography is extraordinary. He has imported into this text the insights of philosophers whose texts are daunting to accomplished academics, and he has done so with a gracefulness that makes it sound as if he were quoting last week's *Economist*. He honors other authors by quoting their insights, but he never falls into academic quibbling. And the insights he derives from books are almost always balanced by anecdotes drawn from his very rich experience. This makes for reading that is both informative and engaging.

One of the authors he honours most is an old friend of mine, Don Michael, a former professor, later consultant, and author of *On Learning to Plan – and Planning to Learn*. During the 1980s Don and I participated in a series of annual workshops on the topic, "Making Heterarchy Work". Our subject was governance. At each of our meetings we did our best to find examples of government agencies or corporations that were challenging a simple hierarchical model without yielding to anarchy. We sought generalizations, but often succumbed to anecdotes. We found it devilishly difficult to make sense of the transition from old governance patterns to ... what? Heterarchy? Networking? But what, precisely, was this new beast?

Now we can both rejoice, and so can many others, that Gerard Fairtlough has combined scholarship and experience, mastery of the large and the small, sensitivity to emotions and respect for intellect, to come up with a biological perspective on governance through creative compartments.

– James A. Ogilvy
Vice President, Global Business Network

Preface

There are supposed to be two types of person. The first, the specialist, goes through life learning more and more about a smaller and smaller field and ends up knowing everything about nothing. The second, the generalist, learns less and less about more and more until he or she comes to know nothing about everything. A glance at my *curriculum vitae* would put me into the second category.

I worked for twenty five years in the Royal Dutch/Shell Group of companies, in a variety of technical and commercial posts, and through my work became interested in many things. One of these was the way human beings behave in organisations, the field now known as Organisation Behaviour. A Shell colleague, Geoff Wheatley, introduced me to a firm where he had previously worked, the Coverdale Organisation, which is a leading consultancy in this field. After I had attended a week's training with Coverdale, the course director, Peter Harris, was kind enough to say that I was the only person who had been on the course and learned nothing. That wasn't true. For one thing I learned how perceptive and knowledgeable the people at Coverdale were. Later I came to question that, because they made me their Board chairman. But what is unquestionable is that I now have as friends Peter Harris and a good few others at Coverdale.

Another field in which I learned a lot through being at Shell was planning. At least planning was what Shell called it. But as practised by the amazingly talented Pierre Wack and other creative people, 'planning' became an attempt to understand the political, economic, technological, social, ideological and intellectual forces at work in the world; what sort of effects these forces might have on Shell's business in the future, typically over the coming decade; and what Shell could do to prepare for them. If gaining some kind of understanding of these forces was hard, what was even harder was using that understanding to influence the organisation, particularly if the message was an unpalatable one. The achievements of Shell's planners in preparing the minds of managers, throughout that giant organisation, for uncertain and threatening futures were remarkable. They were, in fact, achievements in organisational learning.

Through Shell's planners I met Donald Michael, a consultant to Shell. Don scans the world from a small, spare and beautiful room in San Francisco and he has taught me a great deal. Some of the debts I owe him will be evident from reading this book. Others will not; for instance, he introduced me to the work of Michael Polanyi, which started me thinking in several fruitful directions; and a good number of the books which have helped me in writing this one were Don's recommendations. Later Don introduced me to Peter Schwartz who runs an organisation, Global Business Network, which develops views of the world in a way which follows the tradition of Shell's planners, a tradition which Peter has himself enriched. I am now a Network Member of GBN, another spur to learning. This brings membership of GBN's book club, a further mine of new ideas.

A time came when I decided to leave Shell because I felt there were more urgent things to do than work in an organisation so full of able people. Often in agreeable company and after a glass or two of wine, I heard myself pontificating about what was wrong with Britain's industry, economy, society, climate and so on. It occurred to me in due course that if I knew so much about how to put it all right, I had better put my self where my mouth was. I thought it vital that the country's scientific strengths be used to create new, advanced industries and this would need new kinds of organisation which made better use of people's creativity and energy. The result was that I became the founder Chief Executive of Celltech Limited, later Celltech Group plc, a research-based biotechnology company which we located in Slough, twenty miles to the west of the centre of London. Celltech took over much of my life for the next ten years, until I retired in 1990. During this time I and my colleagues built Celltech into a company carrying out research, development and production of specialised proteins, mainly for pharmaceutical use, employing the techniques of recombinant-DNA and monoclonal antibody production which had been discovered in the mid-1970s. In this book I tell part of the story of Celltech, especially the part about its people and how they worked together.

I learned all the time I was at Celltech. I had to, if the company was to survive. I learned from trial and error, from books, from kind and wise friends around the world and from my colleagues in the firm. Norman Carey, David Gration and Ed Lennox taught me a great deal. While I was at Celltech, Mark Dodgson of the Science Policy Research Unit at the University of Sussex did a study on Celltech. SPRU is a leader in the study of innovation and the link with Mark and others at SPRU has been of real value to me. Celltech was a prototype for the creative compartment. Working there was full of excitement, anxiety, pain and joy. I shall try to convey some of that in this book.

Twenty years ago the founding of the Open University showed that really good things do still happen in the UK. I took a short course with the OU and later taught at the very stimulating OU summer schools. The subject was Systems, an approach to solving problems in organisations and in society; West Churchman is a founding father and Peter Checkland its current leading light. Systems has introduced me to several friends, John Hamwee, Chris Atkinson, Bob Flood and Werner Ulrich among them, who have given me many ideas which have helped in writing this book. I am especially grateful to John Hamwee for making sure I took proper notice of Robert Axelrod's work, and to him, to Don Michael, to Mark Dodgson and to Lisa Fairtlough for reading earlier drafts of the book. All have made valuable suggestions for correcting my mistakes and strengthening my arguments. Of course they are not responsible for the remaining errors.

Others who have given me help with this book include Scilla Elworthy, Janine Nahapiet, Sheila Moorcroft and Bunny Pal.

Lisa Fairtlough was one of the first students at the OU. Being married to her means that I am never without intellectual, and other, challenges. I have learned more from her than from anyone.

Introduction

Part One – Chapters 1 to 6 – of this book develops its central idea – the idea of the creative compartment. The creative compartment is a group of a few hundred people who work together in a completely open way. The growing effectiveness of communication within a compartment gives it an amazing capability and adaptability. How this happens in the creative compartment is best understood by reading Part One, but any reader who wants a summary of the idea can turn to pages 89 and 90 in Chapter Five.

Part Two – Chapters 7 to 9 – looks at the compartment in context – at its external interactions, including networking with other compartments and the discipline of external critique.

Part Three – Chapters 10 to 12 – uses the concept of compartmentation in organisational design, taking both top-down and bottom-up approaches. Top-down design is the redesign of large organisations to give them the advantages of compartmentation. Bottom-up design starts with independent compartments – small businesses, for example – and shows how they can associate to their mutual benefit. Although top-down and bottom-up design have different starting points, their end results are pretty similar.

Throughout *Creative Compartments* I use my own experiences, and the published experiences of others, to tell stories about the working of human groups and organisations. In most cases the setting is identified, in a few it is disguised. In some cases the stories are fiction – credible fiction, I hope.

I have included suggestions for action which people, in most positions in most kinds of organisation, can readily adopt. In the earlier parts of the book these suggestions are fairly simple. Later on they get more complex but I have always tried to provide clear guidance, on which anyone can act. These suggestions for action are indexed as 'practical advice'.

There are notes and references at the end of each chapter and suggestions for further reading at the end of the book.

1

Openness and Trust, Empowerment and Commitment

As a child I went with my parents to see a competition between teams of artillerymen. Each team had a gun which could be taken to pieces for transport in mountainous country. In the competition, the teams had to dismantle their guns, take the pieces over an imaginary ravine, reassemble them and fire a blank shell. The winner was the team which fired first. All the teams had practised for months, each member of the team knew exactly what he had to do and communication between team-members followed a preestablished pattern of reports and commands: "Wheel secured", "Fire !" and so on. The task was precisely defined and the more a team's actions were like a machine's, the better that team's chances of winning the competition.

But behaving mechanically is unusual for human beings. Perhaps the scene of this competition is memorable because, for a child, it was so unfamiliar. More common are situations in which there is a defined task but the means of carrying it out are not specified. In a game of football, for example, the physical location, the number of players, the rules of the game and the aims of the teams are all well defined but play requires instant decisions and constant attention to other players' actions and capabilities. Some of the skills of a good footballer, like accurate passing of the ball, have been learnt by constant practice and are carried out unthinkingly, but others, like deciding who should get the pass, cannot be called mechanical. Nor can abilities like helping to lift the spirits of the team, when it finds itself two goals down and with only twenty minutes more to play. Sporting success usually needs a combination of reliable skills, imaginative tactics and great motivation.

Most organisational settings need a similar combination. Success often depends on contributions from many different parts of the organisation, from many different people. These contributions depend, in turn, on the skill, creativity and motivation of the people involved. Creativity and motivation develop when people have autonomy and responsibility. But there must also be coordination. If there is no over-arching plan which individuals have to follow, then the task may not be successfully completed because one or more contributions may not be delivered on time. On the other hand, if the plan is too rigid, individuals may come to feel like cogs in a machine and therefore lose enthusiasm and inventiveness.

Much of our thinking about the world uses machine metaphors, derived from science, particularly pre-twentieth century science. Certainly my own thinking used to be like that and in this book I describe my own journey away from mechanistic thought and from a management style depending on it. The book is based on my own experience in organisations of various kinds and sizes, on my reflections on that experience, on other people's reports of their own experiences and on their reflections. I have written it because I think personal experience and reflection are highly relevant to the problems of business and of human society as a whole, and because I think we can help each other to learn.

But can people ever really learn ? Might it, unfortunately, be true that the more things change, the more they remain the same ? My answers to these questions are: humans can learn, individually and collectively; change is possible, enduring change, change for the better. These optimistic answers stem from my own experience of learning and changing and from seeing others do so. They depend on a comparison between today's society and that of my young adulthood, which, in Britain at least, was in most ways narrower and more complacent. I believe there is now much more adaptability, concern for quality and acceptance of responsibility for other people and for nature, than there was forty years or so ago. We have started to learn how to learn and to learn how to change.

There is obviously a long way to go. The problems on this planet – conflict, poverty, disease, environmental degradation – are gigantic. There is justifiable doubt about the human race's ability to learn quickly enough to survive, which makes it easy to fall into a gloomy cynicism and to see anyone with an optimistic view as unrealistic and dreamy. But I do not see it that way. Experience tells me that it is possible to find better ways of doing things and to pass on to others your enthusiasm for these better ways. I know that I have been able to learn and change, quickly at times, and I think I now have some idea about how to keep on learning and changing. That is the reason for my optimism. And that is the reason for this book.

The relevance of the personal to the general, of the small scale to the large scale, of the local to the global, is part of what is meant by small is beautiful. One of the aims of the book is to make the idea of smallness more concrete and more usable in practice. In his extraordinarily influential book, *Small is Beautiful*, E.F. Schumacher set out to overturn the "almost universal idolatry of giantism" which prevailed when it was written. Twenty years later we can see that in this he has had great success, since unthinking praise of size has now almost stopped.

But that does not mean that we are particularly sure why small is so good, or that we have a clear idea of how small and large can complement each other. Schumacher thought that smallness and largeness each had their place and said that "If there were a prevailing idolatry of smallness, irrespective of subject or purpose, one would have to try to exercise influence in the opposite direction." Schumacher's vision was not about remote communes struggling for self-sufficiency, nor was it based on a nostalgic longing for times when life was less complicated than now. *Small is Beautiful* engages with the world of complexity. For instance, it has a chapter on the theory of large-scale organisation and the book's study of Buddhist economics recognises that "it is not a question of choosing between 'modern growth' and 'traditional stagnation'. It is a question of finding the right path of development, the Middle Way between materialist heedlessness and traditionalist immobility, in short, of finding 'Right Livelihood'." I hope to provide some examples of Right Livelihood in this book and, by doing so, to help the implementation of the idea that small is beautiful.

This book is written mainly for people working in, or with, organisations of all kinds – in business, government and elsewhere. I will make use of my experience in large and small businesses, in government agencies, in universities and in research institutes. Also I hope to build on current ideas in organisation theory: ideas about openness, trust and empowerment, ideas about personal and organisational learning.

A distinction is frequently drawn between, on one hand, gradual changes for the better in human institutions and, on the other hand, their replacement by completely new institutions. This distinction is not always useful, but where it is drawn, I intend to straddle it by discussing both minor, immediate, incremental innovations and major, long-term, radical ones.

The aim of the book is, therefore, to use analysis and experience, theory and practice, to show:

- firstly, why doing things on a small-scale is efficient, why it is morally right and why it is beautiful, and
- secondly, how to obtain, for organisations and for society, the blessings of smallness, some of them immediately and more of them in future years.

Learning to be a Chief Executive

Although its huge central office buildings in London and the Hague might suggest otherwise, the Royal Dutch/Shell group of companies is highly decentralised. The group is generally known as 'Shell' but its operations are carried out by autonomous national companies, which trade with each other as well as with the outside world. Central control is largely through the setting of standards, for example, for product quality or for health and safety; through authorisation of major investment projects, like new off-shore oil platforms; and through the appointment of the senior staff of these companies. In the early 1970s I was given one of these appointments. I became Marketing Director of Shell Chemicals UK Ltd., the company responsible for Shell's business in chemicals in the UK. I joined a team of six executive directors, led by the Managing Director, Eric Mackay.

Mackay had been appointed about eighteen months before I joined. His task was to put right some serious failings in the company and to get it to adapt to the turbulent business environment of the mid-1970s, with its uncertain oil supply and gyrating oil prices. He was intelligent, forceful and full of energy. He saw that lots of changes had to be made and he set about making them quickly. He replaced the baronial chiefs who had previously kept marketing and manufacturing separate and built a cohesive management team. He set about revamping the whole management information system. He stirred up people in sleepy corners of the company. I admired his courage and drive and knew I could learn a good deal from him. And I did learn from him, but not for very long; just over a year after I joined Shell Chemicals UK, Mackay left the Shell group and I was given his job.

I was 42 when I got this unexpected promotion. I'd had difficult jobs in the Shell group but I'd never been the chief executive of any organisation. To be responsible for a company with over 4,000 people, some very large petrochemical plants and a big share of the market for several key industrial chemicals and plastics raw materials was both exciting and frightening. I had to learn some new skills quickly. As my predecessor had been a good chief executive, the natural thing was to use his management style as a model, partly because many of those around me expected me to behave as he had done, even though my personality was different from his. But I soon realised that everyone is better off with his or her own style, and, although I didn't appreciate it at first, there was another reason not to copy my former boss. This was because the company had moved on, partly due to Mackay's efforts. There was no longer an urgent need for firm action to correct obvious faults, the company's financial performance had improved and a bit of stability was now needed rather than a further spate of new ideas or more initiatives for change.

I realised this one day when talking to a colleague about problems in a particular department. I'd thought up a list of possible actions, but my colleague said: "We've got a good guy in charge there. Why don't we show him we're backing him and leave it at that?" This was the right answer for this particular problem and the remark also altered my perception of the job I was doing. From then on I started to listen to others rather than feeling I must produce a lot of clever ideas myself. I started to let people solve their own problems, although if asked for help I gave it readily. I started setting two or three key objectives for the company which had to be achieved over the next six months, and then went on talking about these objectives so that everyone understood them and had no doubt about their importance. In doing this, I started visiting groups throughout the company, 'walking about' as it's now called, although I did more talking than walking and even more listening.

I learned that, even though change is necessary if things are to improve and if organisations are to respond effectively to external threats and opportunities, change is never cost-free. It needs a lot of work, it creates uncertainty, it may result in the loss of unappreciated competences. I learned how to ration change in an organisation, to treat it as a scarce resource, to examine the purposes for any proposed change and to work for widespread agreement on the priorities for change. I learned how skill in communication and interpersonal process lead to success in organisational change. I learned that supporting and empowering others was what a senior person mainly had to do.

Five years later, when I was moving on from the job of chief executive of Shell Chemicals, I wrote an account of the management practices which my colleagues and I had established in the company. One part of this account was about the role of the top team, including the chief executive's role and those of the other directors. The tasks of the top team were these:

- Articulating a vision for the long term future of the company.
- In the light of this vision, setting each year a challenging budget for the company, monitoring progress against it and taking corrective action if need be.
- Encouraging the various sub-units in the company (departments and so forth) to work constructively together.
- Communicating with the wider systems of which the company was a part. In the case of Shell Chemicals UK, these wider systems were the Shell group's chemicals business as a whole, Shell's UK businesses as a whole and the UK chemical industry as a whole.
- Developing the skills and capabilities of the company, including the skills of sub-units and of individuals.

There was nothing out of the ordinary about this list, even in the 1970s. What was unusual was that the top team really stuck to these tasks and did not try to do a whole lot of other things. Of course, if a member of the top team had a particular kind of expertise, that was available to the company and if a particular task needed a senior person's guidance, that was given, but we found that by concentrating on these five tasks the top team empowered the rest of the organisation, releasing people's energies and innovative talents. The team then had time to make sure that the short-term priorities and the long-term vision were properly understood throughout the organisation. By sticking to their own tasks and leaving the rest to more junior people, team members could more readily provide constructive criticism and coaching to their juniors and could help to develop networking between them.

One of the best features of this style of management was the way in which it developed the self-confidence and resourcefulness of people working in the company. Quite a few people whose capabilities were extended through this style of management went on to take senior jobs in various parts of Shell. Which was, for me, the strongest confirmation that empowering others was the right way to manage.

Open Management

At the same time as I was learning how well empowerment worked as a management style, I was learning the value of openness in an organisation. By openness I mean a willingness to share information widely and to keep secrecy to a minimum. In business, as in all human activities, it is necessary to have some secrets but I think that, in most places, secrecy is ridiculously overdone, partly out of habit and partly because knowing things that others don't gives one a spurious thrill.

In Shell Chemicals, as I spent more and more time walking about and listening to people, I found that secrecy got in the way when I wanted to show why achieving a particular objective was so important; why, for instance, investment in one part of our operations had to have priority over investment in another part. I could have said, politely or not, that I had decided on certain objectives and, as I was the boss, that was the way it was going to be. But I didn't need to take that line. There were very good reasons for all of the objectives we had set and I thought I ought to be able to convince anyone in the company that we had made the right choices. If everyone understood and believed in our objectives, there was a much better chance that they would be achieved. To explain how these objectives had been chosen, I had to talk about parts of the company's strategy. Too much secrecy would have stopped me doing that.

The group of people responsible for the company's solvents business might have worked out a way of expanding a solvents plant, which would considerably increase its output by making a relatively small investment. They might have done a lot of work on the proposal and have calculated that the expansion of the plant would give a very good return on that investment. Our manufacturing director and his specialist staff might agree that the proposal was completely sound from the technical point of view. And yet the management team might have given the proposal lower priority than an alternative project for spending money to improve the reliability of the polyethylene plant, even though the financial return on the polyethylene investment was calculated to be a lot lower than from the solvents one. Justifying decisions like this was not easy, especially to people who didn't like them, in this case the solvents people. To justify the decision convincingly, I would have to show why a reputation for reliability in supply of all our products, polyethylene as well as solvents, was critical, both with external customers and with companies within the Shell group. This would mean talking about past failures and the bad effects these had had on our reputation. These were subjects which many managers would have preferred to forget, but being open about them was the only way to be convincing.

Once openness started to become a way of life, it could not be confined just to more senior managers within Shell Chemicals. These managers had to be able to talk about many of these issues to everyone, in plants and offices in all parts of the company. My senior colleagues and I had to be able to talk about them to employee representatives, to shop stewards representing unionised employees and to groups of middle and junior managers. We had to be just as open with the top brass of the Shell group and with specialist staff in Shell's central offices.

We had to be consistent in the things we discussed, since if we talked about a particular area of the business when things were going well, but kept away from it when mistakes had been made, then our credibility would be reduced. We tried to achieve consistency by sticking to a consistent pattern when giving information about the company. The management team gave formal presentations each quarter on the financial results and operating performance of the company. We did this with the aid of a set of good quality 35 mm slides. For each quarter we had a standard set of slides and we used the same slides for all audiences, whether in the boardroom, to the shop stewards at one of the production sites or to a group of staff specialists. The basic presentations were the same for each of these audiences, although the kinds of question asked and the focus of the discussion usually turned out to be quite different.

Adopting a policy of consistent openness fairly quickly brought its rewards. Once it became accepted that the management team was willing to justify its decisions openly and on occasions to admit its mistakes openly, demands for justifications were reduced. People began to believe that the management team was fair and reasonable and got things right most of the time. Communication became more rapid and, once a decision had been taken, there was less tendency to try to change it or get round it. Openness led to trust, to increasing understanding of the company's business situation and to a reasonable degree of commitment to the objectives we were pursuing.

Trust in the motives and competence of the management and understanding of the business meant that hard decisions were accepted more constructively than might otherwise have been so. If a plant had to be shut down because its products were unable to compete in the world market, there was less of the opposition or sullen resentment usually provoked. When openness is the norm, it is not easy to represent such decisions as arbitrary. If the tradition in a company is secrecy, then rumours will flourish, people will try to trade information with each other and a lot of energy goes into the stupid game of 'who knows what?' We were able to avoid most of that.

Switching to a tradition of openness means that everyone starts to think about the few things that really must remain confidential, not about which tidbits can be revealed. This helps to ensure that these few important things do remain completely secret and avoids the cloud of gossip and half-truths which surrounds many things in a secretive organisation. It is said that in totalitarian states everything is forbidden except those things which are explicitly permitted. In secretive organisations everything is supposed to be concealed unless approval for its release has been given from on high. In contrast, in an open organisation it is the decisions to keep something confidential which are the deliberate ones; it is assumed that everything else can be openly discussed.

Clearly in a company the size of Shell Chemicals there must have been areas where old ways persisted, where increased openness was seen as a fad of the current management, where people kept their heads down and hoped it would all go away. But I do think these were the exceptions. Mostly the open climate was welcomed as a real aid to doing a better job. Mostly people liked being treated as adults. Naturally, openness did not mean an end to personal ambition. Nor did it stop people wanting promotion or pay increases, or more power or influence. Openness did not bring conflict to an end, because differing interests remained. It genuinely was a bad thing for people in the solvents business if it were decided that the polyethylene business had to have priority at a particular time. Quite properly, people continued to lobby for their patch and to present their cases as expertly as they could. But openness moved the game away from intrigue towards debate. It meant that personal interests could be acknowledged openly, often in a way which raised a laugh.

We avoided the alternative in which people would keep a facade of company loyalty, while pursuing skullduggery on the back stairs.

Shell Chemicals UK was a big company on its own and was part of a huge group. It was not possible to be open about everything with everybody since there would not have been time to exchange all that amount of information and since there is a limit to the amount of information anyone can absorb. Company-wide communication had to concentrate on the most important and interesting aspects of the business. And, as I have said, some things were still kept secret. For instance anything which might affect the price of Shell's shares quoted on various stock exchanges could only be disclosed in an approved manner. As another example, it would have been foolish to reveal the company's objectives and tactics for any kind of negotiation. Personal data on individuals had to remain confidential and there were legal constraints on releasing other kinds of information. These areas of secrecy were important but they were selective and, outside the selected areas, openness ruled.

Linking-up the Concepts

The most memorable lessons are those of experience. You really believe what those lessons teach you. I suspect that confident action is always based on experience. My experience at Shell Chemicals certainly gave me confidence in a style of management centred on openness, trust and empowerment, which I have used pretty consistently ever since. I now find that, if I don't keep to this style, I always regret it.

Today the concepts of openness, trust and empowerment are more widely accepted than they were in the 1970s. So if it stopped there, the story of how I learnt about these concepts – on the job, not in the classroom or through reading – might only be interesting as an example of learning through experience. However, the experience of learning made me think a lot about these concepts, about their interaction and about developing them further. I read widely, so as to discover some relevant psychological and sociological thinking. I began to construct theories of my own and found that my theorising and my practice began to nourish each other. One outcome was that my management practice became more successful. Another outcome is this book.

Let us start with the interaction between trust and openness. Openness is a combination of honesty (telling the truth) and frankness (telling the whole truth). Frankness is the more difficult to practice, since it can reveal your own weakness or, when it reveals the weaknesses of others, it can provoke hostility. This is why it is usually easier to keep quiet about difficulties rather than to be open about them. So to be open is to take a risk. And in dealings with other people, a willingness to take risks is to demonstrate trust in them. When you show someone that you trust them, that person is likely to reciprocate, to trust you in return. Such trust then makes it easier for you to be still more open. You can more readily admit your mistakes, and this admission again shows that you trust the other person not to take advantage of your openness. This is how trust and openness develop between individuals, or between groups of people, creating virtuous circles.

Let us now look at a second virtuous circle: the one which develops between empowerment and commitment. When you empower someone, you give her the responsibility for achieving something, together with any help needed. By giving somebody a responsibility and by supporting her in carrying it out, you are showing that you think her worthy and capable of carrying the responsibility. When someone is entrusted with a responsibility in this way, it links that person to the task, or, in other words, generates commitment to the task. A willingness to give responsibility creates a willingness to accept it, and vice versa, establishing a virtuous circle between empowerment and commitment.

The two virtuous circles are connected. Empowerment demonstrates trust, which, as we have seen, encourages that trust to be reciprocated. Empowerment generates commitment, and you are likely to trust someone who is really committed to a task. Full empowerment requires that the person empowered understands the situation fully, or at least as fully as possible. And a full understanding is only possible if there is complete openness, which means that empowerment demands openness. Figure 2 illustrates the interaction of the two circles.

Getting these virtuous circles going, and keeping them moving through difficult times, needs one further driving force and that is communicative competence. Skill in communication derives from several sources, apart from the innate abilities and temperaments of individual men and women. General education is obviously important, at the basic level of reading and writing, for skills like putting together an account of a topic and to supply all kinds of factual knowledge.

Specific training is valuable for developing interpersonal process skills, like making good use of the talents of the less forceful or less articulate. Membership of groups which communicate well is perhaps the best of all ways to learn. Naturally, communicative competence depends on more than these skills. Without a climate of openness and empowerment, people will not say what they really think, will not share their hopes and fears, will not probe matters which could upset the powerful.

Skill in communication is bound up with skill in interpersonal process, with understanding how other people react to what you say, with being able to put yourself in their shoes, with good listening, with appreciating that everyone can contribute to problem-solving if their help is sought in the right way, with learning from mistakes and building on successes. To take an example: if someone agrees with a suggestion you make, his agreement can be at a variety of levels. It might be that the person is prepared to go along with your suggestion because the matter is unimportant to him. Or his agreement may mean that he is anxious to please you. Or it may mean that he agrees because everyone else has, even though he really doesn't like the idea. Or that he quite likes the suggestion, although he doesn't properly understand it. Or that he fully understands the idea and enthusiastically supports it. Someone skilled in interpersonal process will understand that there can be different levels of agreement and be able, when necessary, to bring out the particular differences within a group.

Communication has to cover a wide range: reaching agreement on factual matters, problem-solving by a group, making ethical judgments, expressing feelings sincerely. Some people will have more skill in one of these, other people in another. So communicative competence depends crucially on the skills within a group being complementary to one another and on the ability of the group to draw on these varied skills, as well as on group norms supporting openness and on the willingness of the power structure around the group to permit competence to flourish.

What I learned from experience at Shell Chemicals, and from reflection on that experience, was this:

● Openness and trust, empowerment and commitment are valuable on their own in organisations, but they are much more valuable when they interact to reinforce each other. When this happens, virtuous circles start, which have a vigorous life of their own.

- Communicative competence is vital if these virtuous circles are to be sustained. This competence can be built by training, by example and by the right support.

Applying the Lessons

I soon had the opportunity to apply these lessons in a different context. In 1980 I was given the task of building from scratch a biotechnology company, Celltech Limited. There were few directly relevant models to follow. The other research-based biotechnology businesses founded around the same time in the US gave some guidance but they were in parts of the world where high technology start-up companies were not rarities and where cooperation between university researchers and commercial enterprises was common. This was not so at that time in the UK.

So, drawing on the lessons I had learnt at Shell Chemicals, I proposed a few basic principles to guide us in the management of Celltech. My colleagues, sometimes reluctantly, sometimes enthusiastically and sometimes because they were too busy to argue, went along with these. The company was small (after two years we were about one hundred people, mostly scientifically trained) and we had to make this an advantage. The field of science was new and needed the integration of several disciplines like molecular biology, immunology, cell culture and biochemical engineering. People in the company had some of this expertise; for the rest we depended on collaborations with academic workers, those in research institutes and universities.

Because we were small we had to be unusually productive and creative, otherwise we would get left behind. But being small made communication easier and the first principle therefore was to have superb internal communication, communication between different scientific disciplines and between scientists and business people, communication which was completely open. There were to be no secrets within the company, at least on company matters, and we would trust each other to keep all this information from leaking into the outside world.

Because we had to draw on the skills and knowledge of academics we needed to communicate very well with them, despite the mutual incomprehension and often the mistrust which there then was between academic and industrial scientists. Learning how to close this gap (or, to use a concept introduced later in the book, *to span this boundary*) became the second principle on which Celltech was built.

Here are two examples of the practices which evolved to give expression to these two principles: Firstly, in the early days of Celltech a file was made up at the end of each week which had in it all the correspondence of the company, in and out, and on all subjects which were not of a personal kind. This file was put in the library and anyone working in the company could ask to see it. When a hot issue emerged, the file was consulted by lots of people. A few people read it regularly every week. After a couple of years, the size of the company made this practice too cumbersome to continue, but by then it had helped to establish an attitude of openness. Secondly, like most biotechnology firms, we had an advisory council of distinguished academic scientists and we gave this group the task of overseeing our relationships with academia. The council had to approve the collaborations we had with academics, the grants to them and the terms on which these were made. The council saw the reports which company scientists made on their contacts with academic scientists and if there were disputes, or if things did not seem to be developing well, the chairman of the council would be asked for help in sorting out the problem. Here we were being open with some semi-outsiders, whose scientific reputations made them forceful critics, and this was uncomfortable at times. But, again, openness prevailed.

Large and Small Organisations

How much did the things I learned at Shell help me at Celltech? How much do the lessons from a huge company apply in a small one? The answer is that without the Shell experience I would not have foreseen that a project management system of the kind we developed, with its combination of well-informed support and stringent criticism, would be so good at stimulating creativity at Celltech. I would not have known how to create Celltech's open management style. Without having seen the good effects of a less extreme version in Shell Chemicals, I probably would not have risked a policy of almost total openness at Celltech. Perhaps I would have realised neither the extent to which openness and trust reinforce each other, nor the mutual reinforcement there is between the empowerment of individuals and a supportive critique of their performance. Experience as chief executive at Shell Chemicals gave me the confidence to adopt an empowering, open style and the knowledge that I ought to work ceaselessly for excellent internal communication at Celltech.

Giving people autonomy and empowering them to do their jobs was a management style that had worked well for me in several settings. Its success must have been due to the enthusiasm and the feelings of responsibility which were generated in individuals when they were treated in this way. It must also have been due to the opportunities it gave for people to learn and innovate. And it must have allowed those actually working on a task to interact closely and openly, since they knew they had the backing of their management, leading to an integration of all their efforts and thus to successful working.

When starting Celltech, my colleagues and I knew that we should not build a conventional firm. The scientists we would have to attract to work for Celltech were mostly in their twenties or early thirties and had skills which were in short supply. To get them to join us we had to show that their talents would be used to the full, their voices would be heard, that their successes would be recognised and that life would be fun.

The academic scientists with whom we had to work because they had unique knowledge, knew very little about industry and were often contemptuous of industry. We had to show them that collaborating with Celltech would be helpful to their research, that we would treat them absolutely fairly and that they might enjoy the experience. In our relations with academics, we strove to get virtuous circles going, circles like those I've described in this chapter.

We knew too that we would have to work closely with large firms, particularly in the pharmaceutical industry, who would be corporate partners in projects which were too large for us to do on our own. They would have suspicions of a different kind about Celltech: that we were too small to be effective or that our close association with academic science would make us unconcerned about getting commercially important results.

Superb communications seemed to us to be the answer to most of these difficulties. We aimed for completely open and free communication within the company. We would make sure that everyone knew all the time what was going on and that everyone was involved in key decisions, such as the choice of priorities among the projects on which Celltech was working. Communications with our partners would be excellent too. Of course these could not be as open as within the company. It was vital that we kept our own secrets secure and that we did not reveal to one partner what we were working on with another, but within well defined areas we would be as open as possible–we would always be straight with our partners. These were our standards. They were sincerely sought, but we did not always succeed, because there was a normal quota of human failings among people at Celltech.

The Effects of Openness

Open communication depends on trust and trust depends on open communication. In a newly formed organisation the two could grow in parallel and this is what happened at Celltech. My senior colleagues and I started this process by sharing information, including doubts and difficulties, with junior people. This was straightforward when there were only twenty or so people in the firm, although it was a novel experience for most of us since in our previous jobs there had not been this kind of openness. We all made mistakes but in an atmosphere of trust we could admit them, learn from them and avoid repeating them. Openness and trust reinforced each other and by the end of our first year, when Celltech had around fifty people, it was fair to say that a tradition had been started which was strong enough to involve newcomers quite quickly, stifling any temptation to withhold information as a power-play or to generate a petty scandal, and once established the tradition continued.

Let me give one example which shows how strong the tradition became. In 1989 Celltech's largest shareholder got into financial difficulties and was forced to offer its shares for sale. This could have triggered a take-over bid for the whole company which would obviously have had a great effect on everyone working in it. Although we did not want to lose our independence, the board of directors decided that the proper course of action was to cooperate with potential bidders for the company. In this way we could seek a price which would be acceptable to all shareholders, not a 'distress' price which the largest shareholder might have been willing to accept.

It was necessary to keep this development secret from the outside world for about three weeks while various preparations were made. Some members of Celltech's board felt that it should also be kept secret from people working in the firm because, as one of them put it, "if we tell the staff it's bound to be in the Financial Times tomorrow". I managed to persuade the board that this was not likely. I first asked whether any member of the board could point to an occasion on which a confidence had been abused. As no one could, I said that it was therefore unreasonable not to put our trust in our people. I then said that I felt the secret would be kept and that I was willing to stake my own reputation as a chief executive who knew his company on this. Fortunately for me, I was right, as everybody in the company was given the information in confidence and kept it secret until a public announcement was made. At that time there were about four hundred people in the company. Although several large companies looked carefully at the possibility of buying the company, in the end none was prepared to pay the asking price and Celltech remained independent.

A Context for Virtuous Circles

In Celltech we kept personal data secret, we obeyed the law, a few bits of technology were known only to a limited number of people and the Board of Directors asked that an equally limited number of matters discussed in their meetings should also be confidential, but almost everything else was open. When I tell this to some people unbelieving looks come over their faces. However, we really were that open and I'm sure all those who worked at Celltech would confirm that. In a firm with a few hundred people it is possible to keep everyone well informed and the benefits of openness are soon very evident. It is possible to build up the mutual trust and the self-control needed to keep secrets within the company. In my ten years at Celltech I made quite a few decisions that I later regretted but the decision for openness was never one of these. I think that openness was invariably right.

In our first couple of years, when there were under a hundred people working in the company, openness became a pattern. This was sustained as we grew. After four years sales reached nearly £2 million and staff numbers were up to 130. Because of a heavy spend on R&D, profits were slower to arrive, but we told our shareholders that we expected to be profitable in year seven and I'm glad to say that we achieved this. In this year – 1987 – Celltech had sales of over £11 million, with 230 people working in the firm.

Visitors to Celltech often remarked that it did not feel like most other organisations. Perhaps this was because we had been lucky enough to get into a virtuous circle, not a vicious one, which meant that trust and openness supported each other's growth and that competence in communication grew with practice.

I hope what I have said about Celltech has given you the idea that everyone in the company was treated as a responsible adult with a stake in the company's success, as someone who could be trusted with confidential information and whose voice would be heard on any issue. I certainly believe this was so. One more instance of the respect with which people were treated in the company is the commitment which we had to developing everyone's personal potential to the full, by training on an almost Japanese scale, by coaching on the job and by regular counselling of individuals.

Conclusion

In this chapter I have told the story of my own discovery of what organisations can achieve if they become dedicated to openness and empowerment. I have described how these concepts link with one another and how they generate trust and commitment. And I have shown how theory and practice interact in the process of learning and how I could apply the lessons I learned in one organisation in another, very different, one.

To anyone who is thinking: what are the lessons for me from all this? I would say: try it for yourself. Be open, show trust, empower others, seek commitment. Don't be discouraged if the prevailing attitudes in your organisation are against openness or empowerment. The people in your organisation are waiting to be treated as responsible, capable human beings and they will respond if you treat them so. Be bold, be persistent, you have human nature on your side.

Notes

Page 3. *Small is Beautiful : A Study of Economics as if People Mattered* by E.F.Schumacher, was first published in 1973. The quotation on the idolatry of giantism is from p. 64 and that on Right Livelihood from p.60 of the Sphere paperback edition (1974).

Celltech, pages 14-18. For anyone interested in more detail about Celltech the place to start is Mark Dodgson's *The Management of*

Technological Learning: Lessons from a Biotechnology Company.
Walter de Gruyter, Berlin. (1991). Some of the material in this book
also appeared in the same author's *Celltech: The First Ten Years of a
Biotechnology Company.* Science Policy Research Unit Discussion
Paper Series, University of Sussex, February 1990. The following
also contain material on Celltech:

(a) Gerard Fairtlough. Creative Compartments. *London Business
School Journal* Summer 1986.
(b) Gerard H.Fairtlough. Systems Practice from the Start: Some
Experiences in a Biotechnology Company. *Systems Practice, 2,*
4, (1989).
(c) G.H.Fairtlough. Exploitation of Biotechnology in a Smaller
Company. *Phil. Trans. R. Soc. Lond.* B **324**, 589-597 (1989).

2

The Blankets of Hierarchy

It was a gathering of the powerful. The heads of a dozen of Europe's larger companies were talking together about the future of the continent. All were white, middle-aged males but, despite the cartoonists' stereotype, none of these capitalists had much of a stomach and none smoked anything, let alone a cigar. Topics of discussion ranged from the formidable strength of Japanese competition to the turmoil in Eastern Europe left by the collapse of the Soviet empire. I suppose each was trying to understand how the huge changes taking place in the world's economic and political landscape might affect his business. Each must have known that the future was unpredictable but also knew that its threats and opportunities could make or break his company.

As I watched this group of people I asked myself why they were so concerned about what Europe would be like a decade or more in the future. The future was uncertain and most of them would be retired within ten years, but the light in their eyes, and the alert set of their heads and shoulders, showed that for them this was a really serious subject. Interesting, of course, but why had it gripped these people? Sitting there, I guessed that whatever gripped them must have something to do with power, since people who get to the top of large organisations have this in common: power turns them on. And then, I thought, successful attention to the future leads to power. Ancient astronomers got their prestige through accurate forecasts of the year's longest day or of an eclipse of the sun. Modern business people with a reputation for strategic vision get accolades from their shareholders and their pictures on the cover of *Business Week*.

From watching this group of people, it seemed to me that most, if not all, of them had a strong sense of what could be useful in influencing their organisations. They paid the closest attention to those things which would enhance their power and influence. No doubt, this was one reason why they liked discussions with their peers. They would have learned a lot more about politics in Eastern Europe or about Japanese manufacturing productivity by listening to a university professor or some other expert in the field. But in a gathering of business leaders they were able to concentrate on the problem of turning knowledge about the world into organisational power. They might have found an expert presentation 'rather academic', while describing a discussion in their peer group as 'really practical'.

I am not denying that an organisation has to pay attention to what is happening around it. Careful thought about the future, the ability to spot opportunities and threats, and superior strategic vision are all great contributors to enduring business success. Nor am I saying that the head of an organisation should stay away from these things. In fact, support from the top is essential if strategic thinking is to have value to any organisation and I have sometimes seen how a percipient CEO can personally provide part of this thinking. Rather, the point I want to make is this: when senior people are involved in activities of this kind, the power dimension is always present, and often dominant.

Long-term strategy is not the only power-dominated activity in business. If the top people around that beautifully polished table, with their cut glass tumblers of mineral water, had been discussing quality circles or performance-related pay, the link to power would have been yet more obvious. For more or less every business topic, it would have been the same. Even a discussion of golf or the weather can, subtly or crudely, have overtones of power.

The head of any large organisation has a special view of power, because he or she wields it mainly within that organisation. Mostly, those at the top of large organisations have risen through its ranks, or through the ranks of a similar one. They have been trained to perform in an organisational environment and selected on their ability to do so. After twenty or thirty years in that environment, establishing and using organisational power becomes second nature. Creating the levers of control, and pulling them deftly, develops into an unconscious skill, a skill which pleases when things are going well and reassures in a crisis. Without those levers to grasp, many holders of such offices would not know how to act as a Chairman, a CEO or an administrator of a large government agency. For them, the exercise of hierarchical power has become a way of life.

Power and Hierarchy

Hierarchies are instruments of power. First they were instruments of religious and state power, the means through which the will of its ruler could be made manifest throughout a land or the means through which the infallible decrees of its head were transmitted within a church. In Europe during the eighteenth and nineteenth centuries, state hierarchies became increasingly formalised, sinecures were abolished, corruption decreased, nepotism withered and talent, rather than birth, became the means of advancement. The military and administrative hierarchies of Prussia, and then of Germany, are good examples, the models from which Max Weber derived his classic analysis of bureaucracy. States with efficient hierarchies of this type were feared by other states, who tried to copy this new way of increasing state power, resulting in the spread of the type all over the world.

In the USA during the nineteenth century, the hierarchical corporation was developed, first in railroads, then in meat packing and mass-production engineering products, notably automobiles. Again, this efficient means of enhancing the power of the owner of a business was feared and copied, and again it spread, with modifications, all over the world. Paradoxically, although the systematic hierarchy became such a potent instrument, it did not always benefit the actual people whose power it was supposed to enhance. Kings and queens became less powerful, being moved to one side, or becoming totally redundant, while professional politicians and civil servants gained control of the hierarchy. A similar thing happened in business, as individual owners and family firms became less important, and professional managers gained control.

Systemisation was desirable as a way of getting rid of nepotism and corruption. It also made for greater certainty in the execution of the wishes of the ruler of the state, the commander of the army or the owner of the business. It made good use of scarce strategic skills, such as those of a military commander, which could be used to full advantage only if orders were transmitted rapidly and accurately and instantly obeyed. It made good use of scarce scientific and technical skills, too, and allowed complex operations to be carried out in a coordinated manner. Systemisation, through the adoption of standard operating procedures in which people could be thoroughly trained, meant that the best way to perform a particular task did not have to be rediscovered whenever a group of people needed to perform it for the first time. Instead, they could draw on the

experience of others. Organisational learning was helped by systemisation, since one group's improvements could easily be handed
on to other groups because their practices would be identical to the
innovating group's.

For nearly a hundred and fifty years in government and nearly a
hundred years in business, the professional hierarchy has seemed
the best, the most modern way of organising things on a large scale.
This applies, too, in spheres outside governments and corporations,
like churches, charitable foundations and universities. Hierarchies
were, and still are, effective instruments of power. They got, and
still get, results. Sometimes they become dysfunctional, and then we
pejoratively call them bureaucratic. Often they work quite well, and
then we hardly notice them, because they seem the ordinary way of
the world, even though we believe that they give extraordinary
power to the people at their head. Efficient, systemised, professional
hierarchies, those well-oiled, responsive machines, are, if you think
about it, miraculous inventions. (Sociologists call them
bureaucracies, but as that term carries, for many people, the
implication that they are inefficient and self-serving, I will stick to
'hierarchy' as a way of describing them. Strictly speaking, hierarchies need not be systemised and professional – think of the
inherited hierarchy of feudal ranks, for instance – but that is not the
kind I am talking about).

Hierarchies work particularly well when there are only a few well-
educated, knowledgeable people available, whose knowledge is clearly
advantageous for the organisation, or when the people at the top have a
clear vision, which for some reason cannot easily be shared with the rest
of the organisation. This was certainly the case a hundred years ago,
when hierarchies were starting to proliferate. It was also the case more
recently than that. I can remember the business situation in the 1950s,
when in Europe advanced technological and organisational skill were
short. Organisations, like the one I worked for, which could get hold of
relevant knowledge, often from the USA, and apply it throughout
Western Europe, had a great advantage. This was the golden age of the
large multinational corporation, when its expert central staffs were
really welcomed by the operators in the field. The top-down policies,
set by senior management, were readily accepted amid the confusion
which still remained from the war. But the experts from the centre
quickly taught their colleagues on the periphery and as a result the
experts became less valuable. By the 1960s the central office started to
be resented and its staffs started to hoard knowledge or to refashion it,

so as to retain their (formerly unquestioned) influence. By the 1970s the operating units had gained even more experience and often knew more than more than the so-called expert staffs. They started communicating among themselves on some subjects, ignoring the centre. Whether at the centre or on the periphery, knowledge was power, because of the material gains knowledge made possible and because those who controlled knowledge, by creating it, gathering it together, standardising it and distributing it, gained influence over others.

To sum up what I have been saying in this section: firstly, the systemised, professional hierarchy was a key invention of modern times; secondly, it was so effective that variants of it have been adopted all over the world, in government (civil and military), in business and in religious and other non-profit, non-government sectors; thirdly, when it works well we hardly notice it, because today it seems the natural and ordinary way of arranging things on any scale larger than that of the family; and finally, at least since the 1970s and at least in business, the hierarchical mode of organisation has come under pressure, mainly because of the spread of knowledge.

Giving up the Blankets

As a way of organising things, the hierarchy may be past its peak, but there are still plenty around. Powerful people are acting to retain them for as long as possible. In fact, as with most human inventions, hierarchies bring disadvantages as well as advantages. Even the best accepted inventions have their bad aspects – we need only think of the car and the telephone. This means that all inventions should be used with discrimination. Even when they are, circumstances can change, shifting the balance of advantage and disadvantage.

Imagine someone living about a mile from her place of work. The advantage of making the journey by bicycle, rather than on foot, is to save ten minutes each morning and evening. The disadvantages are the cost of owning a bicycle and the work of maintaining it. Suppose that traffic on the road to work builds up and the journey by cycle gets slower and more dangerous until the balance of advantage becomes negative. Then walking becomes the better option and she changes the way she gets to work. But cycling and walking are still the same in themselves and the bicycle remains a remarkable human invention, although for that particular journey the invention is no longer valuable.

Today, hierarchies have generally lost the balance of advantage. Systematic, professional hierarchies remain an important human invention but they do not drive all before them as once they did. Their first major defect is that they stifle initiative. Since the hierarchy is a means for ensuring ordered behaviour, sticking by the rules must come first and after many years of sticking to the rules, anyone's originality and flexibility will atrophy. As the creativity of individuals disappears, so does the creativity of the organisation as a whole. It becomes incapable of doing new things, of responding to changes in its environment. It is inflexible, it cannot adapt, it suffers from stasis. Sometimes, problems are ignored, because the rules do not specify what should be done about them. At other times, problems are approached by different parts of the organisation in a segmented way, without any overall coordination. Or if top-level coordination is provided, it is usually too remote from the problem to be effective.

The second major defect of hierarchies is that they inhibit commitment to the goals of the organisation as a whole. Since hierarchies are a means of executing the wishes of the people at their head, other people's views become irrelevant. If your wishes are irrelevant, your commitment to hierarchical goals becomes far from passionate. You start to say: "It's not my job to look after that". As Gareth Morgan puts it: "Defining work responsibilities in a clear-cut manner has the advantage of letting everyone know what is expected of them. But it also lets them know what is *not* expected of them." Commitment develops towards local or departmental goals, not to those of the organisation. Inter-departmental rivalries burgeon, empires are built, projects are pushed because they suit personal or departmental interests, all to the disadvantage of the whole.

I will not go on with this list of the disadvantages of the pure hierarchical form, because what I am talking about must be depressingly familiar to every reader. We have all had a laugh at those bureaucrats who blindly follow an obviously absurd procedure because that's what's laid down. All of us must have had our own areas of blindness when we have unthinkingly followed the rules of some organisation or other, because that was the easy option. If we have worked in a hierarchy, we must have been guilty, if only in a minor way, of indulging in inter-departmental squabbling. Living in the twentieth century, we all have plenty of experience in the faults of bureaucracy.

So why do hierarchies continue? I believe the reasons are, first, the love of power and, second, the fear of change. Even if a hierarchy is no longer, on balance, the best way to get something done, it remains a very good way of giving power to those at the top. The people at the top will usually have got there because they love hierarchical power and know how to acquire and retain it. So it will be a hard job to get them to give up the kind of power they know and love. Power corrupts, often unconsciously, and the corruption results in the stifling of creativity and commitment.

Hierarchies continue to work, however imperfectly, and if what might replace them is unfamiliar and unproven, resistance to change must be expected, and not only from the top but throughout a hierarchical organisation. In good times, when experiments with new ways of doing things might be less risky, the pressure for change will be weak. In bad times, even though the need to do things differently may be very clear, the temptation will be to stick to well-known ways and to try to make them work better. The loss of the familiar is threatening, which turns the hierarchy into a child's security blanket, into something which gives the illusion of protection in a difficult world.

If hierarchies are security blankets and if, to change the metaphor, they are also blankets which stifle people's initiative, then we should seek ways of giving up these blankets. Because hierarchies have been so successful in the past and are still successful in some present-day circumstances, and because of the forces of power and fear which support them, it will not be at all easy to give them up. The men and women at the top will often fight to keep them. So we need continuing analysis of their defects. We need imagination and the courage to experiment in the development of alternatives. We have to search for power and security of new kinds, to replace those we lose when hierarchies vanish.

Signs of Change in Business

In the sphere of business, during the last twenty five years, it has become clearer and clearer that the heyday of the hierarchy has past, that the balance of advantage has turned against this kind of organisation, at least in its pure form, and that modified or novel kinds of organisation are wanted. For many, hierarchy stays in the memory, washed clean of its faults, as what *ought* to be, especially in the memory of those in positions of power. Their hope remains that by improving the hierarchical machine it will regain the balance of advantage, or perhaps that circumstances will shift and that the good old days (now seen through a golden haze) will return. But the signs of change are pretty clear all the same. Probably there will be no going back.

In the 1960s, it was the development of inter-personal process skills which led the move away from machine-like hierarchical organisations. Ralph Coverdale, founder of the Coverdale Organisation, was one of the pioneers. Through his insights, individuals found they could increase their capability in working with others. They did this by discovering how to listen properly, how to tackle cooperative tasks in a systematic way and how to learn both from successes and from difficulties. Coverdale training gave individuals the confidence to define their aims and to communicate these aims to others. By being clear about the purposes of cooperation, it became easier to achieve 'cooperation to mutual benefit'. The next step was to build teams in which everyone had got to a good level in these kinds of skills, and then to develop cooperation between teams, again to their mutual benefit. Many others joined Coverdale in teaching inter-personal process skills.

Greater understanding of inter-personal process, and higher levels of skill in this area among individuals and teams, made a machine-like organisation easier to operate. In the 1970s, 'organisation development' became the focus, with the intent to change not only the way people behaved within organisation structures, but also the structures themselves. One of the ways in which the rigidity of hierarchies might be softened was by concentrating on the ability of organisations to learn and to adapt. 'Planning to learn' was helpful for, and was helped by, 'learning to plan'. This directed attention towards creating a desirable future and away from the rules of the organisation which had been established in the past. In a 'learning organisation' the actual learning is done by individuals, however much each person's learning is influenced by the learning of others. This means that organisational learning will be greatest when every individual has responsibility and therefore the incentive to learn. Learning and empowerment go hand in hand.

Both personal skill development and organisation development started from within the organisation. Another approach was to look at whole societies and at the part which organisations play in them. During the period I am discussing, the world's major political contest was between socialism and capitalism, which naturally led to a comparison between hierarchical mechanisms and market mechanisms as means for coordinating, or integrating, the activities of society. Hierarchies and markets could be compared not only at the global and national scales, but also within corporations, which as well as the traditional mechanism of the hierarchy, were increasingly using internal market mechanisms, such as arms-length trading between profit-centres and competition for funds for capital investment between divisions of the corporation.

William Ouchi suggested that, as well as markets and hierarchies, there was a less mechanical method of integration, which he called the clan. His clans were small, cohesive work-groups which recruited members holding similar values to those of people already in the group. Clans needed stability of membership for trust to develop between their members. There was little division of labour within a clan. People did not specialise much and everyone was supposed to be able to do the work of everyone else at a reasonable level of competence. Ouchi identified what he called Type Z organisations, whose internal structures were clan-like and which fostered collaboration between and within work-groups. The trust built-up between people in Type Z organisations reduced the time, effort and cost of working together, which enabled clans to compete economically with markets and hierarchies as a means of achieving of social and economic coordination.

In parallel with these ideas about individual, organisational and societal development, new ways of thinking about the world were being discovered. One of these was 'the systems approach', which took abstract models and sets of concepts, together with methodologies which organise their use, and applied them complex problems such as arms proliferation, schooling in urban ghettos and city-centre traffic jams. The systems approach was thus an attempt to answer in a practical way the question "How can we design improvement in large systems without understanding the whole system?" The answers were not always successful, but several decades of careful work have produced some rigorous thinking. It is now possible for individuals to learn to increase their capacity to think in systems terms. There are also several well tried methods to use in tackling complicated problems. In many of these, there is an emphasis on 'learning to learn' and on the creative use of metaphor in making sense of complexity and in finding new ways of looking at a situation.

In the 1980s, there were even more ideas for change around. These included changes in the nature of work, blurring the distinction between employees and others, and between full-timers and part-timers, and spreading the use of sabbaticals and job-sharing. They included the 'hollowing out' of the corporation, by sub-contracting everything for which the corporation lacks distinctive competence. They included 'flat' organisations, with fewer layers in their hierarchies, and 'federal' organisations, which practice the dispersion of power. The study of corporate culture became the rage, concentrating on symbolic events, on value systems, on leaders who walk about and who listen to the views of people at any level in the hierarchy and on inter-firm and international comparisons of cultures. Metaphor was used in an organised way for understanding organisations: organisations were viewed as living organisms, as political systems, as systems of oppression, as well as mechanisms, the early metaphor used to describe hierarchies and to design them. Latterly, the empowerment of all those working in an organisation has become an influential idea.

The Flux of Ideas

The flux of ideas which I have just outlined was concentrated in the Anglo-Saxon countries. Possibly the strongest sign of change in these countries is their growing realisation that the rest of the world has better practices to offer. The Japanese model is the most widely studied, admired, feared and copied. Ideas like 'quality circles' and 'total quality management' have been directly influenced by Japanese practice. If we can overcome the tendency to make out that Japan has too different a national culture for the West to be able to learn from it, there will be many further lessons to be drawn. Countries with a Chinese ethnic tradition and continental European ones, like Germany, Sweden and Switzerland, also have plenty to teach English-speaking countries.

Some of the signs of change suggest that, instead of tinkering with the hierarchical form of organisation, we should scrap it and find a better form. Other signs suggest that the hierarchy can be modified enough for it to recapture its former advantage. For instance, the Japanese example says that hierarchies do work. In Japan, the size and position of people's offices, the way in which they bow while greeting someone, the titles on their name cards and where they sit during a meeting, all show that hierarchy is carefully nurtured. One of the early preoccupations of a junior executive is to learn all this behaviour and I must confess that, as a foreigner visiting Japanese companies, I enjoyed trying to learn a very small part of it.

If Japanese businesses can have such a strong attachment to hierarchy and be so successful, surely there must be a lot of life left in the hierarchical form? Well, yes, but it is a quite different form from hierarchies in the West. Japan is a society where mutual obligation is most important and the respect, to us exaggerated, shown to senior people because of their position, creates an obligation for the seniors to return that respect and to give help and support to junior people in doing their jobs. Couple that with a system for widespread consultation before key decisions are taken, plus a more subtle attitude towards differences between individuals and there is a lot of empowerment evident in the Japanese corporation.

The concepts of the learning organisation, of the organisation aware of and proud of its own distinctive culture, and of the flat hierarchy, help to modify the hierarchical form so that it can continue to compete. The use of market mechanisms, for instance for hollowing out a large organisation by contracting-out all but its key activities, reduces the hierarchy to its bare essentials, allowing these essentials to receive the dedicated management attention which, it is hoped, will make them function properly. Ouchi's Theory Z organisations also reduce hierarchy to its essentials, but by substituting clans, rather than markets, for many of the former hierarchical mechanisms. Russell Ackoff's design for a circular organisation, whose executive officers are responsible to a Board of Directors composed of representatives of its major stakeholders (including employees) is an example of change through corporate governance. Continental Europe supplies further examples of different modes of hierarchical governance. Charles Handy's federal organisations have "a variety of individual groups allied together under a common flag....combining autonomy with cooperation."

Although it is useful to distinguish between moves which start with the aim of reforming the hierarchical organisation and moves which aim to replace it with a novel form, the end results may converge. If the wishes of those at the top are no longer paramount, if market-like and clan-like areas of activity are spread throughout a formally hierarchical organisation and if empowerment applies to all who work in it, then the result will hardly be recognisable as an old-style hierarchy. And novel organisational forms will certainly have to work alongside the old ones, resulting in societies which combine markets, hierarchies, clans and other means of integration in varying proportions. However, the signs of change are strong and it is entirely reasonable to expect that businesses will look very different one or two decades from now.

A hundred years ago business followed the example of the state when starting to use hierarchies on a grand scale to achieve its ends. Today the position is reversed. Government agencies are learning from business in all kinds of ways: in marketing, in financial management, in the use of human resources and in total quality management. The hollowing out, through sub-contracting and privatisation, of government organisations is growing rapidly, sometimes too rapidly to achieve the best results. Some of the transfer of business experience is difficult to reconcile with the kind of accountability which is rightly necessary for the spending of public money, but no doubt adaptations will sooner or later be made. Even empowerment and openness, which do not fit with civil service traditions in Britain, are now being talked about in this country.

In armies, which used to epitomise hierarchy, there are moves towards flexibility. The Israeli Defence Force is a good example. The level of general education and the comprehensive military training of its members, at all levels, provides the basis. Add to this very high motivation and a tradition of independent action, and the result is a force whose units, small and medium-sized, already have a good idea of what to do in war, before they get their orders. In deciding on strategy, the top commanders know that their overall intent will be very well understood further down, and that there will be resourceful pursuit of that intent rather than slavish attention to every detail in the orders from on high. The results have been amazing. Just before the 1973 Yom Kippur war, the Israeli chief of staff, David Elazar, remarked about the northern front with Syria, "We'll have one hundred tanks against eight hundred – that's enough." This turned out to be a piece of overconfidence, but in that war Israeli forces did defeat a numerically much larger armies.

Biotechnology

How big an advantage an open and empowered business organisation will have depends in part on the nature of the industry in which
it operates. As I'm drawing so much on my experience at Celltech to
illustrate the thesis of this book, it may be helpful to describe the
industry in which Celltech operated – which is biotechnology.

One definition of biotechnology is the use of biological science in
industry. By that definition, it has been around for a long time –
certainly since the middle of the nineteenth century when Louis
Pasteur discovered microorganisms, a discovery which arose from
Pasteur's work for the fermentation industry. Today, 'biotechnology' is often used to refer to the advanced techniques which were
discovered in the early 1970s, particularly recombinant-DNA
techniques, used to modify genes and move them around, and cell
fusion techniques, such as those used to make monoclonal
antibodies.

The rapid expansion in biological knowledge which has taken
place during the past twenty years is largely based on the techniques
of biotechnology. This has, in turn, led to many important new
therapies, to valuable diagnostic tools and to the transformation of
pharmaceutical research, with a much more rational approach than
before. The potential for further advances is in no way exhausted.
Research is likely to transform the treatment of inherited disorders
(like cystic fibrosis), of cancer, of viral diseases (like AIDS), of
cardiovascular disease and, in due course, of mental illness.
Improved diagnostic methods will help to forecast individual
susceptibility to many diseases and to choose the best individual
treatments.

Advances in understanding of the biology of crop plants, and the
ability to improve these plants through biotechnology, are having
major effects on world agriculture. These advances will influence
industries supplying agriculture, such as the seeds business, and
industries supplied by agriculture, such as food and drink. Animal
health and animal breeding are benefiting too.

Here are some of the ways in which the nature of the biotechnology industry influenced the organisation of the firms within it:

• To start with, the new techniques of recombinant-DNA and cell
  fusion were available only in a limited number of laboratories.
  This gave a wonderful opportunity for scientists from these labs

to collaborate with business people in starting new firms. A new industry sprang up and everyone in it had to be a pioneer, since there were no established rules to follow. Firms which knew how to learn had an advantage.

- Key scientists were often young. They knew the value of their skills and weren't going to work for a hierarchical organisation, in which the older people at the top, who lacked these skills, were not prepared to listen to the recently recruited people who did have them.

- The pace of advance in biomedical science became very rapid and it was hard to predict which laboratories would come up with the key discoveries. Companies could gain a real advantage by being the first to spot important new discoveries and then persuading the discoverers to cooperate with them.

- Advanced biotechnology had a large impact on the way existing industry organised itself, particularly on research and development in the pharmaceutical industry. The new techniques were discovered in universities and research institutes, not in the pharmaceutical companies, and many of these companies found it difficult to bring the techniques in-house. The response of nearly every company was to build-up in-house expertise gradually, and to add to it a great range of external collaborations with universities and with specialist companies, the latter often formed as spin-outs from academic research. With the arrival of each new wave of discovery – in protein-based drugs, in drug targeting, in gene therapy and in neuroscience – new specialist companies have been founded, because the environment of a new company has proved to be best for putting the new science into practical use.

Celltech was one of the earlier companies in the field, and it remains an independent company, with long-running collaborations with several major pharmaceutical firms. Other specialist companies have been acquired by one of the pharmaceutical majors. Life is hazardous for a biotech start-up company. Many millions of dollars have to be raised from investors on the basis, not of current profits because there are none, but through the promise of important drugs to come. University scientists have to be attracted as collaborators or to work in the company, there is a race to file patents ahead of competitors, good working relationships have to be established with pharmaceutical majors. Sometimes things go wrong, but over half of the start-ups of the past fifteen years have succeeded, by one means or another, in giving their investors a good return.

Specialist biotech companies have been able to do things which large firms could not. This is, in large part, because the new firms were not smothered by the blankets of hierarchy. Ten years experience as CEO of Celltech taught me how effective a non-hierarchical organisation can be. The biotechnology business provides some useful examples in this book.

What We Can Do

Hierarchy is being modified or replaced, but it remains a very potent feature in business and in other spheres. Anyone working in, or with, an organisation would be foolish to ignore hierarchy. But if empowerment is the wave of the future, we ought not to be lying on the beach, waiting for it to sweep us into the sea. Empowered people should start swimming on their own. In this last section I will make some suggestions about good places to swim.

If you are in a junior position in a hierarchy there will probably be little you can do about changing the hierarchy as a whole. You may also feel that even locally you are pretty tightly constrained. But the signs of change in the world are now so strong that most organisations will surely have some people in the middle ranks who are trying to do without the security blanket of bureaucratic hierarchy and trying to empower others. These people may not be in your department and may not be your direct superiors, but that does not matter. Go ahead and ask someone to give you authority to use your initiative, over a small matter to start with. Then use the authority sensibly, avoiding the temptation to boast about the freedom you've been given or to exaggerate your achievement. If someone tries to slap you down, defend yourself by saying, quite quietly and matter-of-factly, that you have been given authority and that in any case your actions were for the good of the organisation as a whole, which should take precedence over departmental interests. These are not sure-fire recommendations but in nearly every organisation they should work most of the time. Finally, I suggest that you should give support and recognition to anyone who is working to empower others. This person may be senior and much more experienced than you, but he or she is probably feeling the loss of that security blanket, is probably taking quite a risk by going against the prevailing culture and may be unsure about the success of what they are trying to do. So back them up as much as you can.

If you are in the middle ranks of a hierarchical organisation, you can follow the advice I have given for junior people: as far as your relations with more senior people are concerned, draw authority from them and give them your support in return. In your own area of responsibility you can act directly and boldly to empower, to inform, to coach, to train and to help in the longer term development of everyone reporting to you in the hierarchy. You can do the same, but perhaps a bit more cautiously, for your peers and for others outside your direct responsibility. You can help to articulate the idea of empowerment and the reasoning behind the need to throw away the blankets of hierarchy. And then you can spread these ideas throughout the organisation.

If you are at the top, don't think you can abolish the old habits of hierarchy by giving an order to that effect, although naturally your advocacy of the principle of empowerment will be very influential. You must practice empowerment, you must be free with information, you must coach, train, advise, develop and support. You must get out of your office and walk about. While you are doing so you must spend a lot of time in telling stories about the organisation – what is happening in various places, how plans are working out, what was the rationale for a particular decision, where you personally have made mistakes and how you have learned from them. Listening to people is equally important, really listening and responding in such a way that you can test whether you have understood their messages. You may not agree with these messages, and if you don't you should say so clearly and politely and explain why. But you must do all you can to understand the messages sent to you and to show the senders that you have understood them.

Above all, if you are at the top, don't panic when times get difficult, when you might long for the blankets of bureaucracy. Instead, ask for help in getting you and your organisation through a hard patch. In doing this you will be taking a risk. There may be people around who will interpret your call for help as a ruse or as a sign of weakness. You will need time and effort to convince them otherwise. There may be people who will suggest that if you need this help, you are not up to your job. If this happens, I think you should show that you know what is going on but that you are going to ignore these ignorant insinuations. The ability to ask for help shows strength and competence, not weakness or lack of grasp. In any case, when times are turbulent, the blankets of hierarchy, however comforting, probably won't save you. It will be safer to rely on the forces of empowerment to renew your organisation.

Finally, there is something that everyone, junior and senior, experienced and novice, can do all the time. That is to note successful practices, to analyse why they are successful, to talk about them, to spread success in empowerment throughout the organisation.

Notes

Power, pages 20-21. Oliga, drawing on Giddens' work, writes that power, while not inherently noxious, oppressive and exploitative can be noxiously exercised and on the other hand, while it can be positive and enabling, it is not inherently positive. See John C.Oliga, Power in Organizations: A Contingent, Relational View. *Systems Practice*, **3**, 5, (1990) and Anthony Giddens, *The Constitution of Society*. Polity Press, Cambridge. (1984). Clegg thinks that power, rather than efficiency, was the driving force behind the growth of the hierarchical, or bureaucratic, organisation. See Stewart R. Clegg. *Modern Organizations: Organization Studies in the Postmodern World.* Sage, London (1990), especially Chapter 3, entitled 'Why and Where did Bureaucracy Triumph?'

Hierarchy, pages 22-24. For some of his work on bureaucracy, see Max Weber, *The Protestant Ethic and the Spirit of Capitalism.* Translated by T. Parsons and with an introduction by A. Giddens, Allen and Unwin, London (1976). Clegg (*op cit* Chapter 2) gives a good survey of the rise of rationalised organisations. For the history of American corporate hierarchies see Alfred D. Chandler, Jr. *The Visible Hand: the Managerial Revolution in America,* Harvard U.P., Cambridge (1977).

Giving up the Blankets, pages 24-26. For the defects of hierarchies see Gareth Morgan, *Images of Organization,* Sage, Newbury Park (1986) Chapter 2 'Mechanization Takes Command: Organizations as Machines'.

Signs of Change in Business, pages 26-29. The Coverdale Organisation plc can be contacted at Dorland House, 14-16 Regent Street,

London SW1Y 4PH. A pioneer in the field of organisation development was Rensis Likert (*The Human Organisation: Its Management and Value*, McGraw-Hill, New York (1967).

On organisational learning see Donald N. Michael. *On Learning to Plan – and Planning to Learn: The Social Psychology of Changing Toward Future-Responsive Societal Learning*, Jossey-Bass, San Francisco, (1973) and Mark Dodgson, *The Management of Technological Learning: Lessons from a Biotechnology Company*, De Gruyter, Berlin (1990).

The study of markets and hierarchies from the point of view of transaction-cost economics was originated by Williamson. See Oliver E. Williamson, *Markets and Hierarchies*, Free Press, New York. (1975) and Oliver E. Williamson and William G. Ouchi. 'The Markets and Hierarchies program of Research: Origins, Implications, Prospects' in Andrew H. Van de Ven and William F. Joyce (eds.) *Perspectives on Organisation Design and Behavior*, pp 347-370. Wiley, New York (1981). Ouchi added clans to make a trio of coordination methods. See William G. Ouchi and Raymond L. Price. Hierarchies, Clans and Theory Z: A New Perspective on Organizational Development, *Organisation Dynamics*, Autumn 1978 and William G. Ouchi, *Theory Z: How American Business Can Meet the Japanese Challenge*, Addison-Wesley, Reading, MA (1981).

West Churchman and Peter Checkland were influential exponents of systems thinking. See *The Systems Approach*, Dell, New York (1968) and Peter Checkland, *Systems Thinking, Systems Practice*, Wiley, Chichester (1981). A recent book with a good presentation of systems thinking is Peter Senge's *The Fifth Discipline*, Doubleday, New York (1990).

On flat and on federal organisations see Charles Handy, *The Age of Unreason*. Century, London (1989). On corporate culture see Charles Hampden-Turner, *Corporate Culture: From Vicious to Virtuous Circles*, Economist Books, London (1990). On the use of metaphor in organisational analysis see Morgan *op cit*.

The Flux of Ideas, pages 29-31. For Ouchi's and Handy's novel organisation forms see their works cited above. Russell Ackoff's circular organisation is described in his article 'The Systems Revolution' in *Long Range Planning*, December 1974 pp 2-20. My information about the Israeli Defence Force comes from Eliot A. Cohen and

John Gooch *Military Misfortunes: The Anatomy of Failure in War,* The
Free Press, New York (1990). For a particularly insightful analysis of
the parallels between empowerment in military organisations and that
in industry, see Roberto M. Unger, *Plasticity into Power: Comparative-
Historical Studies on the Conditions of Economic and Military Success,*
Cambridge U.P., Cambridge (1987) Chapter 3.

3

The Size of the Clan

In my dictionary, one of the definitions of 'clan' is: "a family holding together, whence clannish". This gets close to the sense in which I want to use the word, with its suggestion of close cooperation, mutual support and special mutual understanding. Charles Hampden-Turner pictures clans as:

> "....groups of enthusiasts united around the potentials of a technology, product and /or service. The clan is resilient, with deep, lasting relationships, which are capable of transmitting complex information in many forms. Yet this culture is also fluid, kaleidoscopic, flexible and fast. (Note that it is not "clannish" in the sense of deliberately excluding others.)"

In this book, I will describe groups, organisations, modes of communication and methods of coordinating tasks as *clan-like* if they depend on shared enthusiasms, lasting relationships and subtle communications. As Hampden-Turner puts it, organisations with these features have a 'clan-culture'.

Clan-like interactions need not be only within an organisation. A network of people with a shared enthusiasm for a particular kind of computer software, or for the growing of prize vegetables, can develop clan-like interactions. So too can an extended family, even if they generally meet only for the weddings and funerals of family members. In this chapter I want to explore how clan-like interactions differ, depending on the size of the clan and on the frequency of interaction between its members.

Frequency of Interaction

There is a limit to the number of people any of us can count as friends. Think of your address book or your Christmas card list – neither can go on expanding indefinitely. You make some new friends and lose touch with some old ones, but the total number probably remains roughly the same, unless there is a big shift in your way of life. The size of the group no doubt depends on your talent for friendship and your desire for sociability, but even for the friendliest and most sociable, there must be a limit somewhere. If you have lived in the same village for a long time, you will probably know everyone else in that small community pretty well. A particular fellow villager may be a friend, but you will know just as much about some other villagers who are not really your friends. If you live in a city, you won't know people in quite this way. The place is too large for there to be a natural group of familiar acquaintances like that of the village. You may not even get to know the name of a person living in the next house. But, whether in the smallness of the village or in the largeness of the city, there is always a limit on the size of the group of people you can know well.

The same goes for the people you know at work. Openness and trust need a virtuous circle if they are to develop fully and no circle will be effective if it is too dispersed. If the circle is closed only occasionally and if it takes a long time to turn, the mutual reinforcement of trust and openness will not happen. The memory of past openness may die away, trust may not get the renewal it needs. You cannot have more than a certain number of close associates, because closeness implies frequency and depth of contact and this needs time. There are only so many hours in the day, which puts a limit on the number of people you can keep close to. Openness doesn't mean being open on one occasion and then hoping that will suffice for ever. Novel situations and new tasks demand renewed openness. When meeting friends or close colleagues who you haven't seen for a bit, you spend time in catching up with their news, in chatting about what has happened in the world since you last met. This kind of exchange has an important social function: it sustains openness and rekindles trust. Without it you lose touch, you forget other people's special characteristics, former friends and colleagues become strangers. But you can't keep up with the whole world. Open relationships can be maintained only with a certain number of people.

Doing business in Japan requires a lot of polite exchange. There, business depends on mutual obligation and mutual trust, which develop through conversation as well as through action. To Westerners, the time spent on politenesses may seem to be a waste of time. But Japanese business avoids Western over-reliance on formalisation of relationships, on legal documents and litigation – this is highly cost-effective. Nevertheless, this desirable way of doing business takes time, in Japan or anywhere else. Time must be available to maintain an open style and to build mutual trust. This places a inevitable limit on the number of close business contacts you can keep up.

Energy and skill can expand this limit. A good sales representative can build close relationships with a larger number of clients than someone less skilled or less experienced than he is. The abilities of an effective consultant allow her to keep up-to-date with the business of many client firms and enable her to give them the help they want. A virtuous circle of openness and trust can be started more quickly and reliably by people skilled in interpersonal process. The skilled can participate in a larger number of virtuous circles than the less skilled. A school or a hospital whose teachers or nurses are blessed with communicative competence will have a wider, as well as a deeper, set of interactions with its students or its patients. But the logic of time will eventually restrict the number of virtuous circles in even the most competently communicating organisation.

People are complex. So are many of the problems we are faced with in our lives. Because of this complexity, it will take time for any pair of people to understand each other reasonably fully, regardless of the level of openness between them. Wide-ranging mutual understanding is the basis for a robust cooperation and a steady trust. This comes through seeing someone in a series of different situations, in varying moods, in the best and in the worst of times. That, in turn, needs a good many hours of close association. And as our hours are limited, so too are the number of close associations we can maintain, at work or anywhere else.

While there can be clan-like interactions between people in a wide variety of situations, the points I have just made suggest that these interactions develop a special quality when they take place within a small and stable group. In order to learn more about the characteristics of such special tight-knit groups, I now want to look at communication of two kinds – codified and uncodified communication – and at the shared languages, worldviews and practices which arise within these groups.

Codified Communication

Imagine yourself at a large international airport, waiting for your flight to be called. You listen to the announcements, in two or three languages, of departures to places around the world. These are deliberately unemotional and impersonal. This is partly because emotion might add to the fear which some people have about flying, or to the anxiety of those unfamiliar with that airport, or to the frustration of travellers whose flights are late. It is partly because the announcements have to be heard through the noise and distractions of a very busy place, so keeping them simple and in a standard format will help. The announcements are so standard that they are often prerecorded.

Airport announcements are *codified* communications. They are supposed to give precise information to many different people, who may have little in common except the need to know where to board a particular plane. Irrelevant information is pared away from a codified communication, it should be as sparse as possible, overtones are suppressed, clarity and relevance are everything. Codified information need not be audible; there are signs around an airport which give information in a single word like TAXIS, or solely through a symbol.

Now imagine a couple who have been together for many years. They can guess each other's thoughts on a great range of things. A raised eyebrow can suggest ideas which might need half an hour of talk to make explicit to someone without their shared background of life together. Their communication can use references to past events, or to novels or films which they both know well. A grunt or a twitch can change instantly the moods of both.

Between this long-wedded couple communication is mainly *uncodified*. It does not have to be lengthy or verbose, but it is not deliberately simplified, nor is it unemotional. It does not follow publicly accepted forms, rather it is complex, often subtle, sometimes ambiguous, sometimes deliberately misleading to outsiders. It can vary, a similar message being given in different ways at different times. Uncodified communication is rich, not bare; personal, not standardised; elliptical, not direct. Psychological studies have shown that, within a close-knit group, up to eighty percent of information exchange is by non-verbal means – signs, tone of voice,

body language and so on. Non-verbal communication is mostly
uncodified.

I am not saying that the codified/uncodified distinction is clear-
cut. Most human communication uses a blend of codified and
uncodified information, but the make up of the blend varies from
time to time, from group to group, from situation to situation. The
distinction between the pure forms is an abstraction, but one we can
use in everyday life, and use in the kind of argument I am putting
forward at the moment.

Information is essential to economic activity but is often taken for
granted. Thus the economist's model of perfect competition
assumes that economic actors are always sufficiently well informed
to make the right choices. No doubt there are cases like street
markets where this is a reasonable approximation; in Adam Smith's
time they would have been the norm. Economic folklore has some
celebrated examples of the value of information, such as the
exclusive early knowledge which the house of Rothschild had about
the outcome of the battle of Waterloo, but these are often forgotten
when it comes to the construction of theories. The reality is that in
economic activity, as in most human activity, information is always
problematic and that acquiring it in a reliable and usable form is vital
and takes up a great amount of time.

The codified/uncodified distinction can be applied to flows of
economic information. A street market relies largely on codified
information; apples are twenty-five pence a pound on one stall,
thirty pence a pound on another. Thirty pence per pound means
very much the same on one stall as it does on another stall and it
means the same from one day to the next, at least if inflation is not
horrendously high. This single measurement says nothing about
quality, but there is no doubt about its simplicity and clarity. Of
course, things get lost in the process of codification. Codified
information lacks perceptual texture and richness and there is no
place for what Michael Polanyi calls 'tacit knowledge'. Codification
is a social rather than an individual process, because the whole point
is that pence per pound means the same to everybody. Obviously
codification is a matter of degree; information about a particular
situation can be more codified or less codified depending on the
purposes or the habits of those involved. I want to suggest that
communication using codified information is quite different from

communication using uncodified information and that economic institutions organise themselves to take account of this.

The huge volume of information about currency exchange rates which now sweeps around the world at all hours of the day is a much larger example of codified information than the street market. The news of a fall in the value of the US dollar in terms of the Japanese yen is received virtually simultaneously in Tokyo, New York and a dozen other financial centres. Having this financial information allows currency traders to work out at once whether a change of this kind is due to a fall in the dollar against all other currencies, to a rise in the yen or to a more complicated set of adjustments in currency cross-rates. The change can instantly be seen in the context of a continuing series of information about currency rates codified in just the same way. And traders know that all other traders everywhere else have almost the same information as they do. The codified information is precise, its implications are clear to those familiar with its areas of use and its diffusion is extremely rapid.

Uncodified Communication

But of course not all economic information is codified. In a street market regular shoppers will get to know which stallholders sometimes have their thumbs on the scale and which might put a bad apple in the bottom of the bag, which are responsive to a smile and which enjoy haggling for its own sake. Codified information, like the price per pound, is obviously still important for these shoppers and is blended with all kinds of uncodified information when they decide what to buy. Market traders have the same sort of blend of information as the shoppers; for example they can guess that a low price on a competitor's stall is nothing to be worried about, because that particular stallholder always has a small stock and likes to finish early on cold days.

Once we leave the fairly simple world of street trading the significance of uncodified information grows larger. Take the example of an airline deciding what type of aircraft to buy for an expansion of its fleet. Which of the many (codified) indices of performance are relevant to the particular routes the airline flies, or rather is likely to be flying in the future, since there is often a few years delay between the purchasing decision and the delivery of the planes? How consistent are the various suppliers of aircraft in their reliability and service? What will the passengers of the future like or dislike about the different types of plane on offer and do these preferences matter enough to them to cause them to travel with one airline rather than with another? Although codified information, such as the amount of fuel the aircraft uses per mile, is of course very important, making a good decision needs a huge amount of uncodified information, all of it weighted and compared, considered for its relevance and its accuracy, clarified and deepened by discussion.

Working at Shell taught me that communication can work on the large scale, even using uncodified information. But on the scale of a small firm the use of uncodified information is much more pervasive and complete. To understand how people feel about a proposed change, to influence their shared understanding of a business situation, or to develop mutual trust, requires the exchange of uncodified information. It is far easier to exchange this face-to-face, between a small group in a single room, than through the complex systems of a large organisation.

As I have said, both kinds of communication, codified and uncodified, have their place in the modern world, but to increase the opportunity to use the uncodified kind provides a very valuable resource for problem-solving, for innovation and for empowerment. A small scale is needed to gain the full advantage of this resource. Uncodified information evolves through use in a particular situation. I hope I have been able to describe for the reader the general idea of uncodified information. But we can only learn its special value for communication in actual cases, because uncodified information, tends by its nature to be specific to the situation in which it develops. Someone's involvement in a situation, with what can be called a particular sub-culture, does not happen overnight. It needs continuing interaction with the members of the sub-culture. Indeed, you can only use uncodified communication to the full by becoming a member of the relevant sub-culture.

Shared Worldviews and Languages

One person's life can span several sub-cultures. Let us imagine Catherine Grey kissing her mother goodbye on a Friday morning and getting into her father's car. He is dropping her at the station on his way to his work as Director of Quality Assurance in an aircraft components company. Catherine does not know whether her father's job is a sinecure which he retains because everyone likes him or whether he is really is playing a vital role in keeping his firm at the cutting edge of aviation technology. They pass through the village of Barton All Saints, which was in Domesday book, as its mainly retired residents love to tell you. At the station her father gets his goodbye kiss, she buys the *Independent*, says hello to one or two other commuters and smiles at a couple more. On the train she reads about famine in the Sudan and about a smallish earthquake in California. Then she scans the financial pages to see whether any of the people she takes calls from are being investigated by the Serious Frauds Office.

Waterloo station is crowded and bad-tempered but in the City the sun is shining, so she doesn't mind being met at the office with "Oh Cat, thank God you're here. I want calls to Frankfurt and Geneva right away". Her boss is described in the City as number two in corporate finance at Schneiders, which is a merchant bank with a more cautious tone than some. Cat is his personal assistant. She likes the well paid job and as she is attractive, cheerful, sensible and willing to work long hours in a crisis, the bank likes her. She has a patchy knowledge of banking. She can spot when a shift in a market is important enough for her to interrupt a meeting to give her boss the news, but she doesn't yet understand why some things the bank does are regarded as risky while others of much the same kind are sound. She quite enjoys a crisis.

It is quiet that afternoon at Schneiders so Catherine is glad to hear Tom's voice on the 'phone. "Katy love, I'm back from Houston". Tom was her boy friend when they were students together and she finds it convenient to go on calling him that. Her degree in botany and most of the rest of her life at university seem to her to be pretty unrelated to what she is doing now. Tom is the only steady link, the only person who still calls her Katy. But as he works on Teesside, and visits London when films by Godard or Rivette are showing, this link is weakening too.

That evening Tom is not coming to London and Catherine is not going to the cinema. Instead she and someone she has just met will be at the Salsa Verde club in Bethnal Green. She finds the music they play there compulsively alluring. And Monica is unconventionally beautiful. When Catherine is at the club the sound and the scene enclose her. Until the next morning, they wipe from her mind her mother and father, Barton All Saints, Schneiders, movements in the FTSE index, earthquakes in California and Tom's 'phone calls. Most of the time, Catherine Grey moves easily through the different pools in her life's river, carried by currents of affection, habit, money, status, sex and aesthetic pleasure. But tonight the Salsa seems the only pool to swim in.

In late-modern societies, differentiated lives like Catherine's are quite usual. We take for granted that very different worldviews and languages may apply in each of the separate sectors of a life like hers. We tend to forget that if someone has, by the age of twenty five, already been a part of six or seven distinct sub-cultures, she (or he) will not be fully familiar with any of them. She will have learnt to use parts of the special language which each sub-culture has. She will have some of the common experiences which allow participants in the group to communicate rapidly with each other, making subtle distinctions clear in a flash. She will feel the power of some of the symbols which bind the group together. She will share some of the mental models which members of the sub-culture use to make sense of the world around them. But the sharing will only be partial. The language, the experiences, the symbols, the mental models, will not be fully hers.

If most of a group members have only been there for a year or two, if most of them are also members of several other groups, and if the group is not particularly tight-knit, then the depth of shared experience will be limited and the potential advantages of a common worldview and a common language will be mainly lost. Unless the individuals who make up the group have an extraordinarily high level of competence in inter-personal communication, the group will not be able to move quickly in coping with novel tasks or in solving unfamiliar problems. They will not be able to get their collective act together.

The standard Western response would be that lack of cohesion in a group doesn't really matter, providing there is a strong-minded individual there to tell the others what to do. Leadership will solve the problem of coordination. The leader has the vision; the others follow. Often this will work; things can indeed get done by this means. But the countries of the Far East are now showing us that relying on leadership is not the best way.

Cohesive work-groups can achieve far more. It is the depth of their shared experience, their development of a common language, their collaborative work in understanding the world, the richness of their collective worldviews which makes work-groups into sub-cultures and which underpins their achievements. Clan-like interaction, especially within a stable group of limited size, has a power absent in other methods of coordinating work.

Shared Practices

Let us suppose that Catherine Grey has a sister who is a doctor, a registrar in a cancer hospital. Susan Grey learnt about human illness and about what it is to be a doctor in an old-fashioned London teaching hospital. Both were learnt by observation; illness by observing patients, doctoring by observing doctors. Of course there are books and lectures, but example and experience were her real teachers. Once Susan could observe, decide and instruct in ways which satisfied her mentors, she herself became a doctor of medicine. By then she knew how to use the power which that title required and provided. The training for her speciality of oncology was no less rigorous. Dr. Grey watched and listened to consultants who had themselves had many years of watching and listening. She watched them looking at X-ray photographs and through micro-scopes and taught herself how to look in the same way. This was the start of her lifetime project of observation and decision and of her contribution to the slow advance in the field of medicine she had chosen. In the hospital her colleagues now rely on her diagnostic skill and appreciate her judgment in finding the right therapy for each particular patient, which comes from her deep thought about patients' real interests. She is trusted by patients because she tells them the truth and does not claim omniscience.

Susan's life is in many ways a narrower one than her sister Catherine's. Caring for her patients and trying to understand the disease she is treating make severe demands on her time and on her mental and physical powers. When she and Catherine meet they happily recall their childhood, mildly criticise their parents and chat about trivia. But if one life is narrow and the other shallow, both are conducted with good sense. It is still possible with a bit of effort to imagine their roles exchanged, to imagine Catherine with the clear purpose of a dedicated clinical oncologist and Susan as an assured and sensitive hedonist.

If asked which is the better person, most of us would choose the cancer specialist and as a reason for our choice we might say that she is more obviously serving her fellow beings than her sister. We could also point to the arduous training which Susan completed successfully and to the single-mindedness which she needs in her job. This is not to say that Catherine is without virtue. You might guess that her parents find Catherine's company a blessing and that although they are very proud of Susan they hardly ever see her. You can see that the comparison is not easy to make. My point in making it is to introduce the idea of a 'good' life.

Knowing what you should do in order to live a good life is the central problem of personal morality. Today it is a problem for which solutions are not easy to find.

But in ancient Greece it was not so difficult. Then, you could say a human being lived a good life and mean much the same as you would by saying that a harp-player played well. The relation between 'human' and 'living well' was the same as the relation between 'harpist' and 'playing well'. The Greeks thought they could tell a good farmer in the way we can tell a good watch. The good farmer gets a high yield of crops from the land; a good watch tells the time accurately. In these examples 'good' and 'well' are judgments about human beings and at least in the case of 'living well', the judgment is a moral one. The Greek view (actually Aristotle's view) of morals ties them to function and to the contribution which success in carrying out that function makes to society. But a 'good farmer' in Nepal will work differently from one in Nebraska, so these Greek moral judgments are valid only within a particular social framework and its tradition. In his book *After Virtue*, Alasdair MacIntyre develops Aristotle's view, proposing that moral virtue has meaning only in the context of a group of people with shared lives, work and tradition. In particular they must share a *practice*.

Practices are the established ways of doing things which groups of people come to adopt and to foster in order to pursue a common project or to achieve their common ends. "As modern examples of such a project we might consider the founding and carrying forward of a school, a hospital or an art gallery; in the ancient world the characteristic examples would have been those of a religious cult or of an expedition or of a city."

The qualities which people bring to a practice and which ensure the success of a project are the moral virtues. Practices must have a certain complexity; planting turnips is not a practice, farming is. So are chemistry, chess or party politics. Practices involve standards of excellence, obedience to rules and achievement of common purposes. To join in a practice requires that its rules and standards are learnt by the newcomer; practices are to that extent disciplines, like the discipline of medicine or of historical research. To enter into the discipline and tradition of a practice is to submit oneself to it, not totally, as in due course anyone engaged in a practice can begin to criticise it and thus to take part in the evolution of the tradition, but all the same wholeheartedly, so that the practice becomes part of one's life. To speak a language properly one must accept its conventions and its idioms even though by speaking it one can change these, usually infinitesimally but in rare cases noticeably as with great orators or poets. The result is that the practitioner can change the practice, as well as the more obvious effect of the practice changing the practitioner.

If you follow MacIntyre's proposal, it only makes sense to describe someone as living a good life, or a bad one, in the context of a living tradition or a continuing practice. Shared traditions and practices lead to shared standards of conduct and achievement. With these it is also possible to make sense of an individual life, to give a coherent account of one person's evolving capabilities, choices and activities and to evaluate this account by reference to the accounts of others' lives within the same tradition. This means that a good life is not the same for everybody; the lord of a medieval manor was good or bad in a very different way to a twentieth-century oncologist. On this view, right and wrong depends on the circumstances, but in well-defined circumstances there is no problem of knowing which is which. The extent to which it is possible to tell right from wrong depends on the strength of the tradition and the coherence of the practice within which the moral judgment is being made.

Compartments

There is an important common thread running through the varied aspects of organisational and social life which I have been discussing: many benefits are only to be had by limiting the number of our human associations. By keeping within a limit and by retaining continuity in our interactions, associations become deeper and more productive. Let us look again at the points I have made:

- Non-hierarchical, clan-like organisations depend on continuing and skillful communication between clan members. Clans need to be maintained in proper working order, by active effort. The skill needed to communicate well comes partly though this effort – it is partly learnt by practice.
- There is a limit, imposed by the time requirements for real openness, and by the number of hours there are in a day, on the number of people with whom anyone can develop a fully open and trusting relationship, even though this limit can be expanded by greater communicative competence.
- Uncodified communication can bring great benefits to people's mutual understanding – extending the depth and the breadth of mutual comprehension. But this, too, takes time to evolve and needs continuity of association.
- Shared languages and shared worldviews enable people to cooperate and to solve problems without hierarchical direction. The richness of these languages and worldviews depend on closeness and continuity in association. Too diverse a set of personal interactions will impoverish these shared resources.
- Standards of excellence arise within shared practices. This is so for a skilled craftsperson, an expert professional, a talented sportsman or woman, an artist, or someone trying to live a good life. Practices are on-going activities of some complexity, shared by a group of people who learn from one another, often over many years. Within a practice, it becomes possible to judge someone as a good or a bad practitioner.
- Empowerment is not an act of abdication, which dumps problems on someone else. It is an process of active support, requiring mutual understanding and continuing energy.
- Empowerment, clan-like coordination of tasks, fully open communication, extensive use of uncodified communication, shared languages and worldviews: all these need time and need continuity of association to grow to their full strength.

How can this be generally achieved? The central idea of this book provides the answer: compartmentation, or the building of organisations around compartments. What are compartments? Compartments are groups of people of a particular kind. They are groups small enough to allow interaction between group-members to be frequent. They are groups stable enough for this interaction to continue over a considerable time. Compartments have reasonably clear boundaries. These can be a physical boundaries, for instance when a compartment is a village surrounded by hills. Or they can be legal boundaries, for instance when the compartment's members are all the employees of a small firm.

Most importantly, all a compartment's members can readily tell who is a member and who is not. Boundary conditions do not necessarily exclude the odd borderline case. But if there is a lot of uncertainty about membership, there isn't a real compartment. I will be saying a lot more about compartments in the rest of this book. For the moment, let me summarise the idea in this way: *compartments are groups of people who stick together for a long time and who talk to each other a great deal.*

Compartments contain and concentrate virtuous circles, such as the circles of openness and trust and of empowerment and commitment. Within a compartment, interaction is continuous and strong, avoiding dilution and dispersion. The circles are kept closely together. Compartments are therefore a way of raising virtuous circles to new heights. This is why I believe that *compartments will be the key to organisation design in the 21st century.*

The Limits on Size

It is often remarked that groups, such as schools, villages and firms, where everybody knows each other, have a different 'feel' about them than bigger examples. This is especially so where, in addition, clan-like communication is the norm. Groups of a limited size and with clan-like interaction between their members are what I call compartments. How can we find the limits on size ?

The test seems to be whether each member can recognise all the others by name. If everyone had lifelong membership in a single compartment and met very few outsiders during the course of a year, then by this test the upper limit for size might be something under a thousand people. This might be the case in a remote mountain settlement. But if there is some movement in and out of a compartment and if there is quite a lot of interaction with people external to the compartment, then the upper limit would be less –

perhaps be two or three hundred people. We can check this with a simple calculation. To know someone as an individual requires that there is at least a minimum of face-to-face contact with him or her. The minimum might be a meeting of half an hour every three months or so. Most of us are unlikely to be able to have contact of this sort with more than ten people a day and therefore to meet more than 900 different people in a three month period. The upper limit for an isolated community of less than a thousand therefore seems reasonable.

Is there a lower limit on the size of a compartment? If cooperation brings the kind of benefits I have suggested then we should seek to have as much of it as we reasonably can. If coordination in a business or other organisation is to be achieved mainly by clan-like means, then the bigger the clans, the less the requirement for inter-clan coordination. And if the projects which an organisation is undertaking are complex, many of them will need a good deal of resource, which argues for as many people in a compartment as possible. The ideal compartment will therefore be as large as possible consistent with retaining excellent communication. Perhaps this means that normally we would not talk about a group of people smaller than a hundred or so as a compartment. We might sum this up by saying that the number of people in a compartment should be enough to provide variety and resource but not too many to dilute the frequency of their interaction, and that this number is likely to be a few hundreds.

I have said that the compartment has to have a clear boundary and a high level of interaction between its members. The architecture, geography and other physical aspects of the places where the members of a compartment live and work should define the compartment and should promote communication between the people in it. The attraction for us of villages which retain some of their medieval buildings and street patterns may be the sense that they are the places where human interaction is strong. Why did C. Northcote Parkinson remark that organisations which fit easily into their buildings are probably in decline? Perhaps because crowding gets people to meet and meeting leads to communication, to communication of a random and informal kind rather than the planned kind. The details of buildings are important too, with stairs and halls being the areas where informal contact most easily happens. Courtyards are better than long passageways and offices should be shared or of minimum size. The smaller the office and the shorter the walk to it the less the psychological distance to the people in it.

Research laboratories where the most creative work is done are often quite cramped and messy. Obviously messiness in the wrong places can be a safety hazard or a source of microbiological contamination or to be avoided for other reasons, but it doesn't matter if people's work-spaces are rather small or if a generally heterogeneous appearance is generated. When I have been involved in the design of laboratories I have usually concentrated on the flux of people during the working day. Where will people pass as they go to the fume cupboard, to the photocopier, to the coffee machine or to the lavatory? Will there be a mind-broadening environment, where the unexpected crops up, is noticed and is talked about? Will the surroundings be likely to make people smile at each other as they pass. Can the place be clinically clean in a literal sense, if that is what is necessary, without being cold and forbidding to people?

Conclusion

On a global scale, hierarchy seems to be losing badly, with the failure of communism being only the most dramatic manifestation of hierarchy's defeat. As a means for economic coordination, markets are faring better than hierarchies, but the Far East's combination of clan-coordination with market-coordination seems to be the most successful formula. Might there be lessons from this for the design of organisations? Could the future of the corporation, of the government agency, and of other large organisations lie in some combination of markets and clan-like coordination? It is surely worth looking closely at this combination. To do so, we need to explore how clans connect with markets, and with hierarchies. To make progress in this direction we can use the concept of the compartment, as outlined above. I believe that the idea of the compartment is vital in understanding how the clan can best interact with the other coordination mechanisms.

In this chapter I've tried to show why there are limits on the size of the clan. Beyond a certain size, human groups cannot have the close-knit character of the compartment. I have suggested that clan-coordination works in a special way when it is on the scale of

hundreds of people – not tens and not thousands. Compartmentation, which recognises this limit on size and emphasises the
distinction between internal and external communication, is the way
to foster close-knit human groups. A compartment should have a
definite boundary, within which open, intense, subtle and varied
communication grows and evolves, a style of communication not
available on the larger scale. Compartmentation can be helped by the
architecture of the work-space or living-place. When compartmentation is effective, it is the scene of cooperative problem-solving, of
shared practices, of pride in self-generated standards of excellence,
of common purposes and of worthy life.

Notes

Definition of the 'Clan', page 39. The dictionary I quote from is *The
Concise Oxford Dictionary*. Charles Hampden-Turner's description of
clans and clan-culture is taken from his *Corporate Culture: From Vicious
to Virtuous Circles*, Economist Books, London (1990) pp 19-20.

Uncodified Communication, pages 42-46. The important idea of
distinguishing between codified and uncodified information comes
from the work of Max Boisot and John Child. See their paper 'The iron
law of fiefs: bureaucratic failure and the problem of governance in the
Chinese economic reforms', *Administrative Science Quarterly*, 33, (1988)
pages 507-540. On 'tacit knowledge', see Michael Polanyi, *The Tacit
Dimension*, Doubleday, Garden City, New York (1966). On information and coordination, see also Gerard H. Fairtlough 'A Model of
Capitalism Derived from Communication Theory', *Futures*, Jan/ Feb.
1990, pages 69-77.

Shared Practices, pages 48-50. Alasdair MacIntyre. *After Virtue: A
Study in Moral Theory*. Duckworth, London. (1981). The quotation is
from p. 141. MacIntyre develops the idea of a practice in pp.175-189.
On the relation between individual moral reflection and the moral
language of a group, see also Richard Rorty. *Essays on Heidegger and
Others: Philosophical Papers Vol 2*. Cambridge U.P., Cambridge, UK
(1991) pp 158-163.

Compartments, pages 50-52. If I were to use the language of systems
thinking, I would describe compartments as human activity systems,
partially closed from their environments. Within the compartment,

there is multi-order feedback and broadcast communication. The
density of the internal communication flow is much greater than the
external flow. The compartment is a system with its own internal
dynamic, which evolves over time as a result of internal interaction.
The relative impermeability of the compartment's boundary enhances
internal interaction.

4

Compartments and Communication

When I was Chief Executive of Shell Chemicals UK, I left one day for a meeting at one of our manufacturing plants. I was giving a report on the company's progress to an audience of employee representatives and had for my presentation a specially prepared set of 35 mm slides. Instead of taking these, I picked up the set of slides I'd used the previous week when reporting to Shell Chemicals' board of directors. I realised my mistake a few minutes before my presentation but decided that I'd go ahead and use the slides designed for the board. Some of my management colleagues who were present were a bit surprised at the kind of information I was presenting. However, the audience were interested in the slides and in my explanation of them, and seemed to understand it all perfectly well. I realised that there was merit in giving information in the same form to all audiences, since this avoided discrimination and added to the credibility of the message. So from then on using a single set of slides became Shell Chemicals' communicative practice, in the boardroom and on the shop-floor. It was a small, but helpful, contribution to openness in communication, because it reduced the likelihood that we might be tempted to tell each audience a somewhat different story, slanting the message in whatever direction was pleasing to that audience.

Frankness is a key feature of open communication and giving the same message to every audience helps to achieve this. (Of course, it does not always ensure frankness. The politician's trick of putting things in a way which can be interpreted differently by different groups of people, is an example where it does not.) If you give a message to different, but overlapping, audiences and if the message is part of a regular series of reports to these same audiences, then it becomes pretty difficult to distort your story. You find that it is easier to tell the whole truth, to admit your mistakes and to treat all your audiences as adults, capable of accepting bad news. This is how broadcast communication encourages openness.

Broadcast Communication

Broadcast communication uses messages which can be picked up by many people – radio and television broadcasts being obvious examples. It is worthwhile looking at another example in a little detail. Imagine that a proud owner reluctantly decides to sell his sports car and places an ad in a magazine read by sports car enthusiasts. He is making a broadcast communication, because he has no idea which individuals may read his ad. This is an example of a *selective* broadcast, since the advertiser hopes he has chosen a medium which will ensure that most of those reading it will be seriously interested in buying a sports car and fully able to appreciate his wonderful vehicle.

Here are some real-life examples of selective broadcast communication, using a number of media. The first example is the on-going electronic conference of the Global Business Network. GBN is an organisation which brings together around fifty major corporations and around a hundred individuals. These individuals have a great variety of talents and are located throughout the world, in different countries, in different time-zones. GBN helps the individuals and the corporations to use their joint skills and knowledge to make sense of world-wide change – technological, social, economic and political change – and to devise ways in which corporations can respond effectively to this change. One of the ways in which GBN members keep in touch is through a continuous, unstructured electronic conference, with several hundred different topics. A member asks for help on a particular topic, another chips in with a problem-solving idea, someone else gives a reference to a book or a journal article, someone might then re-conceptualise the issue, and eventually the originator thanks the other members for their help and summarises his or her conclusions. Then someone starts a new topic.

GBN's members tend to be highly imaginative and to think laterally, and it is hard to guess which of them might contribute the most valuable idea to the discussion of any particular topic. So broadcast communication is a good way of drawing on the rich resource which the network of members represents. It is a selective broadcast – to GBN members only – but all members are potentially involved in all topics.

The second example is the Coverdale Organisation's Weekly Information Sheet. Coverdale keeps in touch with its eighty consultants, living all over the UK, by mailing them this two-page bulletin. As far as possible, the WIS is used in place of separate memos or notes to individuals, so that everyone can read what is going on in the organisation. Each consultant can read the messages exchanged by other consultants. Thus broadcast communication preserves openness, as well as keeping the flow of paper economical and tidy. Although this means everyone has to read some apparently irrelevant messages, it has proved worthwhile for the sake of the unexpected insights often provided by this form of broadcast communication.

The third example comes from Celltech, where nearly everyone worked in the same location in the town of Slough. Even with several hundred people in the company, it was possible to gather all together in one large room. We did this at least once a month, usually soon after each monthly meeting of Celltech's board of directors. At these meetings with Celltech's staff I gave a report on what happened at the Board – not a blow-by-blow account, but a frank one. If my executive colleagues and I had asked for advice from the non-executive members of the Board, I reported the advice we received. If the non-executives had criticisms to make, we told everyone what they were. If there was praise, this was also reported. In fact, my monthly report at these meetings was not only an account of Board discussions, but also a report on the company's progress in general, since every Board meeting included a report on progress.

In one meeting the Board was pretty critical of a decision, made about eighteen months earlier, to clone the gene for an enzyme called chymosin. The project had been successful technically and we had got a useful patent out of it, but the commercial payoff, although in the end positive, was less than what we might have achieved from an alternative project, one which I had earlier rejected in favour of chymosin.

Some members of the Board accused me of being too cautious over this choice of project, since chymosin had been technically rather easier than the alternative. I think that this criticism was justified, even though the Board members who made it did so only with the benefit of hindsight. At any rate, I reported the criticism and my reaction to it, to the Celltech staff, using the broadcast communication medium of the company meeting. Since this was quite early in Celltech's history, open communication was still a novelty. The room buzzed with interest. I saw some looks which suggested a suspicion that I might not be telling the whole story. And there was probably a little glee at the thought that I'd been put through the mangle. The excitement generated by items of this kind did make sure that most of the staff came to the company meetings.

Of course, more conventional communication is used by GBN, Coverdale and Celltech as well as broadcast communication. But all these organisations take broadcast communication seriously and try to choose an efficient medium for it and one which ensures openness internally, while being able to retain secrecy externally.

Broadcast communication - through electronic mail, paper mail, or face-to-face meetings – scores highly for its openness and it can be very efficient, but for everyone to try and broadcast everything everywhere would clearly result in massive overload, with a huge and chaotic bombardment of conflicting messages. So for most broadcast communication selectivity is needed and this is where compartmentation is so important. Inside the compartment, broadcast communication can remain the general rule, because the volume of internal communication will be small enough to avoid the problem of overload. Everyone will expect internal communication to be broadcast and will contribute to making this effective. Outside the compartment, where openness not nearly so necessary, there is no need to use broadcast communication unless it is efficient. Another form – directed communication – can be used instead.

Directed Communication

Directed communication is the kind which goes only to a limited number of people, and often to a single person, as in the example of a personal letter. Directed communication is sometimes more economical, and it is usually easier to be sure that the message has been received, but it goes against openness. You will recall my earlier distinction between codified and uncodified information. This is a different distinction from the one between broadcast and directed communication. Broadcast communication can use codified information, as in a weather forecast, or it can be uncodified, as it would be if there was some subtle comedy on television. Likewise, directed communication can use both codified and uncodified information – in a letter to a family member, for instance. Of course, in organisations like Celltech, Coverdale and GBN there is directed communication. But organisations dedicated to openness use broadcast communication whenever they can.

A Biological Analogy

All life on earth, whether plant life, animal life or life in single-cell microorganisms such as bacteria, is organised around biological cells. These cells can only be seen under the microscope and are typically a hundredth of a millimetre across. Cells have outer membranes which retain the cell's contents. Membranes allow only limited traffic of materials in and out of the cell. Within the cell is a solution of enzymes, nutrients and other molecules, which is known as the cytoplasm. Also within the cell is an information-carrying system which provides the instructions for the cell to manufacture its various components and to reproduce itself. The information-carrying system is made up of molecules of DNA. (Viruses might appear to be an exception to the rule that all life is made up of cells, since they are simply collections of molecules and lack the membrane and cytoplasm of a cell. But viruses cannot live on their own. They have to be parasites. They cannot do anything, including their own reproduction, unless the have invaded a cell and subverted its machinery for their own purposes.)

Within the cell, molecules diffuse around in an undirected manner. Because the cell is small, molecules spreading out from any point in the cell quickly reach any other part by this random diffusion, so a directing mechanism is not needed. This is just as well because there is no room in the cell for a plethora of specific directing mechanisms. Thus if the cell is making a certain kind of molecule at one point, examples of that molecule will soon turn up everywhere else in the cell. For a medium-sized molecule, the time taken to get from one side of the cell to the other by random diffusion is about a thousandth of a second. A molecule which is made at one site and has to be further processed at another site, is not sent there by any kind of conveyor belt (at least, not in the simplest cells). Molecules diffuse everywhere and go on moving about in a random way until they meet the enzyme which can do this further processing. Sydney Brenner describes the organisation of communication in the biological cell in this way:

> "....unlike a standard digital computer in which signals are sent from one physical location to another by a wire connecting the two, the bacterium does not have physical addresses but implements a broadcast system with logical addresses; each enzyme ignores irrelevant chemical messages and only those fitting into its binding site are retained and used. It is this special hardware that allows the bacterium to act effectively as a

multiple parallel system without paying an enormous tax in wiring connections."

Biological cells therefore use broadcast communication. There are plenty of examples of directed communication in biology – the best is the nervous system of vertebrate animals – but cells, with their small scale, prefer broadcast to directed communication. On the scale of the cell, broadcast communication is efficient. It avoids the complication of special wiring or conveyor belts and provides a useful redundancy or duplication in communication: if one molecule fails to reach a particular point in the cell, another will travel that way shortly after.

Let us take these ideas from biology and see how they apply in human communication. There is a good analogy between the biological cell and the human compartment. In both cases, a 'membrane' acts to ensure that interconnections are much stronger within this boundary than across it. In both, broadcast communication is the main means for internal communication. In both, broadcast communication means that the same information flows everywhere – there is total openness in communication. And in both cases, there is redundancy in internal information flow – if you fail to get the message by one route you'll soon get it by another.

Redundancy in information flow is what makes uncodified information so readily usable in a compartment. The vocabulary of uncodified speech becomes familiar as it is repeatedly encountered. In the compartment, a stock of shared stories is there for everyone to allude to, there is a wealth of well-understood non-verbal signals to use and if a message is not understood the first time it will probably be repeated in a slightly different form before long. All this provides the means whereby uncodified information, with its subtlety and variety, can be freely used in the compartment. Outside the compartment, codified information often does perfectly well; an extended vocabulary is not needed when buying a railway ticket or cashing a travellers' cheque. Inside, the richness of uncodified information is readily available and is the normal mode for communication.

Having been trained in biological science, I like the analogy between the biological cell and the human compartment. I think the analogy helps one to appreciate the value of broadcast communication in a small, partly closed, compartment, and to understand the economy, openness and advantageous redundancy which it provides.

Unconstrained Communication

In totalitarian states it can be dangerous to say what you think. In hierarchical organisations in the West it can be dangerous too – you won't face the firing squad, but you might get fired. Everywhere in the world you can find powerful people who wish to suppress dissent. Constraints on openness not only arise from this kind of fear. The constraint of tact – leading, for instance, to insincere praise of your uncle's new tie – is generally harmless. Other social constraints are more serious – such as those which leave wrongs unchallenged because no one wants to make a fuss. More subtle constraints are imposed by our upbringing and training, or to put it more emotively, by conditioning and brainwashing. There are constraints resulting from lack of imagination and lack of skill in communication. Given all this, complete openness must remain an ideal which will never be fully attained – perhaps never should be fully attained. Nevertheless, I think an understanding of the constraints on openness and a vision of what really unconstrained communication might be like, are both needed if we are to move towards much greater openness in human association.

So let me try to define what I mean by unconstrained communication. I think it is communication undistorted by the influence of power, whether the influence is perceived, as it is when people are 'afraid to speak out' or concealed, as it is by ideological distortion. Because power is pervasive, and because power corrupts, the distortions it gives rise to are complex and sometimes hard to see. We should note that power is not only hierarchical; it can arise from a forceful personality, from intellect or from physical attractiveness. Someone with power may not always be aware that he or she is using it.

Jürgen Habermas says that the only permissible power is the power of the better argument and that this must be the basis for unconstrained communication. With unconstrained and undistorted communication, there is complete sharing of information, there is no holding back for fear of the consequences and there are no unchallengeable ideas which prevent free debate. No doubt this will strike many people as hopelessly out of touch with reality. How can we ever avoid numerous preestablished ideas? How can we challenge everything? Certainly these are reasonable objections. But as the norm today is so far from the ideal of unconstrained communication, I believe we can set these objections aside while we try for complete openness, for free challenge of assumptions and for human communication undistorted by power.

J.K. Galbraith, following the Pulitzer rule that you should not only comfort the afflicted but also afflict the comfortable, gives the name 'institutional truth' to those stories which serve the needs of large institutions, like the Pentagon, the State Department and Wall Street firms. Institutional truth, he says, "bears no necessary relation to simple truth". An example is the story that all financial operations are inherently benign. "In these last years corporate raiding, leveraged buy-outs and the mergers and acquisitions mania have increased the debt structure of our industries dramatically and dangerously....That this is good, that laissez-faire, laissez-passer will always provide, is the institutional truth that awaits you even at Morgan Guaranty." Intelligent people working for Wall Street banks are seemingly required to hold as an article of faith this totally unfalsifiable theory. They are pressed to do so by their own firm and by by the mores of the world they work in. This is an excellent example of constrained communication.

If institutional truth, as described by Galbraith, is normal, then unconstrained, undistorted communication is indeed abnormal. But in fact something approaching this rare state can readily be achieved given real commitment to achieving it and the necessary skills. In my experience, it is a lot easier than might be imagined to create a climate in which openness flourishes and in which communicative skills develop. The right thing is to try it out, for someone to take the lead, not necessarily the formally appointed leader of a group or an organisation. There are risks involved, but also great rewards.

Communicating about Facts, Ethics and Feelings

Unconstrained communication does not come easily. It needs openness, which in turn needs skill in communication – skill in dealing with facts, ethics and feelings. Dealing openly with factual matters might seem to be fairly easy, at least if there is a common problem to be solved which requires some factual analysis for its solution. But the facts are often inconvenient and it may need hard thinking to get at them. The circumstances may be confusing, it may not be clear just which are the relevant facts and even if it is clear, those facts may still be difficult to discover. We have at least two models for getting at the facts, the scientific and the legal, and the former has the advantage of not always being adversarial. In science those who have studied something closely get a full hearing and if they can also produce a cogent theoretical argument which ties in with their observations their view is likely to prevail. But in science theoretical models are subject to rejection if they fail to account for new observations or if simpler or more comprehensive models come along. The proponents of a model are supposed to accept this gracefully and the mores of the scientific community help them to do so. This may seem too elaborate a method for reaching most of the factual conclusions we want in everyday life but the spirit of open-minded scientific enquiry is a good one for us to keep as a guide.

Take the example of a group of people deciding the quickest route for a car journey. The knowledge of a commuter who regularly travels the route will carry a lot of weight in the discussion. But if the planned journey is to be on a Sunday and if someone objects that the commuter's knowledge applies only to weekdays, when the pattern of traffic is different, this objection to the relevance of the first person's observations could well be accepted. If there is an authoritative source like a reputable map, once again everyone's first reaction might be to agree with the evidence it provides about the shortest way or about the best roads. But whoever produces the map as an argument for a particular route will have to be ready to accept that a more up-to-date map might overturn that conclusion. In a case like this, a comparison with the scientific method is reasonable. I certainly think that communicative skills relating to factual matters involve listening to anyone who has experience of the area, forming and testing conclusions and being ready to reject conclusions in the face of new evidence or better ideas.

In the Western tradition, communicating and making judgments about ethical matters, that is about matters of right and wrong, is thought to be different from communicating and making judgments about factual matters. I think that the distinction has been overdone and that there are, in fact, close parallells between the two. Firstly, it is important to pay attention to those who have thought carefully about the ethics of a particular situation – they will probably have identified the key issues even if they have not made a generally acceptable judgment.

Secondly, the group of people concerned should seek a judgment tested by debate among themselves. In such a debate there may well be appeals to universal norms, or moral laws, specifying which are good and which are bad actions. It will be found that these norms are often difficult to apply, because one norm may lead to one conclusion and another norm to a different conclusion, or because the norms can be interpreted differently. This is why a practice-based morality is best, since it ties ethical judgment into the life and work of an actual community. Within a particular community, skill in judging cases has to be learned by communicative practice.

Communicative skill is even more needed in dealing with ethical matters, because they often raise an emotional response, making constructive debate more difficult than when dealing with facts. I have found that it helps to start with a calm acceptance that emotions will probably surface during any discussion on critically important issues. If it is clear that a particular issue is indeed an emotional one, but that it has nevertheless to be openly discussed if things are to progress, the heat starts to go out of the situation. In fact it is better that emotion does come to the surface at the time it is aroused, rather than being suppressed and emerging later in a different guise. Education, particularly a scientific or a business education, tends to play down the importance of emotion, teaching us to act rationally and coolly. But committed people rightly have strong feelings, and to ignore this is to ignore an important fact about the situation. We need an approach which recognises that emotions are always around and that they should be welcomed, not treated as an embarrassment.

Once a group of people finds this approach successful, its repeated use becomes easier. It then becomes an ordinary thing to question whether the set of norms in use by the group is coherent and whether they are being used in a consistent way. When this has become commonplace, the group has acquired part of the skill needed to deal with matters of right and wrong.

Everyone's authenticity and sincerity must also be open to question. It must be acceptable within a group for someone to say of another's remark: 'it doesn't sound to me as if you really mean that' or 'that's not how you felt about it yesterday,' providing he or she gives reasons for these doubts and providing the doubter is also open to challenge. Once again, with practice this gets easier to do, since an expression of doubt will not then be taken as an insult and the value to everyone from getting things clear will be well appreciated. Making and responding to these challenges help us to clarify our own opinions and feelings. Thus communicative competence grows within a group when it becomes capable of testing the sincerity of its members' expressions of feeling.

When people develop sufficient trust in one another, it becomes possible to deal equally well with the factual, ethical and subjective aspects of a subject and with the mixture of all three which is needed in any fully open discussion. If the wish to cooperate is strong then there will be an active desire in a group to reach a complete understanding about the situation and about what should be done. If the skills in open communication which I have described become widespread not only in a small group of, say, half a dozen people, but within the whole membership of a social compartment then the speed with which a mutual understanding can be achieved and a common purpose agreed, becomes remarkably high.

This account of what is required for excellent communication is based on my experience of how people actually start to behave as communicative competence develops in a community. The process of challenging reported facts, values and feelings may seem a difficult and lengthy one and it certainly needs time to get established. But once it is established, it is an economical way of going about things, especially when compared with the situation of a group racked with uncertainty and suspicion where so much time and energy must be spent in making it possible to function at all. Communicative competence should give rise to a virtuous circle in which the skill and confidence generates success in solving problems and this success leads in turn to a greater commitment to open communication.

When you visit a place such as a factory, a research institute, a school or a university, it is worthwhile looking out for signs which point to the effectiveness of human communication in that place. Here are some good signs: a board with passport-size photographs of *everybody* who works or studies there, arranged in a non-hierarchical way; groups of people talking animatedly together; an untidy and lived-in look but a clean one (litter is a bad sign); colourful posters about social events; pinned up clippings from recent newspapers; attractive places to sit and talk.

The Compartment as a Democracy

While effective communication opens the way to better problem-solving and decision-making, it changes many other things too. Intense, repeated, uncodified and unconstrained communication has an enormous influence on the thinking patterns, the vocabulary, the beliefs, the values and the habits of the members of a social compartment. These form the basis of future communication as well as being generated by it. The compartment can become a learning system and the commonality of its language and values is an evolutionary achievement. This achievement has instrumental, practical and aesthetic features, by which I mean that it is useful for getting tasks done well, that it leads to fairness and to justice and that it can be perceived as beautiful.

An empowered and creative human compartment becomes a democracy. By engaging the talents of every member of a community the positive contributions that all can make will be forthcoming and the deadweight of non-contributors will be avoided. Groups facing only routine problems can perhaps cope without the active help of all members, but in situations where a great deal of creativity and adaptability is needed success depends on decisions being influenced by everybody. If this does not happen the most creative and flexible solution will not be found.

I earlier defined clan-like communication as that depending on shared enthusiasms, lasting relationships and subtle communications. But the relationship between master and slave can be a lasting one, and one with subtle communication. Perhaps I need an expanded definition, if I mean clan-like interactions to be democratic ones. For this we can draw once more on the work of Max Boisot and John Child, taking up their distinction between clans and fiefs. As they describe them, fiefs are smallish groups of people who use mainly uncodified information in their lives and work. But they are not democratic. Power-holders keep a grip on their fiefs by fear of violence and other punishment. This ever-present threat is supported by patronage and by power ceremonies and the cultivation of myths of power. Communication is limited to what the power holders want their followers to hear, debate is restricted and deference is required. The medieval village was a fief, with the lord or lady of the manor controlling the lives of the villagers as much as he or she could, helped by the parson's contribution of ideology. The Victorian family business was run in much the same way, with long-serving retainers coming to believe that this was the way the world had to be. And there are plenty of fiefs in the world today, in the Mafia and elsewhere. Clans, on the other hand, have unconstrained communication, freedom of information and democratic decision-making. They are characterised by informality, trust and interpersonal communication skills. Communicative competence is high and its improvement is constantly sought by all. Like fiefs, clans have common values but these come from free debate not from conditioning imposed from above.

The ideal clan, without any trace of patron-to-client relationships between its members, which always has unconstrained communication and which is fully empowered and democratic, is unlikely to exist, certainly in the world today. Some fief-like features will usually persist. But it is possible to approach the ideal. I have seen this happen. When it does the results are startling. People's expectations change, cynicism drops away, behaviour becomes open and trusting, positive and challenging. Respect for every individual develops. Each individual is known by all the others and appreciated for his or her varied personal characteristics and opinions; in a community of a limited size it is genuinely possible to do this.

Among millions only a few individuals can be in the limelight, but in a compartment everyone can play a part. The compartment, with its limited size, can be ordered so that this happens. The compartment is where clan-like communication can flourish, although the danger of fief-like characteristics developing must never be forgotten.

What's Special about Compartments?

There is nothing new in the appeal of community. Both conservatives and radicals have drawn on this appeal for centuries. Conservatives see communities as the preservers and transmitters of old ways, as the best means for saving traditional values, as the settings in which strife is muted and individuals reconciled. The conservative view holds that loyalty to and affection for the nation, the township, the church or the local pub allow us to forget the inevitable injustices of the world and to accept its natural hierarchies and inequalities. On the other hand, radicals see communities as the means for replacing competition by cooperation, self-assertion by mutual help, individual isolation by sisterhood and brotherhood, domination of others by love for them. The radical view is that it is the support of our communities which allows us to face the difficult changes brought by modernisation and enables us to seek a better life for humankind.

My arguments in support of the compartment, being based on communication theory and on biological analogies, may sound novel. But do they really add anything to the old ideas of community? Might they simply provide help either to conservatives or to radicals in the pursuit of their familiar ends? Can there honestly be something new in a vision of organisations, or of societies, based on compartmentation? What's special about compartments?

The special thing is the break at the boundary of the compartment. The boundary of the compartment signals a significant change. Within the compartment broadcast communication is the standard mode, there is a commitment to complete openness, the skills of unconstrained communication are practised, collaborative problem-solving is the norm. However, outside the compartment things are different. Outside, it is just not possible to use more than a limited amount of broadcast communication. Openness about everything is just not feasible, since openness needs time and there are far too many matters to find time for. Fully unconstrained communication depends on shared practices and it is only on the scale of the compartment that practices can be fully shared. Collaboration beyond the scale of the compartment needs other methods of coordination than those of the clan. Compartmentation lets everyone know where open, broadcast, unconstrained communication can no longer be the rule. This kind of communication has to be concentrated within the compartment's boundary. Within a community of up to a certain size – a few hundreds of people – it is entirely possible for most communication to be this way. To try to make it the rule on a larger scale is impracticable, although openness and lack of constraint are, of course, still desirable. *Thus the clarity of the boundary and the distinctly different quality which communication has within it, are essential features of compartmentation.*

Clear signalling of the limit of community is what's special about compartments. Traditional pleas for community, both from the political left and right and mostly driven by an unreal nostalgia, leave out this limit. An image of community derived from collective worship in a rural church, or from the village cricket team, is evoked in support of the idea of community on a national, or even an international, scale. The concept of the compartment suggests that this is an invalid extension. Face-to-face communities have special features and this should be clearly acknowledged. Compartmentation means that this must be acknowledged. For small to be beautiful, it needs to be different. Compartmentation demonstrates the difference and reinforces it.

Practical Steps

The unavoidable limit on the size of the compartment, and the vital need to recognise the difference between the practices which work within the compartment and those which work outside it, together bring a notable advantage. The limit on size and the need for difference mean that organisational change must mainly be sought on the small scale. The concept of the compartment may be global, but practical steps to bring it about cannot be anything else than local. So this is the big advantage: compartmentation must start at the grass roots. Local action is both necessary and sufficient.

A group of people who like the ideas of openness, unconstrained communication and empowerment can start applying these ideas on the smallest of scales, without feeling that they have embarked on a project which will only make sense when the whole world changes. Sometimes there will be an obvious boundary within to work; sometimes a boundary will have to be invented by the people involved. Sometimes people will have a wealth of interpersonal process skill and a deep understanding of clan-like communication; sometimes these will have to be learned while the compartment is being built. Sometimes the existing hierarchy will support change, sometimes not. Always a bit of luck will be needed to help the project along.

To suggest how a compartment might come into existence, let me tell another imagined story. Coming from a family with a literary tradition, Frank Arabin chose education as his field, and in his thirties got a lectureship in the Faculty of Education at the University of Barchester. A few years later, he took the unusual step for a faculty member, of studying part-time for a master's degree in business administration. At that time, his university didn't have an MBA course, so Frank became a distance-learning student with the Open University Business School. One of his aims in taking the course was to discover at first hand what distance learning was like, and he certainly found how tough it could be to study for a degree while doing a full-time job. He also learnt some useful things about education in general, partly from being a distance-learning student, and partly because of the surprising parallels he found between teaching and management. He gained a new perspective on the process of learning.

Soon after getting his MBA, Frank reached the conclusion that Barchester ought to have a business school. It was the late 1980s and business education had, at last, become widespread in the UK. Barchester taught commerce and accounting at the undergraduate level and the Faculty of Engineering had combined degrees in engineering and management, but there were no post-graduate business courses. Many people working in organisations in and around Barchester seemed interested in post-graduate study. The difficulty for the university in trying to meet this need was that it couldn't easily recruit experienced teachers in post-graduate business studies, because the current boom in business education had led to a shortage.

Frank thought that the solution was to use the resources of the university's existing faculties. Since his experience suggested that teaching people to teach might not be so different from teaching people to manage, his own faculty might play a key part in the project. Some faculties were already teaching aspects of management, and others like Law and Economics could clearly contribute. Instead of taking these ideas to the dean or the vice-chancellor, Frank started to discuss them with the members of staff whose work might turn them into reality. He was pleased to find that many of the people he talked with were keen to be involved. The project for a new kind of business school began to take shape. In some fields, like operations management and business strategy, a few good people would have to be recruited from other business schools. It would be necessary to have demanding external examiners and other measures which would help to build a course of the highest quality. Quite soon, there would be the hard task of raising funds for a building.

Frank, with two others, wrote a proposal and found a dozen people from Education and other faculties who were happy to give it public support. A group of fifteen agreed to meet every two weeks and to copy to each other all letters and papers they wrote about the project. Frank wrote a short progress report each week for circulation to the group. Although nothing was kept secret from other members of the university, this group were the ones who kept abreast of what was happening. They did not always agree on how the project should develop, for instance on the extent to which the MBA course should differ from courses at other business schools. For some of the group, personal ambition played a part, for some the project was important for their faculty, for others it just seemed an interesting thing to be doing. They learned how to resolve these differences and to benefit from them, particularly at a weekend session which most of the fifteen attended and which was facilitated by a member of the education faculty who had considerable skill in interpersonal process. It was unusual at the University of Barchester to open up issues of this kind, so the weekend was quite an experience.

When they were satisfied that their plan had been well thought through and that they would be able to deal with the objections it was likely to provoke, the fifteen asked the vice-chancellor and the deans of their faculties to come to a meeting at which they would present the plan. They prepared carefully and the meeting went well. The project soon got a small development budget and started to make its way through the university's decision-making procedures. A steering committee, including many from the group of fifteen, was formally set up. It looked as if Barchester would shortly have a Business School and an MBA course, both centred on organisational learning.

Although this story is not about an established compartment, I think it can tell us quite a lot about compartments and communication.

- It is the story of a *project*, a vision of something which ought to be brought into being. Although the project was initiated by a single champion – Frank Arabin – it was quite soon 'owned' by a group – the group of fifteen.
- The group was self-selected, but it established a *clear boundary* - the fifteen signatories were members of the group. Others, whether they were supporters or opponents, were not members.
- The group developed shared practices. These included communicative practices, using written materials and face-to-face meetings for *open, broadcast communication* within the group's boundary. Outside the boundary directed communication was used, for instance in the group's talks with the dean and the vice-chancellor.
- Members of the group saw the need for *skill in inter-personal process* and worked to develop this skill.
- The group developed some *communicative competence* and this proved useful in resolving problems arising from differences in viewpoint and conflicts due to personal ambition.

The University of Barchester is a fiction – but one based on actual experience. There are plenty of real-life organisations with scope for self-organising groups to champion many kinds of projects. These groups can succeed through articulating their vision and developing their skills. The group is a compartment in embryo. It shares some of the strengths of the compartment.

Notes

A Biological Analogy, pages 61-62. The quotation from Sydney Brenner comes from a paper presented at a conference in Cambridge, UK, on 'The Present State and Future of Life Sciences' held in 1984.

Unconstrained Communication, pages 63-64. My discussions of unconstrained communication and of communicative competence are largely based on the work of Jürgen Habermas. The most relevant of his works is *The Theory of Communicative Action*, published in 1981. It has been translated by Thomas McCarthy and is available in two volumes with an excellent introduction by the translator, from Polity Press (1987).

John Kenneth Galbraith's remarks are taken from a commencement address at Smith College reported in *The Guardian* newspaper of 26th. July, 1989.

Clans and Fiefs, pages 68-69. See Max Boisot and John Child, The Iron Law of Fiefs: Bureaucratic Failure and the Problem of Governance in the Chinese System Reforms. *Administrative Science Quarterly*, **33**, 507-527 (1988). Their distinction between codified and uncodified information also appeared in this paper.

Boundaries, page 70. Werner Ulrich makes an important point about boundary judgments. The choice of which matters to consider and which to ignore in coming to a practical conclusion may greatly influence that conclusion. His view is that those who set boundaries must be responsible for making absolutely clear why they are drawn in a particular place and that if this is not done we may reasonably expect that there is some concealed power-play around. Compartmentation makes boundary judgments transparent, because everything within the compartment has in principle to be considered. See Ulrich, 'W. Churchman's process of unfolding – its significance for policy analysis and evaluation'. *Systems Practice*, **1**, 415-428, 1988 and Fairtlough, G.H. 'Systems Practice from the Start: Some Experiences in a Biotechnology Company', *Systems Practice*, **2**, 397-412, 1989.

5

The Creative Compartment

A high-technology business is absolutely dependent on the creativity of the people who work for it. Certainly this was so at Celltech. Our success depended on our scientists having novel ideas and on everyone in the firm working together to turn those ideas into reality more quickly than others could do. Ideas were our life-blood, yet we could not follow up every idea; no organisation can do that and certainly not a small, new one like Celltech. We had to have a system for collecting ideas, for appraising them, for choosing the few we were going to work on and for making sure that the ones which were chosen got the necessary resources. This was our Project Management system.

The Project Management system was developed during the first four years of the company's life. Norman Carey, Celltech's Director of R and D, and I thought we knew how it should function, because we had designed similar systems in other organisations. But we also knew that unless people throughout the firm understood the system and felt comfortable with it, unless they had the feeling that it was *their* system, it would be resented. We wanted a system which both encouraged creativity and introduced discipline. And the discipline had to be of a kind that everyone felt was fair and in the real interests of the firm. In short, we wanted the system to be a source of empowerment for people in Celltech.

The system grew through a combination of experimentation and consultation. One part of the system was put in place and, after a few months experience, there was widespread discussion about the way it had worked, culminating in a meeting, open to everyone in the firm, to decide on modifications and on how to move on to the next part of the system. For instance, part of the system was the reporting of costs. We had a satisfactory departmental cost-reporting system and we needed to add a project cost-reporting section to this, since most departments were working on more than one project and most projects involved more than one department. After some months, we found that the degree of detail provided about project costs was too great. The system had started by providing the level of detail which department heads wanted so as to be able to control their costs but it turned out that this detail was unnecessary for project management. By itself, this was no earth-shattering mistake, but if a system had been put in place in one big operation, the combination of a series of mistakes of this sort might well have made it ineffective.

We found that giving the right names to the elements of the system was important. If the name of each system-element clearly described its purpose and if the whole set of names was logical, then it was much easier to understand the concepts behind the system, to remember them and to communicate about them. We found that a system of well-integrated activities should be based on a coherent system of concepts. The key tasks in Celltech's Project Management system were to generate ideas for new products and technologies, to select the most promising of these and to organise their further development. Doing this did not prove easy, but progress was made when two matching sets of names gained acceptance across the company. The first set named the stages of evolution from ideas to products. The second set named the people responsible for organising each stage. These were names of roles rather than individuals; a new individual could become responsible when a new stage was reached, or the same individual could take the project through two or more stages, but the role changed in any case.

Stage	Person responsible
Idea	Idea Champion (Self-appointed and part-time)
Candidate	Candidate Champion (Part-time)
Research Project	Research Project Manager
Development Project	Development Project Manager
Product	Product Manager

Anyone could be an idea champion, simply by arguing for his or her idea. To get attention the idea champion would have to make a good case, which often meant quite a bit of out-of-hours work. Sometimes there was joint championship of an idea by two or more people. To help idea champions, we set up an innovation support group of experienced people who were available to help the often quite young and inexperienced champions prepare their cases. One key rule for members of this group was never to raise an objection to an idea until they had first given two reasons for supporting it. So, the champions were not on their own but it is fair to say that they needed quite a lot of enthusiasm and persistence, since there were many ideas competing for attention. Luckily there was plenty of enthusiasm as well as plenty of ideas.

Once an idea had been defined and the case for it getting support from the company had been developed, it then had to pass through through what we called a 'decision gate', in order to become a 'candidate' rather than just an idea. The gate was operated by the head of Research, who was advised in this task by a small group of people from different parts of the company and who held a budget dedicated to candidate projects, which allowed up to £25,000 to be spent on a candidate. This sum covered both the cost of people's time within the company and external costs like consultancy and the investigation of what rival patents there might impinge on the field. In the candidate phase it was vital to define the risks which a full-blown research project would face and what the rewards could be if the research succeeded. A candidate champion had the task of collecting this data and progressing the candidate project through this phase.

After a few months in the candidate phase there was another decision gate to pass through, this time to reach the status of a full research project with a budget of £250,000 or more and with several people working on it full-time. The move from candidate status to a full blown research project was a critical decision which involved lots of people across the company and often outside advisers as well. Sometimes a new project could only be started if an existing one was dropped, sometimes there were two or three promising candidates but resources for only one project, always it was a tense moment. A champion was often the person who had thought of the original idea and usually he or she felt passionately committed to the candidate. We had to make sure that, in making the difficult but inevitable choice between projects, justice was done and seen to be done. It was a great thing to have several exciting projects from which to choose, but if the choice was ever regarded as ill-informed or unfair, then enthusiasm and inventiveness throughout the firm would be stifled.

I made sure that I found out which of a set of candidate projects seemed likely to be rejected and then started arguing for them. If my senior colleagues wanted to kill a candidate, they would have to produce darned good reasons and if these reasons were persuasive, I could then make sure that they were fully understood in the firm, especially by the supporters of the failed candidates. This open process of decision-taking required some hard work but it did not delay things, since everyone knew that good communication was part of the preparation for a decision. Everyone knew too that decisions had to be taken and that the senior people in the company had to take them. Senior people had to give good reasons for any decision, preferably well-defined reasons, but statements of opinion from an experienced person were listened to. The latter might be like this: "I think it will be very difficult to develop the reliable assay we need to tell us whether or not we are getting near our target." Coming from someone who has worked for years with assays of the kind planned for the project, such a statement carried real weight. Statements which did not carry any weight were: "I'm the boss and this project isn't getting through."

The later stages of the Project Management system were more conventional. Once a full research project was authorised, a new project manager was usually appointed, as the original champion often did not have the experience to take on this job. However, the old champion usually kept some connection with the project, carrying out some parts of the laboratory work, for example. Occasionally we arranged training for someone so that he or she was able to continue through from project champion to project manager. A research project had to get through further gates in its progress towards becoming a product and decision-taking at these gates followed the pattern I have described for the early ones.

A key purpose for Celltech's Project Management system was to appraise projects rigorously and to manage them in a disciplined way, while keeping a vital innovative spirit in the firm. We achieved this by:

- Testing each part of the system and modifying it as a result of feedback from all those involved.
- Making sure the basic concepts underlying the system were clear and that the names given to its various elements were logical and memorable.
- Giving strong support to everyone's novel ideas in their early stages, even though at later stages these ideas would have to survive strenuous questioning and competition.
- Seeking opinions from everyone before taking the decision about which candidate should get through the gate to become a full

project, taking this decision openly and making sure that the reasons for the decision were widely known.

- Providing well-trained project managers to take projects through their later stages, while giving people who had the original idea every chance to go on being identified with the project.

Did All of This Work?

Did the project management system produce good decisions? My answer is: yes. Of course it is never possible to prove that a particular way of organising things is the best possible. There is no controlled experiment to show that another way of managing projects would have given poorer results. What I can say with certainty is that the decision-making process was at least as fast and economical as the more secretive processes I have experienced in other organisations. At Celltech we did not have the back stairs lobbying and horse-trading which goes on elsewhere and which can absorb a great deal of time and emotional energy.

Furthermore, the openness of decision-making and the real help and recognition given to people with ideas made Celltech a highly innovative outfit and helped us to attract first-class people to work in the company. The problem of combining creativity and discipline is a classic one for high-technology companies. I believe that Celltech's Project Management system went a long way towards solving that problem.

By the end of its seventh year Celltech had grown from nothing to a company of around 250 people. In that year total sales were £11.5 million. Profit was small at £250,000 but this was after spending 37% of sales on R&D. This record of growth, together with the exciting set of projects in research and development and with two or three important collaborations with major pharmaceutical firms, enabled Celltech to strengthen its balance sheet by over £40 million through a placing of shares. I am sure that the Project Management system made a big contribution to this business success.

An example of a project which was initiated and developed through the system I have described was a novel means for increasing the productivity of cell culture. In cell culture, a minute number of animal cells is induced to proliferate in a bottle or a tank, much as yeast cells proliferate during fermentation. Just as yeast cells in fermentation can produce something useful, like wine or

beer, so animal cells in culture can produce useful biopharmaceuti-
cals. But animal cells in culture are in an unnatural situation and
they often produce only very small amounts of the wanted product.
The skill of the biotechnologist is needed to increase the productivity of the cells – by a thousandfold or more.

Dr. Geoff Yarranton, then a department head at Celltech, had an
idea for a novel and general way to amplify the output of products
from animal cells in culture – the so-called GS amplification system.
He championed this project and got agreement to do the experiments which demonstrated this his idea did indeed work, first on a
small scale and then on a production scale. The idea got patent
protection and is now a key factor in Celltech's world-leading
expertise in cell culture. One of the reasons why the world beats a
path to the company's door, when it wants products from cell
culture, is Celltech's unique GS amplification system.

Common Purposes

Suppose that a skilled gardener comes to live in a suburban street.
After a year or two her skill starts to be obvious to anyone passing in
front of her house. Suppose too that her skill is not confined to
gardening: that she knows how to give advice to her neighbours in a
way which actually helps them, rather than in a way which shows off
her superiority. Then, if the weather and other things are kind, it is
probable, as a result of her example and her help, that most of the
gardens in that street will come to look interesting and decorative.

What will most likely also develop will be a collective pride in the
attractiveness of the street and a common aim to keep it that way.
Mutual help in watering others' gardens during absences on holidays
and in the swapping of plant cuttings or seeds will be easy and
unforced. Learning more about gardening, making the gardens on
the street more varied and simplifying the work of looking after
them, will all become shared aims, aims which are supported first by
the pleasure given by working towards them and second by their
achievement. No one set out to teach this group of people to be
skillful gardeners, no one proclaimed an objective of beautifying
their environment, no one sought to use gardening as a way of
drawing the community together. But these joint aims grew as the
possibility of their fulfilment started to become clear. By learning
how to help each other effectively the group was able to do
unexpected things with little or no extra effort.

Nobody sought this result at the outset and things might have turned out quite differently. Had we supposed some other gardener, one equally skilled in gardening but a competitor rather than a cooperator, then his advice to his neighbours might have been patronising instead of encouraging and the habit of giving help to one's neighbours might not have spread in our imagined street. Our second gardener might have induced one or two others to compete against him and he might have been a vigorous member of committees in the county horticultural society, but the street would have looked different to a visitor and in minor ways would have been a different place in which to live.

This group of gardeners is not a compartment; there are too few of them and there is no clear boundary around them. However their story demonstrates the part played by skilled communication in the development of cooperation. The first gardener knew how to share her knowledge and how to create enthusiasm, the second was more concerned with his own ego. Both were skilled in horticultural tasks, but only the first gardener had skill in interpersonal process. The first was the more creative, since creativity usually needs skill in both task and process.

The story also demonstrates how common aims can grow organically. It is not necessary for a group to have a well-defined purpose at the start. Group cohesion and identity can grow together with a group's common purpose. The evolution of a common purpose generates cohesion and can give a group its identity. The shared project helps to define the boundary of the group. As the group becomes committed to the success of its project and increasingly proud of its achievements and its purposes, it raises its standards of performance. It becomes committed to ever-increasing quality in pursuit of its aims. It becomes more cooperative and also more self-critical. With increasing communicative competence, the group gets better at handling the interplay between mutual criticism and mutual support. As in the case of Celltech's Project Management system, this stimulates a wealth of innovation and creative problem-solving.

Groupthink

Donald Michael has written about the significance of what he calls 'sentient groups'. These are groups to which individuals are prepared to make emotional commitments and from which they receive emotional support. Sometimes the sentient group is the same as a work group or at least overlaps with it; at other times the sentient group will be made up of family, friends or perhaps a professional association of some kind. Michael points out that the cohesion of sentient groups may inhibit change. While the emotional support which such groups provide to their members is vital for coping with disorientating change, these groups tend to deny difficulties, reduce questioning and smother proposals for action.

The denial or the exaggeration of difficulties, and the failure to question assumptions, lead to what is sometimes called 'groupthink'. Groupthink happens when group cohesion becomes the main aim and the group's project is sacrificed as a result. Then standards of performance drop, self-criticism is lost and skill in handling tricky issues is no longer demanded. 'Tough love' is needed to face reality, while at the same time preserving a group's mutual support. Groupthink is a manifestation of 'weak love', when fear of disagreement overrides commitment to the group's task.

This can happen anywhere. I have seen it happen at the top of a large pharmaceutical company when the CEO set out to check the in-fighting which had been endemic between R&D and Marketing. He called for less opposition and more cooperation between the two functions. The next time R&D staff made a proposal, the Marketing staff supported it, even though they didn't really believe in it. Later R&D developed doubts themselves, but because of Marketing's support they were now reluctant to abandon the idea. The project continued unconvincingly for months, until it finally collapsed, leaving Marketing and R&D as much at odds with each other as they ever were.

The perils of groupthink mean that a group's aims and purposes have to be openly and rigorously tested by debate in the group, to make sure they are clear to everyone and that there are no hidden reservations. This process should provide a clear vision as the group carries forward its project. It should ensure that there are no misunderstandings about aims and that there is real commitment from everyone.

This is another example of openness and trust, empowerment and commitment all reinforcing each other. It is another example of the need for competence in communication and skill in interpersonal process.

More Biology – The Origin of Life

There is no more intriguing mystery than the origin of life on earth. Creation myths abound and there have been constant attempts to find scientific explanations for this astonishing phenomenon. Theories of biological evolution starting with primitive, single-cell organisms take us only part of the way, as they do not tell us how these primitive living things arose. What is needed to complete the picture is a link between a plausible chemical environment for the pre-life earth and a plausible biochemistry for early life. Neither of these can be known with anything like certainty, and the link between them is even more difficult to investigate, but progress has been made by a combination of deduction and model experiments. Experiments on the chemical side of the gap show that under the kind of conditions which might well have existed on the earth at the time, it is likely that a 'soup' of organic chemicals dissolved in water would have been present. Some of these chemicals are of the kind that make up life today. On the other side of the gap it is possible, by looking at the biochemical features that all kinds of life have in common, to deduce what the biochemistry of the first living things might have been.

Among the scientists who have done work of this kind are Manfred Eigen and Peter Schuster. They started from the realisation that although the primordial 'soup' would have contained the molecules of life, it would have had a great many other kinds of molecule as well, so that there had to be some organising principles which could select out only those molecules which could combine to give the features of proto-life, particularly the feature of being able to reproduce themselves. This is in line with the observation that life, as it has evolved, is very selective in the kinds of molecule it uses. For example, only twenty different amino-acids are normally used to make protein molecules, out of the thousands which are theoretically possible, and the twenty are the same for all forms of life; animals, plants and bacteria alike. Eigen, Schuster and their co-workers set out to find what these organising principles could be.

Firstly they found that in certain conditions, conditions which might well have existed in the primordial soup, molecules can reproduce themselves in the absence of any living matter. Certain configurations of chemicals were found to have greater stability than others and some of these could encourage the duplication of the configuration by acting as a template on which the duplicate would

form. Furthermore these configurations competed among themselves for raw materials, so that eventually one became dominant,
because it had the best combination of rapid self-replication and
stability. Here we have Darwinian selection of non-living things,
with the survival of the fittest molecular configuration. The molecules involved were those called RNA which, together with the
rather similar DNA, are now the basis for reproduction and
inheritance in all forms of life. So Eigen's and Schuster's first
organising principle for the origin of life was Darwinism: competition among and selection of molecules.

Eigen and Schuster discovered that, on its own, the application of
this principle limited the complexity of the self-replicating molecules which were produced. This is due to the fact that replication is
not error-free. In one way errors are helpful because they are the
source of the variety on which the principle of competition and
selection can operate. But in another way errors are unhelpful
because in a large template they accumulate to such an extent that
supposedly 'duplicate' molecules are very far from being like the
original. With this amount of error, it is impossible for replication to
take place in a way which preserves a selective advantage for that
species of molecule. In fact, the chains of units which make up the
molecules of RNA cannot grow longer than about 100 units before
the loss of accuracy in replication prevents any further sustainable
growth, and 100 RNA units is well below the size of the smallest life
forms.

This is why a second organising principle is needed. If two kinds
of molecule cooperate together they can improve their accuracy of
replication by at least tenfold. Eigen and his colleagues studied the
interaction of RNA and protein molecules and showed that they can
indeed assist each other's replication and make it more reliable so
that RNA molecules with more than 1,000 units in their chains can
successfully replicate. This is around the size of today's smallest
living things, the smallest of the viruses which infect plants, animals
and bacteria.

To go beyond this size one further organising principle is
required, which is compartmentation. This builds on the principle
of cooperation and now makes use of the fact that if the two kinds of
molecule which assist each other's replication remain closely associated, they can evolve together. A random change in one kind of
molecule, say the RNA, might confer a potential advantage, say
greater stability. But if the change meant that the protein did not

interact so well with the RNA, the nett effect could be harmful. However, more-or-less simultaneous changes in the protein and the RNA can, with a bit of luck, lead to a nett benefit, because sometimes the two changes are not just compatible but actually helpful to each other's replication. This will only work if the association between the new variants continues, for such changes will most likely be harmful in the absence of the compatible partner. Continuing association can be secured by putting the two kinds of molecule in a compartment which keeps the compatible variants together, and in addition keeps them separate from other, similar molecules in the primordial soup. *That is to say, the compartment is a device for isolating particular varieties of molecule so that they always have good partners around them and for encouraging mutually beneficial evolution of the partner molecules.*

Once a compartment is set up, the opportunities for beneficial association go far beyond the simple pair of molecular types we have been discussing, because other molecular types, like DNA, can join the process of mutual adaptation. Life is everywhere organised in cells, which provides the advantage of co-evolution of compatible molecules, made possible by compartmentation. Once established, the compartments start competing with each other in a Darwinian fashion and the evolution of life forms then continues in the way familiar to biologists.

Cooperation, Competition, Compartmentation

If these ideas about the origin of life are right, then the principles of competition, cooperation and compartmentation combine in a fascinating manner. Competition first selects a certain kind of molecular configuration as having the best blend of stability and self-replicative ability. But this takes things only so far and to go further requires a second organising principle: that of cooperation between more than one kind of molecule. In the next stage this cooperation is enhanced by compartmentation, which preserves mutually beneficial adaptations. Finally competition returns as the compartments, which are by now living micro-organisms, are subject to evolutionary pressures of the classical kind.

Biological analogies prove nothing about the functioning of societies; at best they suggest models which may turn out to have explanatory power. There is no reason why the particular sequence described by Eigen and Schuster, with its alternation between competition, cooperation and compartmentation, should be echoed in social evolution or in social organisation. But it is worth holding onto the idea that these three principles can interact in a complex and fruitful way, as they do in this theory of the origin of life on earth.

On this account, the early history of life depends on the interplay between competition and cooperation. We can find the same kind of interplay in natural ecological systems, where prey populations and predator populations evolve together and some populations interact symbiotically. The success of Far-Eastern economies depends on a similar blend. In communitarian-capitalist countries such as Japan and China, there is fierce competition between firms, but also a lot of cooperation, for example in the long-standing relations between a large manufacturing firm and its trusted sub-contractors.

To combine two apparently contradictory principles, like competition and cooperation, needs another, synthesising principle. Compartmentation can be that principle. As we have seen, it operates at the molecular level in biology. It also operates at the ecological level – niche creation has some similarity to compartmentation. And it operates at the societal level – for example, the business 'family' in Japan, called a *keiretsu*, can be viewed as a large compartment whose members cooperate with each other much more than they compete.

Distribution of Tasks

Let us now return to the clan-like human compartment, with its superb internal communication, its common purposes and its mutual support both in carrying out tasks and in providing for needs. There is a very well-established model for a system of mutual support – the family. An ethic of mutual support exists within families in most parts of the world, at least within nuclear families. But the model may not be an ideal one, especially when we consider how tasks are normally distributed within families: the allocation of tasks is often inflexible and unfair – for example, women get a raw deal in many cultures.

To get the maximum advantage from the intense communication within a compartment, there needs to be little rigidity in internal structure. A salient feature should be equality in the distribution of tasks; everyone should have their fair share of the less pleasant or less interesting jobs as well as of the stimulating ones. The reasons why this should be so go beyond fairness, because without it there

will not be full empowerment. Nor will the advantages of cooperation be fully achieved without widespread knowledge among the
members of a compartment about all the tasks it is undertaking. A
bit of specialisation may be sensible; some people will be more adept
in precise manual work like repairing bicycles, not everybody is
good at book-keeping and some will be physically stronger than
others. Leadership will be needed, and can be rotated, although
perhaps not everyone wants to take the lead; the difficulties in
getting someone to take the chair at an informal meeting are not
always the result of false modesty.

This is what Roberto Unger has to say about the distribution of
tasks:

> "Unless individuals deal with one another in a multiplicity of
> different ways, they cannot discover the organic unity of each
> other's personalities. When another is always seen as the
> performer of a particular role, he must tend to become that role,
> first in his fellows' eyes, then in his own. And unless the
> spectrum of interaction is broad, there will be no basis of
> common experience upon which common ends might develop.
> Or if they do develop, they will do so under the constraints of a
> particular specialised activity and of the outlook it
> imposes....Multipurpose organisation complements small-
> group interaction. Whereas the latter makes persons visible to
> each other, the former expands the variety of their encounters.
> In this way it both fosters the recognition of individuality and
> contributes to a shared experience from which shared ends
> might arise."

The industrial revolution brought task-specialisation because of the
great increase in productivity which it produced – when, for
example, cart-making ceased to be the task of a craftsman and an
apprentice and was organised instead on the principle of the division
of labour. Rotating tasks, as in Unger's multipurpose organisation,
reverses the trend towards ever-increasing specialisation. How can
that be done without losing the high productivity which the division
of tasks provided?

The answer is that the division of tasks works by making it
possible to learn more effective ways of carrying out those tasks and
that if other ways of learning are available the division is no longer
essential. Compartments, with the multi-order feedback generated
by intense communication within them, are innovation systems.
Skill in questioning old assumptions constructively, competence in
drawing on the experience of every member of the group in order to

find new solutions, the confidence which membership of a community gives when experimenting with new methods or when adapting to external pressures, all go to make the compartment capable of continuous learning.

This is how Berth Jonnson describes production at Volvo's plant at Uddevalla in Sweden:

> "The Uddevalla car builders have the very best professional training. They have become well-rounded employees, in some ways like old-fashioned craftsmen but also trained to use computers and to be familiar with the new techniques. They must understand the entire production process, not just fragments of it.
>
> The car builders are divided into groups of teams of eight or ten. Each group has responsibility for a much greater part of each system in the car than at the Kalmar plant....There are no traditional foremen to supervise work and decide who does what. Instead, each group is trained to work cooperatively. Each group is able to access information on the results of their work via a computer placed right in the working area. This goes for quality production as well as for financial information. The jobs and the assignments of white and blue collar workers have been integrated as much as possible. They work close to each other – in order to encourage speedy and informal contact.
>
> In order to promote good social relations in each group, there is a mix of age groups and sexes. The experience from Kalmar has shown that this is the best way to get the most out of the different levels of skill and knowledge among the individuals within a group."

These production groups are not compartments, but their method of working has apparently been successful when compared with the traditional production line. The example shows how group working can generate a learning environment. So the rotation of tasks within a group spreads understanding of task variety and reduces complacency. It therefore helps the compartment to find better ways of doing things.

The Creative Compartment

Whether we call it a clan, a community or a compartment, a group of a few hundred people has the opportunity to generate great creative energy in achieving a common aim, in carrying out a common project, in solving a common problem. Almost any group of this size can assemble a rich blend of skills and knowledge, giving it the potential to produce extraordinary results. To fulfil this potential for directed energy and creativity, certain things must be in place. These are summarised below. When this happens, the compartment becomes so special that it deserves a special name. *I will call it the creative compartment.*

These are the features of the creative compartment:

- Within the compartment there is complete openness about all task-related matters as well as considerable openness about personal matters. This openness leads to mutual trust between all members of the compartment's community.
- Every member of the compartment has a good understanding of common purposes and contributes to the evolution of these purposes. This leads to strong feelings of empowerment and of commitment to these purposes.
- Compartment members give each other support, but they expect others to have competence and diligence in furthering the group's purposes.
- Compartment members can communicative effectively on factual and ethical matters and on matters of feeling. They can give and receive constructive criticism on all these matters. An allied competence is in interpersonal process. Open communication is not constrained by power or manipulation.
- Tasks are distributed fairly between members and rotated, so that everyone has a wide experience of different tasks.
- Members of the compartment share a common language and a common set of concepts, which they develop as communicative and problem-solving tools, in their shared work and life. Communication is mainly broadcast and often uncodified.
- The compartment's membership is a few hundreds of people, which provides enough resource to tackle significant projects but retains a face-to-face communicative style.
- There is a clear boundary marking off compartment members from non-members and a strikingly different expectation about openness, trust, shared purposes and shared language inside the boundary, compared with expectations across it.

With this combination of features, there can be an explosion of innovation, of adaptability to changing external circumstances and of creative problem-solving in the compartment. Intense internal communication allows its projects to be brought to fruition in a timely way, it enables new projects to be started easily, it constantly enhances performance standards and continuously raises levels of quality. *The result is a truly creative compartment, in which the creative capability of human beings is unlocked – perhaps to an unimaginable extent.*

My model of the creative compartment could be seen as an 'ideal type', as a device for analysing social situations, which might be found, in different cases, to approach more or less closely to the ideal. Thus particular groups of people could be said to be more or less like a creative compartment. Or my model could be seen as an ideal in the sense that it is a condition which we should strive to create. In fact I think the model is both a descriptive tool and a goal. Some may think it is a utopian goal. I hope this book will show that it is not an impossible one. In any case I agree with Alasdair MacIntyre's remark "that the charge of utopianism is sometimes best understood more as a symptom of those who level it than an indictment of the projects against which it is directed."

Notes

Celltech's Project Management System, pages 75-79. My article in the journal *Systems Practice*, 2, 4, 397-412 (1989), entitled 'Systems Practice from the Start: Some Experiences in a Biotechnology Company', gives further information about the Project Management system and other systems at Celltech. The information about Celltech's business in its seventh year is taken from the Annual Report of Celltech Group plc for 1987 and about the success of the GS amplification system from the Annual Report for 1992.

Groupthink, pages 81-82. Donald N. Michael. *On Learning to Plan – and Planning to Learn: The Social Psychology of Changing Toward Future-Responsive Societal Learning,* Jossey-Bass, San Francisco, 1973, pp 218-224. Michael's study of human behaviour amid the complexities of 'advanced' society has been a source of inspiration for me.

The Origin of Life, pages 83-85. In 1938 Oparin suggested that life might have begun in globules containing polymerised organic molecules. A much more advanced theory is put forward in Manfred Eigen and Peter Schuster, *The Hypercycle: A Principle of Natural Self-Organisation.* Springer-Verlag, Berlin, 1979. See also: Manfred Eigen, William Gardiner, Peter Schuster and Ruthild Winkler-Oswatitsch. The Origin of Genetic Information, *Scientific American,*

244, 4, April 1981. More about self-organising and self-replicating systems is in Erich Jantsch, *The Self-Organising Universe,* Pergamon, Oxford, 1981.

Cooperation and Competition in Japan, page 86. See Bohdan Hawrylyshyn. *Road Maps to the Future: Towards More Effective Societies.* Pergamon, Oxford, 1980 and Lester Thurow. *Head to Head: The Coming Economic Battle among Japan, Europe and America,* Brealey, London 1993.

The Distribution of Tasks, pages 86-88. See Roberto M. Unger. *Knowledge and Politics.* The Free Press, New York, 1975. Pages 262-7. Also Berth Jonsson. Production Philosophy at Volvo. In Michael Maccoby (Ed.) *Sweden at the Edge: Lessons for American and Swedish Managers,* University of Pennsylvania Press, Philadelphia, 1991. Page 117.

Utopianism, page 90. Alasdair MacIntyre, *Three Rival Versions of Moral Enquiry,* Duckworth, London, 1990. Page 235.

6

Power and Conflict

Building a new organisation from scratch is exciting. There are fewer limitations than usual; for a while all is bright confident morning. When in 1980 I started the task of building Celltech, there were several reasons for confidence. We had a pledge from a group of five investors of a total of £12 million in equity capital; we had the enthusiastic cooperation of one of the best bioscience laboratories in the world, the Medical Research Council's Laboratory of Molecular Biology in Cambridge, where Watson and Crick had worked out the structure of DNA and where Milstein and Köhler had discovered how to make monoclonal antibodies; the scientific opportunities were endless and there was great public interest about the new technology and indeed about the formation of Celltech.

But opportunities bring dangers. In this case public expectations were so high that it seemed impossible to meet all of them however well we did, there was a need to move very fast so as to keep the lead which we had in the technology and there was little tradition of doing this kind of thing in the UK and no really suitable models for the kind of company we had to create. And our good fortune had made some influential people envious.

Like every newly-formed organisation, we had no organisational history, good or bad, and thus had the chance to avoid bad habits. The pressures on us were strong, but if the founding team kept its nerve we could avoid the blankets of hierarchy and start a tradition of empowerment in the company. We could start the virtuous circles of openness and trust, of empowerment and commitment. Of course there was a danger of going in the other direction, of starting vicious rather than virtuous circles. Celltech's high profile could have tempted people to seek individual gain or glory, generating mistrust and lowering everyone's commitment to the company's goals.

The exercise of power in the company presented a particular danger. Writing about vicious circles in organisations, Michael Masuch asks why groups of people so often act in ways that prevent the achievement of their ends. They try to do better, but...

> "... they don't do better. They are somehow trapped in the web of their own actions. The hidden score is their own, but they don't like the music. Unable to stop, they play the unpleasant tune over and over again.
>
> The emerging picture begins to resemble a vicious circle. By trying to avoid undesired outcomes, human actors actually create these outcomes...
>
> An example of the dynamics of expanding vicious circles can be seen in the 'vicious circle of bureaucracy'...The circle has the following general shape. The management of an organisation attempts to bring about some change, such as raising productivity. It does so by rule making, close supervision, or other bureaucratic measures – in short, by increasing formalisation. Instead of helping the organisation reach its goal, these measures trigger apathy, alienation, or other dysfunctional reactions in the work force. Management, unsatisfied with the results but unaware of the real causality, further increases the pressure on the system, and around comes the circle."

We should not forget the temptation there is for managers to get into this kind of circle. At Celltech, the pressure to perform was intense. At times I felt like passing on this pressure by making unreasonable demands on my colleagues. If I did that, I would at least be seen to be doing something decisive. I might have pleased some members of the board of directors. I might even have felt better myself. No doubt I actually did make some mistakes of that kind but, on the whole, I avoided them and so did the rest of the founding team. In due course, visitors to Celltech started to remark that the firm did not feel like most other organisations. Perhaps this was because we had been able to start virtuous circles, not vicious ones, which meant that trust and openness supported each other's growth and that competence in communication grew with practice.

Celltech had a management hierarchy of a fairly conventional kind – the novelty was in the practices, not in the structure. Looking back I am inclined to think that we should have innovated there too, although since no one seemed to feel strongly about the issue, our caution on this matter might have been wise. And anyway the hierarchy was one which listened. My door and those of other senior people were open most of the time, literally and metaphorically, and people came to see us when they felt strongly about something. This was sometimes a personal worry, sometimes a concern about a scientific or business matter. After each monthly board meeting all Celltech staff got together in one room and I told them in some detail what had been discussed and decided by the board. The bolder spirits used that as an opportunity to quiz me in public on policy issues, the less bold preferred not to ask questions in front of several hundred colleagues and instead tackled me during one of the regular visits I made to each section of the firm.

Occasionally, policies the management wanted to adopt were opposed. For example, I thought it a good idea to pay a bonus to the sales staff involved, when we secured a significant contract. But the scientific staff felt that their efforts were just as important in securing contracts and, since sales people were paid to do their job, it would be unfair to give them give special rewards. We had an all-company meeting at which I tried to convince the scientists that it was right to pay these bonuses because salespeople everywhere expected rewards of this kind. The response was that everyone joining Celltech had to learn new ways of doing things and that this should include salespeople. So the proposal was dropped. The sales department was unhappy for a bit but I think they saw the logic too.

In this instance, as well as communication being completely open, there was genuine accountability to the whole staff for fairness in rewards. The management was willing to change its mind as a result of sound arguments. I believe that instances of this kind built trust around the way Celltech was being managed.

As well as direct communication between people in public meetings, groups of twenty or so of Celltech's staff elected one of their number as their representative on a Staff Council which met regularly, both on its own and with senior management. The council provided another channel for communication, which was useful since, even with the utmost goodwill, in a busy world messages can get lost or misread and more than one way of sending them helps to get them through.

Commitment to the success of the company meant there was considerable peer pressure to perform. If a project was not going as well as it should, those working on it were made to feel, sometimes unfairly, that they were letting down their colleagues. There were fierce discussions on issues of strategy, like the balance between risk and reward in choosing projects – appraisals of risk differed between individuals. Mistakes were tolerated but naturally they were not popular. In an ambitious and risk-taking enterprise there was quite a high level of anxiety and the company-wide sharing of information meant that anxiety was widely shared too. Newcomers to the organisation found that it was not easy to give up habits formed in different environments; although we tried to select adaptable people the adaptation required was sometimes a tough one.

Most of the time the circles were virtuous. If communication with individuals is on the basis of openness and equality, and if everyone is treated with respect, individual and institutional aims tend to coincide. And respecting people means having high expectations about their skill, performance and integrity. At Celltech these expectations became self-fulfilling.

Problems of Power

How real was the democracy within Celltech, given that there was a conventional management hierarchy, with greater rewards for senior people? One answer is that in formal terms there was no democracy; Celltech's legal status was that of a Limited Company controlled by its shareholders, who had elected, and could remove, its board of directors, who in turn had appointed, and could remove, its management. In political theory, democracy means that the whole people ultimately have the power to remove their rulers. But the reality in democratic states is that the electoral system gives people only a limited power. Since they usually vote for their government only once every four years or so, the choice people have is effectively restricted – there are numerous ways for those in power to manipulate matters in order to stay there. Formally the voters have all the power, but practically the politicians keep much of it.

I think that at Celltech the reality was to some extent the other way round. Formally it was the outside shareholders who had the power, not those working in the firm (since their shareholdings totalled less than ten percent of the whole). But in actual terms the situation was different. The value of the company lay almost wholly in the skills of the people working there and in the combination of those skills in carrying out research, development and production activities. The portfolio of patent applications and the hardware in the plants and laboratories had a value on their own, but it was much less than the value they had when they were in use by knowledgeable people.

Celltech was therefore a professional firm whose main asset was its people. Because of the long-term nature of the research the investment by the shareholders was essential. Because of the specialist nature of the research the people were not at all easy to replace and their enthusiasm was vital for success. So shareholders and employees had to cooperate if anything was to be achieved. They had to have faith in each other. Power was shared. Once the company had products on the market the situation might change, for example, the shareholders could then sell out to a large firm for a lot of money. But that would quite likely be far in the future and in any case many employees owned shares, not nearly enough to control the company but enough to provide a good financial reward if it were taken over.

Might this balance of power between shareholders and employees have given a lot of power to the management? Well, without management action on organisation and decisions about priorities, not much would have got done. Power can be regarded as the ability to influence events, to make things happen. Anthony Giddens suggests that this transformative capability, this ability to act, is the most fundamental aspect of power. If this is so Celltech's management did have significant power, although by no means absolute power. It was power which was constrained in the long run by the need to satisfy both the shareholders and those working in the business and in the short run by the policies of open communication, of avoiding secrecy and of respect for individuals, policies which were partly initiated by management but, once adopted, were hard to flout or to abandon.

Perhaps the best way of describing management power at Celltech would be to say that I and other senior people had a great deal of influence. In gaining this influence, I think the competence and experience of these senior people counted for quite a bit, as did their willingness to listen properly to everyone and to be influenced by what they heard. Also, everybody in the firm wanted to get clear decisions and were, on the whole, willing to let the senior people take the most important ones. This gave managers influence (a reciprocal concept of power) but avoided dominance (a one-way concept).

The Right to be Heard

A characteristic of democracy is that individuals have the right to be heard. On a national scale this means freedom of speech, freedom of the press and other news media, the right to appeal to an elected representative or to an ombudsman and the right to due process in the courts. For these rights to be effective they must be perceived to be available and the procedures for using them must be reasonably simple. I think that similar rights were there in Celltech, that they were known to be there and that they were freely used. It was the case, and people believed it to be the case, that the force of the better argument would, when necessary, prevail over hierarchical position.

How does this analysis of power fit with the facts of Western economic life? Surely, boards of directors, once they are elected by shareholders, can do what they like, providing they keep within the not-so-difficult constraints of the law? Of course, boards must keep the shareholders happy and they are sometimes far-sighted enough to consider the interests of other 'stakeholders' in the business, employees and customers particularly. Many proposals have been made for institutionalising this accountability to groups other than shareholders, and in Germany, for instance, the system of worker directors and works councils does this. But in the West, even state-owned companies behave in pretty similar ways to the truly capitalist ones, when it comes to relations with employees and customers. Could all this be due to some inexorable laws of organisation, to what Max Weber called the 'iron cage' of bureaucracy? Is it inevitable that large organisations, and even medium sized ones, will develop the same pattern of power relations?

Certainly, different styles of organisation, such as cooperatives, have not flourished. But Stewart Clegg writes of the lack of evidence that the fairly general pattern of power in Western economic organisations really is due to inexorable laws. He suggests that two other factors may offer a better explanation: first, the fact that organisations imitate each other so that once a pattern gets established it is hard for a rival pattern to get a serious trial and, second, that the prevailing pattern suits those in power very well and they will strive to perpetuate it. If Clegg is right, then it would be perfectly possible to break the pattern by changing some of the widely-held and generally unquestioned assumptions about organisation which prevail in Western societies. If open and unconstrained communication became the norm, instead of being a rarity and if there was much greater emphasis on shared purposes in Western organisations, somewhat on Japanese lines, then change could be profound. Until these have been tried, I think we should not be put off by fears of inexorable laws or iron cages.

In view of all this, I believe it is right to say that Celltech had many
of the characteristics which define a creative compartment, particularly the characteristic of unconstrained communication. But
power does indeed corrupt and the price of liberty is indeed eternal
vigilance and these are no less true within a compartment than in a
nation. In the following section, I will look at some restraints which
can prevent influence from turning into domination.

Exit and Voice

Alfred Hirschman offers a most perceptive account of the the
restraints on organisational power. Hirschman imagines a situation
in which an organisation starts to fail in some respect. The
organisation could be a business firm, which fails to satisfy its
customers for goods or services, or it could be a political party,
which fails to provide political satisfaction for its supporters, or it
could be an organisation which fails to attract or retain good
employees. The customers, the party supporters or the employees
can respond to organisational failure in one or both of the following
ways:

> "(1) Some customers stop buying the firm's products or some
> members leave the organisation: this is the *exit option*. As a
> result, revenues drop, membership declines, and the manage-
> ment is impelled to search for ways and means to correct
> whatever faults have led to exit.
>
> (2) The firm's customers or the organisation's membership
> express their dissatisfaction directly to management or to some
> other authority to which management is subordinate or through
> general protest addressed to anyone who cares to listen: this is
> the *voice option*. As a result management once again engages in a
> search for the causes and possible cures of customers' and
> members' dissatisfaction."

Exit is voting with your feet. It is the mechanism on which
economists tend to rely. On this view, the summation of customers'
choices gives strength to the invisible hand of the market. The
summation of their exits puts pressure on the firm to improve.

Voice is telling the boss what is wrong. It is the mechanism studied
by political theorists. The more articulate and widespread the
protest the more an organisation's managers take note. That is not
by any means to say that exit only applies to firms and voice only to
political parties. Hirschman's point is that economists tend to study
exit and political scientists to study voice.

Traditional managements, whether of businesses, political parties or other membership organisations, tend to see exit as treason and voice as mutiny. To preserve their organisational power, they want loyalty from their customers and their members. They may therefore ignore the calls for improvement which exit and voice both make. They try to convert voice into 'letting off steam', hoping that after some protests things will return to normal, that changes uncomfortable to management will be not be necessary. The response to exit may also be to muffle its effects through 'better presentation of our policies'.

In the case of business, the response to exit could be some type of cartel, tacit collusion between firms or perhaps political action aimed at excluding competitors. Sometimes such responses work, which leads management to continue on that path rather than making the changes which customers or members want. The customers or members may then switch to the alternative option in order to get their point across. Which means that the mix between exit and voice changes over time depending on the interaction, possibly a complex one, between moves by managements and moves by customers or members.

Hirschman explores the mix between exit and voice which will most likely get the best performance out of organisations and concludes with a triple suggestion:

> "In order to retain their ability to fight deterioration those organisations that rely primarily on one of the two reaction mechanisms need an occasional injection of the other. Other organisations may have to go through regular cycles in which exit and voice alternate as principal actors. Finally, an awareness of the inborn tendencies toward instability of any optimal mix may be helpful in improving the design of institutions that need both exit and voice to be maintained in good health."

The creative compartment has superb internal communication. Voice is therefore its prime mechanism for improvement. I have no doubt that at Celltech the voice of all who worked for the company was heard. Everyone could have an influence, small or large, on the policies and priorities of the firm. We also listened to our shareholders, our customers, our academic collaborators.

Exit should not be ruled out, even in a compartment where voice is at its the most effective. Maintaining the exit option is essential, both for the health of the compartment and for the freedom of its members. When at Celltech we accepted that certain people, whose full potential could not be realised in the company, might want to leave, and if so that this should happen without any rancour, we were not really being altruistic. In the longer run it suited the company well for people to have the option of exit, because of the signal for improvement which exit sent.

When someone decided to leave Celltech, I always tried to find out why. Sometimes the reason was that the person's spouse had got a job in a far away location, like San Francisco. Sometimes the reason was that another company had offered a more responsible job than we, in a small company, were able to do. We took such a case as a compliment to our ability to develop peoples' talents, even though a rival firm got the benefit. Sometimes the reason was less pleasing: for example, the person had decided to go because he or she felt some lack of recognition by the company. When this happened, we had to make sure we learned from past mistakes, otherwise the message given by the person's exit would not be a force for improvement.

Quiet Leadership

The string quartet is a small work group and communication within a quartet while playing is peculiarly intense.

> "Many players commented in the interviews that the ability to listen and respond to each other was the most important characteristic that differentiated quartet players from soloists."

> "The members of successful groups tended to be friends. As one viola player put it, "We are friends...To play chamber music with someone you don't like – I can't imagine that. How can I play with somebody I don't like? He can be a Paganini for all I care. I think we play more and more to each other." Several described a string quartet as a marriage, not to one person but to three, with the exception that there is no sex (which, of course, is not always true)."

These quotations are from an article by Keith Murnighan and Donald Conlon. Their comments on power relationships within string quartets are:

> "All of the groups except one espoused democracy. First violinists in the successful groups, however, recognised the need for a directive leader more than first violinists in the less successful groups. They took active control of many of the group's activities and acknowledged this in their interviews.

> They did not advertise their leadership, however, within their group. Instead they advocated democratic action and, it appears, did so sincerely. Thus, they preserved the leader-democracy paradox by acting as a leader while simultaneously advocating democracy."

The authors of this paper refer to this kind of leadership as 'leading quietly'. The implication is that because it is done quietly it is not noticed and no doubt this is partly the reason why it works in the setting of the string quartet, and probably in many other settings. But remember, it was the successful quartets which were led in this way, the ones which were achieving their goals. The members perhaps felt that leadership was essential for success but that they also wanted to preserve their right to voice on matters of real importance to them. The continuing espousal of democracy might well have been seen by them as the way to ensure that right.

Exit was also an option: the study shows that there was turnover in quartet membership, with one or two members changing, on average, during a decade. It is important that exit is available, but if it is an option which is exercised too much the damage to the cohesion of the compartment could be serious. In a string quartet, a rate of turnover of one or two players per decade equates, for a larger group, to a rate of turnover of less than five percent per year. Celltech had a rate of turnover of between five and ten percent a year for most of its first ten years, which was not too big a problem and a level of turnover which was on the low side for high-technology firms. (This excludes turnover among the secretaries and clerical staff where the turnover was sometimes as high as 25% a year. Perhaps these people did not feel the same degree of involvement in the life of Celltech as the rest of the staff. This is quite a big issue, but one which I don't have space to explore here.)

To what extent could the leadership by myself and other senior people at Celltech be called 'quiet'? Well, it was not quiet in the sense of being self-effacing; my colleagues and I frequently spoke at all-company and other meetings and paid regular visits to all parts of the operation to talk to individuals or small groups at their work-places. But I hope it was quiet in the sense that we listened very hard and that we did not claim any monopoly of wisdom about the direction the business should be going. If this is quiet leadership, I'm all for it.

Dissent for the Sake of the Task

I've said that, in my view, leadership should involve a lot of listening. Widespread listening will produce a range of views – often conflicting ones. In the extreme, this can be a problem, if polarised positions develop and conflict ensues. But without disagreement a business loses a vital resource. In many ways it becomes a dead business.

No one can foretell the future and yet a view of the future has always to be taken, even if the view is simply that the future will be the same as the past. In most businesses, there is disagreement about the future, whether those disagreeing recognise this or not. And different views about the future lead to different views about what should be done in the present. In making guesses about the future and judgments about current action, everyone draws on his or her experience. Differences in personal experience and differences in individual temperament will lead to different judgments. If a group of people is capable of communicating about these different judgments, and of synthesising them into something better than any one of them, then the group has an enormously valuable resource.

Jane Jacobs suggests that a particular feature of commercial life is a belief that it is right to dissent for the sake of the task in hand. She says that the same applies among scientists. It is easy to understand why this could be so, since without dissent there will be no chance of drawing on different people's judgments. If there is absolutely no dissent, whatever kind of groupthink happens to be around will just continue. Of course, the ability to handle dissent constructively is a vital interpersonal process skill – there will be plenty of creative dissent in a creative compartment, where the power of the better argument is decisive.

Dissent can turn into conflict – sometimes into irreconcilable conflict – whatever the process skills of the people concerned. This happened at Celltech just before my retirement as CEO. I can't disclose the full story – complete openness should be the rule within a compartment, but not necessarily outside it – but here is an edited version. There was one obvious internal candidate to succeed me and also a case for trying to recruit the new CEO from outside the company. As the date of my retirement came closer, rival factions started to form in the board of directors and among senior people: one faction was for the internal candidate, the other for looking outside. Personal ambition played a part in causing this factional split and influenced people to join one faction or another. Differing views about the future of the business also contributed to the conflict. Eventually the board decided to recruit someone from outside, which led to some resignations and to a lot of acrimony.

I realise now that I made several mistakes in this situation, one of which was allowing my own emotions to stop me being as open as usual with my colleagues. Others also failed to be open. The result was undoubtedly damaging for Celltech. Exit was the option chosen by several talented people. Others who stayed, nevertheless felt that, in this case, the better argument was not behind the decision. Business performance almost certainly suffered. However, my successor was a very astute person who has helped the company through a difficult time and, as far as I can see, has preserved its open and creative culture. Celltech's future now looks good.

Personal Goals and Group Goals

Dissent for the sake of the task is usually vital, because of the variety it generates and, through this variety, the problem-solving capability it gives. But, as the story of the appointment of my successor at Celltech illustrates, dissent can degenerate into strife. One reason for this is that group goals and personal goals are not the same. This factor will always be able to affect the life of a compartment. Coping with this disparity is yet another skill which compartments need to learn.

There never can, and never should, be complete coincidence between individual self-fulfillment and the achievement of group goals. Complete coincidence would obliterate differences and suppress dissent, reducing adaptability, creativity and problem-solving capability and producing a 'cloned' set of people. Too little coincidence would, on the other hand, lead to perpetual conflict and lack of common purpose. In fact, it would mean there was no group worth speaking of. In a creative compartment, there should be a good overlap between the goals and values of individuals and those of the group as a whole, but not so much overlap that variety vanishes.

So differences should remain, but it is vital that their nature is clear to all. Differences in goals and values can be challenged, and the result of a challenge will probably be that some differences disappear, but others continue. The group needs a capacity for collective action, action which takes differences in viewpoint into account but is not paralysed by them. By achieving clarity in group and individual purposes, the creative compartment can approach this ideal.

To get close to the ideal requires that each should come to have strong sympathy with all others in the group, which Roberto Unger calls the political equivalent of love. Without face-to-face dealings with each other this will not happen and these dealings should be of a varied type, so as to encourage the recognition of others as whole people rather than as holders of particular roles or as representatives of particular viewpoints.

Power in the creative compartment will inevitably start from some historical basis or other and the more talented of the compartment's members will have a continuing basis for power because of their talents. If there is to be a steady move away from power based on history or on merit, towards the power of the better argument, talented people can be both a great advantage and a threat to the group. Unger quotes Goethe: "against the superior gifts of another person there is no defence but love". If talented people use their gifts to achieve the fairly established goals of the group, then all is well. But if they use their gifts to push group goals too far towards their own, then it is not.

Other threats to effectiveness and fairness in a group are the lack of structure in decision-making, leading to unending debate (a well-known feature of cooperative organisations), and a lack of privacy for individuals caused by too much openness. The decision problem might be solved by having the aims or purposes of the group in mind at all times – what in more technical language is called attention to superordinate goals. The privacy problem might be solved by sympathetic discrimination on which issues to raise when; Unger says that within the group no subject should be barred from discussion but not all subjects should be for discussion at all times. The ultimate safeguard is freedom to join and to leave a group. No one should be forced to join a group or to remain in it. The option of exit is, as we have seen, of great value to the group as well as to its members.

An Illustration

Jack Nelson was a chemical engineer by training. He was also a good systems thinker. In the 1970s he founded a consultancy serving the process industries, such as chemicals, steel, aluminium and brewing. The combination of engineering and systems thinking proved successful, helping Nelson Associates to develop a world-wide practice. As the firm grew towards its peak size of 100 consultants, its expertise became more and more industry-specific and less use was made of the general systems insights of the founder. In any case, by the mid 1980s client businesses had more people of their own who were able to think in systems terms, so this expertise seemed less of an advantage.

In the 1980s Nelson Associates was reorganised into three semi-autonomous divisions, each specialising in an industrial sector, with the aim of empowerment of the consultants in these divisions. Jack Nelson and three other consultants formed a central group, mainly undertaking assignments covering several industry sectors. The Oil and Gas Division became very successful through its skill in evaluating new pipeline proposals. This division's clients were no longer the big oil and gas companies, but investors, government agencies and sometimes environmental protection groups. This meant that Jack Nelson's personal reputation in the oil and gas industry was now less important for winning business.

This gave people in the Oil and Gas Division the feeling that they did not need the rest of the firm. In 1988 virtually everyone in the division unexpectedly resigned and formed themselves into a new consultancy firm. They claimed that the rest of Nelson Associates had been living off their success for too long. "Good bye parasites !" they said. Some of his colleagues tried to persuade Jack Nelson to sue the breakaway group, since there was a strong suspicion that copies of client records had been taken by them. Jack wouldn't do that, partly because he blamed himself for the situation, which showed that he'd been seriously out of touch with a major section of the firm, and partly because he realised that what had happened might not, in fact, be a bad thing for the rest of the firm.

By 1990, it was clear that on the second point he was right. The demand for pipeline studies fell drastically and soon the breakaway consultancy collapsed. Business conditions became tough for Nelson Associates too, but they were much less narrowly specialised and more skilled in general problem-solving than the breakaways, and so were able to get work from new sectors. The task of diversification would have been much more formidable had the former Oil and Gas Division, with its 40 consultants, had still been part of the firm. So their departure had indeed been a blessing in disguise.

What can we learn from the Nelson story?

- Firstly and most obviously, that identity of interests between individuals and the group cannot be taken for granted. Without continuing communication about group, sub-group and individual purposes and interests and a sincere effort to find courses of action which serve all of these, conflict will, sooner or later, emerge.
- Secondly, that the move to create empowerment by forming semi-autonomous divisions did not work very well. Empowerment can be dangerous unless openness and excellence in communication go alongside it.
- Thirdly, that exit can be by a sub-group as well as by individuals, leading to fission of the initial group. If the goals of a sub-group cannot be met within the larger whole, this may be the best outcome. But in the case of Nelson Associates, it was not a good outcome for the exiting group. Had there been a real debate about the advantages and disadvantages of membership of Nelson, the oil and gas people might have realised the advantages of staying, that the goals of the larger group were closer than it seemed to the real interests of the sub-group.

Hiding Conflict

The anthropologist F.G. Bailey describes the negotiations which take place between the families of a bridal couple in the Kond Hills in India. With the aid of a go-between, the families make enquiries about the prospective mates and their families. If these point to a promising match, private meetings are held at which this early information may be confirmed and at which the financial contributions which both parties will make to the couple may be agreed. There then follows an open meeting at which the boy's people go to the girl's village to hand over their contribution, the bridewealth.

> "The two parties sit facing each other, and then the bride's spokesman opens the proceedings by proclaiming that, seeing "the big turbans and strong arms" of the visitors they are afraid. "From what country do you come?" he asks. "From far away", the groom's orator replies and then launches into an elaborate account of how they chanced by this place and saw in the pool a lotus of surpassing beauty, which they have a mind to pluck and take with them. The bride's spokesman replies that

many others have tried to pluck the flower but have gone away because the pool is very deep and contains fierce crocodiles and dangerous serpents....they pass to bargaining. "....if the gold and silver that you bring stand as tall as the flower, then you may take it." Then, the conventions having been duly observed, there is an abrupt shift from poetry to business, and the bride's representative says, "Then fetch it out and get it counted!" and that is what they then do.

...The ceremony is a lie. I do not mean merely that there are no snakes and no crocodiles and no boats and no heaps of gold and silver. The ceremony itself is false in the sense that it is like the facade on a building, presenting to the beholder a front that is more acceptable than the real building that it conceals.

...The ceremony rewrites the history of the marriage negotiations in a form that is not only memorable (because it is both dramatic and stylized) but also is a preemptive exclusion from the *public* record (but not from *all* records) of what in fact happened."

Ceremonies of this type are familiar in Western business negotiations. For instance, as the Shell group is one of the largest in the world its dealings are frequently with smaller companies, and representatives of these companies usually open a meeting with a remark about "the mighty Shell", no doubt meaning the over-mighty Shell. Bailey thinks that 'collusive lying' is a common aspect of social life. Will that be so in a creative compartment? What about my meetings with Celltech's staff?

Well, at Celltech informal discussions did take place outside the public sessions and sometimes this meant that the public meeting had a partly ceremonial air to it. My senior colleagues and I did keep our ears to the ground so we were usually unsurprised by what what was said. But this didn't happen all the time. The reason why the meeting at which the special bonus for sales staff was challenged was such a memorable one was because the strength of the challenge was unexpected and the need for me to climb down was completely unexpected too. That was not a ceremonial occasion.

Bailey's thesis is that there is nothing unusual about collusive lying. It happens the world over and it illustrates the links there are between knowledge, interests and power. This thesis is a useful reminder not to be complacent about communication. Everything may appear to be open, everything to be agreed, but conflict may still be there, hidden by mutual consent, or as Bailey puts it, by collusive lying, and ready to reemerge.

Conclusions

Variety and dissent are essential for creativity and adaptability. The communicative competence of the creative compartment allows variety and dissent to be sustained without harm to the compartment's cohesion. The way to make conflict constructive is to seek clarity about individual, sub-group and whole group purposes, using the compartment's openness and interpersonal process skill. In the creative compartment, conflict is brought into the open and used as a creative resource. In a traditional hierarchy, conflict is suppressed, because the boss's goals are supposed to be the group's goals and any contradictory voice is treason.

However, even with the most constructive possible use of conflict, it can happen that group goals cannot be reconciled with those of individuals or of sub-groups. If so, exit of individuals or sub-groups is the best outcome, best for those leaving and best for those remaining. Sometimes neither the option of voice nor the option of exit is chosen. Then conflict remains hidden, not by the blankets of hierarchy, but by mutual consent, by ceremonials or by paradoxes.

How can we act so as to make conflict constructive?

- We can do everything possible, in organisations of whatever size and with whatever level of empowerment, to make *voice* an effective option. We can continue to show our colleagues that dissent is a wonderful resource for any organisation, provided the skill is there to use it well. If the skill is not there, it is unprofessional not to acquire it, since the lack of it is very damaging to the organisation.
- We must pay careful attention to entry to and exit from groups. The option of *exit* must never be denied, but for organisational health it should only be used if voice has been fully used and if group goals really are incompatible with individual goals. Compartmentation is very valuable here. The well-defined boundary of the compartment shows us where entry and exit should be lovingly considered. It also marks out the area within which compatibility of goals should be diligently sought. Outside the compartment, no problem need arise from a wide divergence in goals. It is inside the compartment that we should strive for open debate and for the constructive synthesis of the group's goals.

Notes

Mark Dodgson writes in *Celltech: The First Ten Years of a Biotechnology Company. (Op. Cit.)* "Although I believe I know the company reasonably well, and have been assisted in this by unlimited and generous access to people and records within and outside the company, I cannot claim that what follows is 'the' Celltech story. Inevitably, it is *my* interpretation of how the company reached its present position." These comments apply just as much to my story about Celltech.

Vicious Circles, page 93. See Michael Masuch. Vicious Circles in Organizations. *Administrative Science Quarterly.* **30**, 1, 14-33. (1985).

Power as the Means to Make Things Happen, page 96. See Anthony Giddens. *The Constitution of Society.* Polity Press, Cambridge. (1984).

Inexorable Laws, page 97. See Stewart R. Clegg. *Modern Organizations: Organization Studies in the Postmodern World.* Sage, London (1990) Chapter 3.

Exit and Voice, pages 98-100. See Albert O.Hirschman. *Exit, Voice and Loyalty: Responses to Decline in Firms, Organizations and States.* Harvard U.Press, Cambridge, Mass. (1970).

Quiet Leadership, pages 100-101. See J.Keith Murnighan and Donald E. Conlon. The Dynamics of Intense Work Groups: A Study of British String Quartets. *Administrative Science Quarterly.* **36**, 165-186. (1991).

Dissent for the Sake of the Task, pages 102-3. See Jane Jacobs. *Systems of Survival: A Dialogue on the Moral Foundations of Commerce and Politics.* Random House, New York. (1992).

Personal Goals and Group Goals, pages 103-4. See Roberto M.Unger. *Knowledge and Politics.* The Free Press, New York. (1975). Chapter 6.

Hiding Conflict, pages 106-7. See F.G.Bailey. *The Prevalence of Deceit.* Cornell U.P., Ithaca (1991) pp 36-9 & 61. Don Michael pointed out to me the relevance of Bailey's work to the description of what happened at Celltech. This is one of many things in this book over which I have had his help.

Part II

The seamless communication and shared purposes within the creative compartment are the solution to the problem of coordinating its internal activities. But this solution cannot extend to the whole world, since the means of the creative compartment work only on the smaller scale. The boundary of the compartment marks the transition point to a different kind of coordination, to coordination which cannot now rely solely on a close-knit clan.

In Part II of this book I explore what kinds of coordination would be needed to link together the activities of two, several or many compartments. Compartmentation will have a huge influence outside the compartment, as well as inside it, so in the next chapter I start by looking at the kinds of coordination available and at which kind will be appropriate in a world of compartments.

I then go on to describe more specific interactions between a compartment and the world outside it. In Chapter Eight I look at ways of spanning a compartment's boundary and at networking between compartments. In Chapter Nine I look at the need for each compartment to be accountable to its outside world, and at how this need might be met.

7

Markets and Hierarchies, Clans and Fiefs

A good way of looking at general problem of coordination outside the compartment is to use Max Boisot's and John Child's model of four modes of coordination – markets and hierarchies, clans and fiefs. Both markets and hierarchies use codified information and they are systematised, impersonal, mechanistic modes of coordination. In contrast, clans and fiefs use uncodified information and are flexible, personal, organic coordination modes.

Although markets and hierarchies are similar in that they are impersonal, they differ in their openness. Markets are open, while hierarchies are controlled and secretive. This distinction applies also to clans and fiefs. This time both are personal, but they differ in that clans are open, fiefs controlled and secretive.

Markets	*Hierarchies*
Impersonal, open.	Impersonal, secretive.

Clans	*Fiefs*
Personal, open.	Personal, secretive.

The Four Modes of Coordination

Markets

In classical economic theory market coordination is self-organising. Traders evolve a way of interacting which gets the results they want. The theory sees deals as being done between selfishly motivated individuals, who react to pressures such as their competitors' lower prices or their customers' refusal to buy. Moral scruples do not enter into this picture, although enlightened self-interest can do, represented for instance, by a decision to choose honesty as the best policy.

The theory supposes that everyone has a choice, so any long term business relationship must go on producing mutual benefit, since otherwise one of the parties will bring it to an end.

This theory is an abstract one, because it assumes that humans are desiccated, calculative economic maximisers. Given the degree of abstraction, it is surprising that the theory is useful at all. But it can be, provided we use it carefully, unlike those economists who fall in love with the models derived from the theory, and unlike the politicians who use it in much the same way that televangelists use religion.

The classical theory can be helpful in understanding how markets promote an efficient allocation of resources between various desired ends. Also, the picture of self-interested entities learning how to work together for mutual benefit, can help us understand how compartments might coordinate their activities. It ties in with the idea that cooperation and competition, rather than being mutually exclusive, often work together to produce novel and useful results. Let us look further at the interaction of cooperation and competition.

In his book *The Evolution of Cooperation*, Robert Axelrod seeks to discover the conditions under which people with no inclination to cooperate nevertheless regularly do so, and do so without being forced to by any hierarchical authority. He thinks that it is unduly pessimistic to accept the Hobbesian argument that people will only live and work together harmoniously when they are frightened of the agents of a powerful government. But he also knows that people are not angels; he has, for instance, studied the behaviour of the United States Senate. So the question is: why should people cooperate, if selfishness looks more likely to pay? Surely good guys finish last ?

Axelrod investigates this by using the game of the Prisoner's Dilemma. In its original form, the game has two prisoners either of whom can get off scot-free by informing on the other, who is then executed. If they both inform, there is evidence against both and both die. If they cooperate with each other by keeping their mouths shut then eventually they will both be released, but can they trust one another sufficiently for both of them to escape death? The variant of the model which Axelrod uses leaves out the execution, which has the advantage of allowing the game to be repeated many times. There are numerical payoffs for each round and these are added up over the whole game to get to a final score. The aim is to get the highest final score; playing endless rounds of such a simple game is very boring but this is just the kind of game computers love to play.

Axelrod arranged a competition to which he invited not players but computer programmes, submitted by experts of many kinds, and set the programmes to play the Prisoner's Dilemma game against each other for round after round. Rather to his surprise, the winner was the simplest programme submitted, one called TIT FOR TAT, which has just this rule: start by cooperating and then do whatever the other player did on the last round. When the outcome was announced many people thought they must be able to design a programme to beat such a simple formula, but in a second tournament TIT FOR TAT won again, in spite of the fact that the people sending in programmes for the second tournament had been able to study the detailed results of the first. From the results of this competition Axelrod was able to work out some rules for success in an iterated game of Prisoner's Dilemma.

The first rule is to be nice, by which he means don't ever be the first to cheat on the other player. This ensures that cooperation gets going as quickly as possible and also reduces the probability of a pattern of continuing retaliation, along the lines of the vendetta. The second rule is to be provokable, that is to repay a defection immediately. Axelrod says he started the project believing that you should be slow to anger but found that it is better to respond at once to a provocation, as otherwise there is a risk of sending the wrong signal, of being seen as exploitable. Thirdly, you should be forgiving; if you have to retaliate to punish a defection, then you should go back to cooperation immediately afterwards. Finally, don't be too complicated. Cooperation depends on others being able to read what you are up to and complications which baffle the other player can induce suspicion and thus reduce cooperation.

More about Markets – Tit For Tat in Real Life

A game like the Prisoner's Dilemma is not real life but Axelrod gives many examples of these principles at work, in the bargaining of elected politicians, in international politics, in biology, and in war, including:

> "The fascinating case of the 'live and let live' system which emerged during the trench warfare of World War I. In the midst of this bitter conflict the front-line soldiers often refrained from shooting to kill – providing their restraint was reciprocated by the soldiers on the other side. What made this mutual restraint possible was the static nature of trench

> warfare, where the same small units faced each other for extended periods of time. The soldiers of these opposing small units actually violated orders from their own high commands in order to achieve tacit cooperation with each other. A detailed look at this case shows that when conditions are present for the emergence of cooperation, cooperation can get started and prove stable in situations which otherwise appear extraordinarily unpromising. In particular, the 'live and let live' system demonstrates that friendship is hardly necessary for the development of cooperation. Under suitable conditions, cooperation can develop even between antagonists."

As shown by this example and others, and by the results of the computer tournament, cooperation does not evolve unless there is a strong likelihood of continuing interaction between the participants. Unless the future casts its shadow on the present, defection may become attractive. In situations like the last round of a game of the Prisoner's Dilemma (providing you know that it is the last round), or in dealings with politicians nearing the end of their terms of office or when businesses are near bankruptcy there will be an incentive to cheat, sometimes counteracted by a desire to retain a reputation relevant to future interactions with third parties. The shadow of the future can be enlarged by making interactions between particular parties more frequent and by reducing other interactions, as birds do when they establish a territory or as happens in small towns, whose people are more prone to cooperation than those in big cities.

Further studies in cooperation theory (which I won't go into here) demonstrate that quite small clusters of cooperative people can initiate stable cooperation, even when all those around them are non-cooperators, and that once initiated, cooperation tends to increase. This is inherent in the mechanics of cooperation, driven by the mutual rewards which cooperation produces. Axelrod concludes that the "foundation of cooperation is not really trust, but the durability of the relationship." Or as Richard Dawkins puts it in the introduction to the paperback edition of *The Evolution of Cooperation* "...we start pessimistically by assuming deep selfishness, pitiless indifference to suffering, ruthless heed to individual success. And yet, from such warped beginnings, something that is in effect, if not necessarily in intention, close to amicable brotherhood and sisterhood can come."

This shows that, with the aid of some simple rules, people can gain a great deal from self-organised cooperation, while keeping a basically competitive stance. The paradox of competition working alongside cooperation can be resolved. We can see that there is no reason why market coordination, which is a competitive mode, need rule out cooperation.

Hierarchies

Although markets certainly do work – especially in allocating resources efficiently, in preserving the 'exit' option, and in achieving coordinated action through a combination of cooperation and competition – that does not always happen. Markets can fail to work for a number of reasons. One example is the 'free rider' situation, arising when a number of individuals or organisations are contributing resource to the achievement of a common objective and one of the number tries to retain the benefits without contributing resource. Another example is when participants in a market have very different levels of information on which to make their judgments about the deals they enter into. Yet another is when certain participants collude together to rig a market.

E.J.Hobsbawm identifies the 1870s as the historical point at which the Adam Smith model of capitalism ceased to be credible.

> "The new era which follows the age of liberal triumph was to be very different. Economically it was to move away rapidly from unrestrained competitive private enterprise, government abstention from interference and what the Germans called *Manchesterismus* (the free trade orthodoxy of Victorian Britain), to large industrial corporations (cartels, trusts, monopolies), to very considerable government interference, to very different orthodoxies of policy, though not necessarily of economic theory. The age of individualism ended in 1870, complained the British lawyer A.V.Dicey, the age of 'collectivism' began; and though most of what he gloomily noted as the advances of 'collectivism' strike us as insignificant, he was in a sense right...."

Driven by enormous changes in technology and demography, by increasing international economic rivalry and by the demands of the poor that they should no longer have to bear the horrors of the industrial revolution, the role of the state grew in economic and social affairs during the late 19th century and the first half of the 20th century. The state was then seen as the only corrective for the ills which capitalism had brought. Rational planning was to replace wasteful competition. Earnest and diligent administrators, such as the Fabian Webbs in Britain, would take over from ruthless exploiters. The complexities of capitalism now required that a different kind of coordination be added to that of market mechanisms. Rational, bureaucratic administration by civil servants and by the staffs of business corporations seemed to be the answer to the chaos of competition. Although there was an intense political struggle between left and right over the extent to which coordination was to be provided by the state rather than by private firms, there was much less contention about the role of bureaucratic hierarchies; for many years, it appeared that modernity needed bureaucracies, either private or public.

Today the appeal of hierarchies is waning, but because market failure is quite frequent, the state still has to intervene to set the rules for markets or to carry out various regulatory functions. Company law, protecting creditors and investors, employment law, regulatory agencies supervising stock exchanges or food safety are all examples of state intervention. So is the law of contract and the ability to enforce contracts through the courts. The pioneers who start markets of new kinds usually regulate themselves. Later, as a market gets established, imagination switches from creating a new market to finding ways to manipulate an existing one. That is the point at which state regulation becomes necessary.

Again less so than in the past, hierarchies remain a big feature of private corporations. This no doubt happens because, in their sphere, they provide a more economic means of coordination than markets. But changes like the 'hollowing out' of corporations indicate that the economic balance is shifting, with hierarchies becoming less effective economically than previously. If compartmentation comes into general use, there might be a much more dramatic shift, which would leave corporate hierarchies as the exception, not the rule. Measured by their sales or their assets, large corporations would remain. But they would have much smaller numbers of people and would rely on sub-contracting and collaborations with smaller firms to a much greater extent. Market and clan-like coordination would then become predominant.

Cooperation to Mutual Benefit

Clan-like coordination does not have to be confined to the creative compartment. Although the intensity of interaction and the excellence of communication will be less, sometimes far less, than within the compartment, some of the compartment's attributes can be very useful outside.

Celltech's business success depended on cooperation with a number of large pharmaceutical companies. Sometimes cooperation extended over many years, in programmes of research which could not be defined in any detail at the start, because of their exploratory nature. We had legal contracts covering the cooperation, which laid down how matters like patenting would be handled, but the progress of the research collaboration depended very much on the goodwill between the two companies and between the scientists involved.

People in the two companies could rely on each other. Of course, each looked after his or her own company first, but the collaboration went further than that. Both sides knew that the partnership would almost certainly be a long-lasting one, and tried hard to make it a success for both. This was cooperation which certainly went beyond contractual obligations. It might also have gone beyond enlightened self-interest, and beyond good professional behaviour, because the scientists liked working together, felt committed to the overall project and felt a personal obligation to help the others involved.

Celltech and the partner company had complementary skills, so together we were able to do things which would have been difficult or impossible on our own. To regulate a complex research collaboration wholly by contract would also have been impossible, so some kind of mutual trust was necessary if the scientific goals were to be attained. In setting up the collaboration, the senior people on both sides had to commit themselves to a trusting relationship. In addition, mutual trust grew as the work went on, as people got to know each other and, mostly, to enjoy working with each other. So the building of trust, or of goodwill, was partly a consciously managed process, partly a natural human process.

I believe that in Japanese, the word for the kind of personal trust or goodwill I have described is *shinrai*, in contrast to *shinyo*, the latter being a more impersonal trust, depending on legal contracts or on the general business standing of the partner. That such a distinction is reflected in the Japanese language is significant, since *shinrai* plays an important role in that nation's business. In the language of economists, *shinrai* is a competitive advantage for Japanese business, since it reduces the transaction costs in a business relationship, producing mutual advantage without extensive negotiation or complex contracts. This kind of trust is part of the reason why subcontracting by major firms works so well in Japan, providing lots of flexibility and adaptability for the economy.

Fiefs

The role of fiefs can best be explained by the example of China. In the 1950s, China introduced the Soviet model of state bureaucracy, but without ever achieving the USSR's level of central control. So it is from a starting point of a long feudal tradition, plus a somewhat superficial application of communist methods, that moves towards a market economy are now being made. Not surprisingly, the result is very different from the market economies of the developed capitalist world.

China's huge size and poor infrastructure of transport and communications have always made central control difficult. Today they inhibit the flow of accurate information, for example about stocks and prices of foodstuffs, which is needed for the operation of a large-scale market economy of a Western type. The well-organised flow of information which takes place in the West is simply not possible in China. In any case the tradition has been for things to be settled locally. Add to this strong preference in the Far East (it applies also in Japan) for doing business on the basis of personal relationships, rather than on the basis of impersonal contracts enforceable through the courts, and the difficulty of moving to a Western-style market economy becomes clear.

As China has loosened central control of the economy, what has emerged is a set of fiefs controlled by local magnates, dealing with each other largely on a one-to-one basis and relying on personal relationships in their transactions, not on legal contracts. This seems very much like an industrial version of the landlord system which existed in China for centuries. If it seems like medieval Europe, that is because medieval Europe and medieval China were similar. China may have enough trained people to run central bureaucracies in a modernised way in the major cities but, somewhat like the old imperial bureaucracy, their influence on the local fiefs is remote and limited.

In China, then, the fief is a particularly important mode of coordination. Within and between fiefs, transactions are face-to-face and based on personal trust or on fear. Secrecy is used to sustain the power of the boss. People who do not cooperate are coerced or driven out. The bosses dispense patronage and give some protection to their followers. Perhaps the boss has one or two people who are well-trained enough to handle any dealings with the provincial bureaucracies, but otherwise his henchmen are bullies and bribers.

China retains a communist hierarchy, with some relics of Soviet-style bureaucracy. In an ideal bureaucracy, transactions are impersonal and decisions are those which an official in a hierarchy is supposed to take rather than those of individual preference. Secrecy and formality prevail. Trained people are needed and conceptual skills are important, especially among people at the top.

Parts of China, particularly in the province of Guangdong close to Hong Kong, are becoming part of the world market system, where transactions are impersonal and competitive and ultimately regulated by contracts. Other parts of the country have important local markets, but the coordination achieved is limited. And then there are, no doubt some clans, in which openness and democracy prevail.

To conclude this picture of coordination in China, we can say firstly that fiefs are the main type of coordination. Secondly, there is trading between the fiefs, but of an informal and often unrecorded kind. Thirdly, there are bureaucracies, but these are remote from the bulk of the population. Fourthly, there is a growing market system consisting of those more advanced industries which trade with the rest of the world using Western-style transaction methods.

The Modes of Coordination – Past, Present and Future

Historical Change in the Modes of Coordination

At the risk of some over-simplification and from a rather Eurocentric viewpoint, I will try to put the four modes of coordination into a historical context.

In *pre-modern times*, such as those of Medieval Europe, fiefs were the main method of coordination. On the small scale, the manor was a fief and one with a certain amount of compartmentation, since at work and at home, at prayer or at play, the manorial village was the setting for the everyday activities of the majority of people.

Political-military coordination was through the feudal system. Feudal codes of 'honour' regulated the interaction of fiefs, with relatively little legal or higher political intervention. When coordination on a national scale was needed, kings, queens and the higher nobility exercised fief-like control over the lesser lords. Educational and moral coordination was through the church.

Particularly in the late Middle Ages, national political hierarchies started to develop, including a legal system and a system for tax-gathering, administered by officials on behalf of the monarch. This brought to society the hierarchical method of coordination. Thomas Hobbes, writing right at the end of pre-modern times, welcomed the emergence of the powerful state as means of controlling the violence between rival fiefs.

At around the same time, societies also started to depend on market methods of coordination. Trading and banking grew in the big cities, chiefly regulated by merchants and bankers themselves, and then spread nationally and internationally. Sea and land transport became easier and more widespread. Legal regulation of commerce, including the enforcement of contracts in the courts, became widespread too.

Modern times, starting in the eighteenth century, are typified by an enormous expansion of the hierarchical and market methods of coordination. Both the private and public sectors were involved. (The idea of distinguishing between these sectors is, of course, 'modern'.) Markets were supported and regulated by the state, corporations used hierarchy for internal governance. Individuals found themselves dealing more and more with the state, as taxpayers, as voters or as citizens with rights. They also found themselves dealing with large corporations, as employees or as consumers.

With the arrival of modernism, market mechanisms grew in importance and sophistication helped by supporting legal devices, such as limited liability companies, and by supporting institutions, such as stock exchanges. Market mechanisms needed improved communications, transport and education. Innovation in the legal, educational and communications spheres was also important for the growth of bureaucracies, as professionalism replaced nepotism in state and corporate hierarchies.

Under the pressure of modernisation, fiefs withered. As fiefs tended to be oppressive, modernisation was experienced by many as liberation. But modernisation means systemisation, because both markets and hierarchies depend on codified information and on standardised procedures. And systemisation becomes dehumanising, cancelling out the liberating effects of modernisation. By the nineteenth century, the damaging side effects of bureaucracy and of capitalist markets were starkly clear. In spite of this, systemisation continued. Huge military machines successfully coordinated the activities of millions of soldiers by means of hierarchies carrying out the commands of the top brass. It seemed that many civil tasks, too, were best done in this way and if they were not, coordination should be left to the market. This was one of the origins of the idolatry of giantism, noted by E.F.Schumacher.

Capitalists hated the dehumanising effects of socialist state bureaucracies. Socialists hated the effects of ruthless capitalist greed. Until the second half of the twentieth century, there were few voices equally critical of both. But now the state and the corporation are together under attack, as the impersonal mechanisms they share are increasingly seen as dysfunctional through their suppression of human creativity. It is possible, therefore, to separate out the two mechanisms of markets and bureaucracies from their customary political or ideological connections, recognising that capitalist societies make widespread use of both mechanisms and that the formerly communist societies did too, although in their case the use of market mechanisms was limited to a small part of the economy or was an illegal way of correcting bureaucratic malfunction.

In theory, both markets and bureaucracies are impersonal mechanisms. People using these mechanisms are supposed to follow the rules, like the law of contract in the case of markets and 'established procedures' in the case of bureaucracies. In practice, neither mechanism would work without certain human relationships, without a degree of trust, without some personal satisfaction, without sparks of humour. In other words, the clan has always been necessary to some extent.

A decisive spread in clan-like coordination is the *post-modern* answer to the impersonal systems of modernity. As the supply of talent grew and other aspects of modernisation progressed, clans became more feasible and the increasing differentiation and complexity of societies meant that clan-like organisations, with their problem-solving capabilities, became increasingly necessary. Clans developed within bureaucratic structures as a way of coping with inflexibility. They also developed out of the fiefs of family businesses, some of which had clan-like features anyway.

Now, in late modern times and in advanced countries, the clan is becoming the key mechanism for integration. Today the clan is seen to be the right means to counter the ill effects on many parts of human life of hierarchies and of markets. Coordination through the impersonal mechanisms of hierarchies and markets is being reduced and replaced by clan-like coordination.

The Four Modes Compared

Markets are driven by competition, particularly by customers choosing the 'exit' option, or by the knowledge that this option is available.

Clans are driven by cooperation, particularly by the exercise of 'voice' made possible by the superb internal communication in the creative compartment.

Cooperation and competition can work together constructively. This is why, outside the compartment, market and clan-like coordination can be harmoniously combined.

In hierarchies and fiefs, neither 'exit nor 'voice' is welcomed. Domination is the desire of the bosses in both hierarchies and fiefs.

Both the clan and the fief can make particular use of self-reinforcing circles. The clan uses virtuous circles, the fief vicious ones. Compartmentation concentrates both these circles, making them more and more effective. This is why a shift from the clan to the fief is always a danger in a compartment.

A Present-day Example – The Coordination of Scientific Research

In the UK, as in other countries of the developed world, the government thinks it a good use of the taxpayers' money to spend a substantial sum on the support of research in basic science. The funds provided are not as substantial as scientists would like (in this the UK is not very different from other developed countries) but they amount to over £1.5 billion a year. (This is the spend on basic science and excludes applied research in specific areas like defence, transport and energy.)

In the UK, the number of high quality applications from researchers is such that only around one third can be funded. This means difficult decisions have to be made. As in other countries, the UK makes these decisions through a combination of bureaucratic and market mechanisms. I have some personal experience of these mechanisms, both through Celltech's close collaborations with academic scientists and through membership of the UK's Science and Engineering Research Council (or SERC, for short). To decide which areas of science to support, governments have a series of bodies, made up of practising scientists together with administrators and industrialists, to advise on policy and to award grants to researchers in university laboratories and in specialist research institutions.

The SERC is the largest of these bodies in the UK. It is one of five Research Councils, and each of these has subsidiary boards below it, and committees below these boards, dealing with a smaller and smaller segment of science. For example, the SERC has three boards, one of which is the Science and Materials Board, which itself has as one of its subsidiary bodies a Chemistry Committee. The eighteen-member Council of the SERC has to make policy and divide its funds between the three boards, the boards have to do the same for their committees, and the committees have to award the grants to the scientists who will do the research. These bodies are mainly composed of scientists active in the field concerned, so the system is one of judgment by peers. Obviously the system is cumbersome, but with several thousand grants running at any time, and many applicants for each grant awarded, something of the kind is inevitable, if justice is to be done, and to be seen to be done by the scientific community. It is also important that the large sums of money involved (over £600 million a year in the case of the SERC) are handled with care and integrity. SERC has a staff of about 500 people to support this work.

It is clear that there is bureaucracy in all this, but where is the market? Well, the market is in ideas. When they apply to the research councils for grants, scientists write proposals outlining the work they intend to do. The novelty and the soundness of the grant proposal, plus the previous track-record of that group of researchers, is what persuades the grant-awarding committee to select it. At the level of an area of science, for example chemistry or astronomy, it is the fruitfulness of current research and the opportunities opened up by recent discoveries, which influences decisions on the split-up of funds, and hence the number of grants which can be awarded in the area. This competition between the proposals from individual scientists or from small groups is what I mean by a market for ideas. The decision makers in this market are those scientists' peers, who have gained their own positions through success in the same competitive system. The bureaucrats administer the complex system and ensure that no decisions are made without proper peer review. The system can thus be described as a market within a framework of bureaucracy.

There is a further feature which emerges in parts of the system, in an informal and unplanned way. This is the growth of communities in many areas of science. Although scientists compete for grants and for the prestige which comes from being the first to discover something important, they also cooperate. People working on, say, the molecular biology of plants are generally enthusiastic about the area and want to help others to make advances, so that the whole area progresses. This sometimes leads to joint research projects, sometimes to smaller bits of cooperation like the supply of plant specimens for use in the experiments of other groups or the exchange of advice on experimental procedures. The fellow-feelings of a scientific community of this kind are built up by attending the same conferences, where plenty of ideas are swapped in the bar as well as in the discussion periods following formal talks. Another contributor to community spirit is the movement of scientists from laboratory to laboratory during their careers.

Peer review helps the growth of these communities. Although peer review is highly competitive, it also leads to cooperation. Reviewers give advice on how a project could be improved and suggest contacts with other scientists which might be useful to it. This happens whether or not the project gets a grant. This kind of cooperation is partly altruistic and partly self-interested. Chemists are interested in the success of chemistry both because they are fascinated by the subject and because they want chemistry to attract more funds from government (and from other sources like foundations). The more successful other chemists are, the greater the prestige of the subject as a whole.

The peer review system applies not only to the award of grants but also to other key decisions like the appointment of university professors. The system both supports, and is supported by, the informal communities I have described. One of the reasons why practising scientists are willing to spend a lot of time in peer review committee meetings (which are not always fun-filled affairs) is that by doing so they are helping to maintain the community to which they belong, and their own places within it. Scientific research thus depends on three types of coordination: bureaucracy, which ensures that public money is spent correctly; competition, which, by peer review, selects the most original and scientifically rigorous projects; and cooperation, which arises informally within communities of scientists.

The Future May Lie with Compartmentation

Bureaucracies use the hierarchical method of coordination. Competition is the distinctive feature of market coordination. Cooperation is the typical means of coordination within communities or clans. In the post-modern world the clan looks likely to play the leading role. *Compartmentation* may well be the next big step towards increasing the role of clans – towards a truly post-modern economic system.

If compartments did become the major means of coordinating economic activity on the smaller scale – on a scale of up to a few hundred people – the effect would be to secure clan-like coordination at that scale. Within the compartment there would be little need for markets or hierarchies and everyone would take for granted that clan-like coordination was the way to do things. Of course, small scale marketing and bartering could continue within the compartment if that was what people wanted, but these would not be essential for economic success. Leadership and management would be needed within the compartment, but these would not be impersonal, codified or standardised.

Compartmentation would therefore have two complementary effects:

- clan-like coordination would be be far the most widely used mode of coordination for activities up to the scale of a few hundred people, and
- markets and hierarchies would continue to be important in the world outside the compartment, but so would clan-like coordination. The huge experience of clan-like coordination, gained within the compartment, would greatly aid the use of this mode in the world outside.

From classical economic theory we can get the idea that, outside the compartment, coordination could be achieved simply by self-organising interaction between self-interested compartments. But this simple pattern of coordination will not work all the time. Today market failure is common and mutual trust often brings real advantages. There is no reason to think that market failure would be any less common, or mutual trust less advantageous, were compartmentation to become widespread.

Coordination outside the compartment is therefore likely to happen through a combination of the market, the hierarchy and the clan. Hierarchies should be used to correct market failures and clan-like coordination used to gain the benefits of trust. The fief is undesirable and a danger which must not be neglected.

The reader may reasonably say at this point: this stuff about coordination is all very well as a theory, but how does it help me in practice? What does it tell me about changing my own organisation? How can it guide my everyday activities?

Getting into Action

In drawing out from this chapter some proposals for action, I want to suggest that the reader considers his or her mental models of how organisations work. Let me first explain what I mean by mental models and by the management of them.

Managing Mental Models

In an attempt to make sense of a part of the world which concerns us, most of us construct mental models. These could alternatively be described as pictures of, or theories about, an area of interest. We hope by constructing these models to choose appropriate courses of action within the relevant part of the world. We then adjust the models through experience and by talking with others. After a number of years, we often come to use the models in an unthinking way, hardly noticing that they form the basis of our actions and of our debates with other people. At any rate, this is my mental model of the way people try to cope with complexity.

To expand on the idea of mental models: I think people get their mental models in two ways. Firstly by working them out themselves on the basis of their actual experience; in other words, through learning by doing. This is often an unconscious process. Secondly by taking them over from someone who is good at seeing and formulating new models, that is, from someone with skill in conceptualisation, who can describe models which are striking and memorable. The models which really influence action are those where good concepts and personal experience reinforce each other. To result in action, any new mental models must be relevant to the business situation of a particular organisation. They should point up threats and opportunities relevant to the organisation. To be able to do this we need practice in managing mental models. Shell started me on this path twenty years ago.

In fact I learned this lesson the hard way. I found I could no longer use the mental models, involving continuing industry growth, which I (along with nearly all my colleagues in the Shell group) had built up to encapsulate my experience of the oil and petrochemical business. The world changed radically in 1973, and not only for the oil industry, making obsolete the formerly valuable models acquired through years of experience.

Although the lesson was a hard one, it was very good that I learnt it, since otherwise my actions would have been based on wrong models and could have been disastrous. That I did learn was mainly due to the understanding which Shell was beginning to have at that time of the importance of mental models. As a result, there were people around me who were working to make explicit the mental models they had, to examine them and to start working out alternative models, since the old ones no longer seemed to be relevant to a changed world.

Peter Senge has recently written that:

> "...new insights fail to get put into practice because they conflict with deeply held internal images of how the world works, images that limit us to familiar ways of thinking and acting. That is why the discipline of managing mental models – surfacing, testing, and improving our internal pictures of how the world works – promises to be a major breakthrough for building learning organisations."

I was fortunate to be in a learning organisation when the 1973 oil shock hit the world. Shell was able to ride that shock better than most because it was better at learning. Through that experience, I learned better how to learn, which has been of huge benefit to me ever since.

So, we all as individuals have mental models which we use to make sense of what is happening in the world and to decide on action. People in an organisation often share the same or similar mental models. Model-sharing is a very important aspect of organisation culture. Making mental models explicit, testing them, improving them and adding new ones is a major part of organisational learning.

Mental Models from this Chapter

Here are some mental models derived from the discussion in this chapter:

- The concept of the compartment is, of course, a mental model. This model prompts us to expect superb open communication and wholly clan-like coordination inside the compartment and to expect a different type of communication and coordination outside.
- The main danger from compartmentation is that the open, democratic clan could degenerate into the coercive, manipulative fief.
- The mental model developed in this chapter for coordination outside the compartment, is that self-organising, self-interested market coordination will play a major role. So too will trust-based, clan-like coordination and blends of it with market coordination. Cooperation and competition can be complementary.

- Some hierarchies will remain, state ones to correct market failures, private ones when their economics are unusually favourable.

Notes

The Four Modes Model of Coordination, pages 113-114. The model originates with Max Bosiot and John Child. I am much indebted to their paper 'The Iron Law of Fiefs: Bureaucratic Failure and the Problem of Governance in the Chinese System Reforms.' *Administrative Science Quarterly*. 33, 507-527 (1988). This is the paper in which the distinction between codified and uncodified information appeared. It also provided most of the information about China which I have used to illustrate the section on fiefs in this chapter. See in addition the following papers which deal with aspects of coordination and the relative cost of the various transaction modes:

Oliver E.Williamson. *Markets and Hierarchies*. Free Press, New York. (1975) 'Williamson's Transaction Cost Economics' in Richard Schmalensee and Robert Willig (eds.) *Handbook of Industrial Organisation*, 1, 136-182. North-Holland, New York (1989). Oliver E.Williamson and William G.Ouchi. 'The Markets and Hierarchies program of Research: Origins, Implications, Prospects.' in Andrew H.Van de Ven and William F.Joyce (eds.) *Perspectives on Organisation Design and Behavior*. pp 347-370. Wiley, New York (1981). William G.Ouchi. *Theory Z: How American Business Can Meet the Japanese Challenge*. Addison-Wesley. Reading, MA (1981).

The Evolution of Cooperation and Tit for Tat, pages 114-116. First and foremost, see Robert Axelrod, *The Evolution of Cooperation*. Penguin, London, 1990. This is the edition with the foreword by Richard Dawkins. Axlerod's book was first published by Basic Books, New York in 1984. TIT FOR TAT is the creation of Anatol Rapoport, one of the pioneers of systems thinking. Recent research has shown that under some circumstances a more forgiving version of TIT FOR TAT will have advantages. A programme called GTFT (generous tit-for-tat) devised by Martin Nowak and Karl Sigmund, can invade populations of competing programmes in a computer tournament of the iterated prisoners' dilemma game. GTFT is more forgiving than TIT FOR TAT in a random one-third of the cases of an opponent's defection. GTFT cannot compete against strategies which always or frequently defect, but once a population of TIT FOR TAT programmes has got strongly established, a more generous strategy like GTFT then has a chance. Axelrod's original intuition that a more generous strategy might succeed better than TIT FOR TAT was not, after all, completely incorrect. See Nowak and Sigmund, *Nature,* **355**, 6358, 250-252 (1992).

Hierarchies, page 117. E.J. Hobsbawm. *The Age of Capital: 1848-1875.* Wiedenfeld and Nicholson, London. (1975) Paperback edn. Sphere Books, London (1985) pp 354-5.

Trust in Japan, page 119. See Mari Sako, 'The Role of Trust in Japanese Buyer-Seller Relationships', *Ricerche Economiche*, **XLV**, 2-3, 375-399 (1991).

Fiefs, pages 120-121. See Boisot and Child, *op cit.*

Historical Change in Modes of Coordination, pages 121-123. My discussion in this section, especially on the impersonal, systematised nature of the market and hierarchical modes of coordination, owes much to the work of Jürgen Habermas. Habermas distinguishes between 'system' (roughly the impersonal modes of coordination) and 'lifeworld' (roughly the personal modes) and deplores the 'colonisation of the lifeworld' by system pressures. See Jürgen Habermas, The Theory of Communicative Action, pages 128-130. Two volumes, trans. Thomas McCarthy, Polity Press, Cambridge, UK (1987). See also Gerard Fairtlough, Habermas' Concept of "Lifeworld", *Systems Practice*, **4**, 6, 547-563 (1991).

Mental Models, pages 128-130. See Peter M. Senge, *The Fifth Discipline: The Art and Practice of the Learning Organization,* Century, London (1992) p 174.

8

Islands and Bridges

If compartments were to become too inward-looking they might well lose their creativity. They might become right little, tight little islands. This need not happen. If compartments are truly creative and cohesive, they will not need to fear contamination by contact with the outside world. And in any case, isolation is pretty impracticable in the interdependent world of late modernity. We are not living in medieval villages.

So, to understand the creative compartment we not only need to consider what happens inside it, how its members relate to one another, but also how compartments relate to the outside world. In this chapter I will look at the ways in which compartments can work with each other, on how bridges can best be built between these islands.

The Pomegranate Collective is a community of designers, craft-workers and traders whose home is in a group of nineteenth century buildings on the side of a steep hill some twelve miles south of Manchester. A small silk mill, two dozen houses for silk workers and a rambling farm have been converted into the workshops and dwellings of the collective. Not all of the 200 or so people who live there are current members of Pomegranate but most are connected with the collective in some way or at any rate sympathise with its values and ambitions.

Liz Grey met and married Frank Maclean while they were both at art school in London. They enjoyed the life of the school and felt the lack of a base for their work when, after graduating, they started free-lancing, Liz in textile design, Frank in graphic design. Liz had a few commissions from Pomegranate, which at that time was small and growing rapidly, and she felt attracted by their artistic style and by their way of doing business. Having learnt that the collective was looking for new members, Liz and Frank spent a weekend there and enthusiastically decided to join. They survived two winters in a mobile home while they constructed a house from a derelict barn, finding that the warmth of the community compensated for the piercing winds of the Pennine hillsides and that they could leave the glitter of London without too much regret. At that time Pomegranate's products were much in fashion in the UK through the sheer inventiveness which they showed and because of the resonance between the styles of their clothes, accessories, gifts, toys and cards. But a few years after the Macleans joined the collective, the public got bored with the Pomegranate look and one dark October day it became clear that the year's sales were going to be less than half of the plan.

The good years had left Pomegranate with some cash, which several of its members wanted to use just to keep the collective afloat until the fickle buyers returned. Others, Liz among them, argued that as the world was no longer beating a path to their door, they should do more to show their wares to the world. This opinion won and Liz found herself, as Export Sales Manager, on frequent visits to Paris, New York, Seattle, Munich and Tokyo. Selling came quite easily to her, she found that the shops started to trust her and she became skillful in appreciating what would sell well in the various markets. She got help from some of the other sales people she met while travelling. A young American, a publisher's representative, told her how he went about selling English language books in France. She exchanged perceptions of US West Coast stores with a New England furniture maker, who seemed to find their ways as strange as she did. She began to build a network of contacts.

But as her success abroad grew so did her problems at home. The ideas for new designs which she brought back were felt to be a slur on the creative talent in the Pomegranate studios, her close attention to the wishes of the buyers was interpreted as neglect of the needs of the community and her trips, often tiring and lonely for her, were envied for their glamour by those left behind in the grey stone buildings on the hills.

Liz had joined Pomegranate because she and Frank wanted security and continuity in their lives and work. She had indeed received these. She had given too; for four years she had worked hard in making original clothes, in caring for others' children, in cooking and presenting the collective's occasional feasts and lately in earning the loyalty of customers thousands of miles away.

But now she felt that the community no longer welcomed her return, she was not comforted but envied, the news she brought from the outside world was resented, Frank was starting to be jealous. In short, by playing a key part in keeping the collective going she had somehow become separated from it. Liz then made a difficult decision. She would try to persuade the members of the collective that she should swap places with the person who was presently her assistant, and who had learned a good deal about the overseas market. He could start by going to Los Angeles next month to find a store which accepted that there was more to British design than pictures of the Queen.

She would have the humbler role of taking the phone calls and rushing urgent orders to the airport. The knowledge and contacts she had built up would be useful in this role, she would not lose touch altogether with the friends she had made overseas, she would have time to convince people in the community that ideas from outside enhanced, not diminished, their creativity. She could make dresses again, even have children of her own. She would stop spending all her time working with the outside world. In other words, she would no longer be a full-time boundary-spanner.

Boundary Spanning

The term 'boundary-spanning' refers to the activity of understanding another culture, to the activity of purposefully connecting two organisations and to the experience of having a foot in both of two cooperating camps. If it is done more than just mechanically, boundary spanning is difficult. If the two cultures, the two organisations, the two camps are very different, formidable pressures are placed on the boundary-spanner. Loyalties are challenged. It becomes hard to maintain personal integrity, to stay truthful when explaining the two cultures to each other.

There are parallels between Liz's problems as an international sales person and the problems of a police officer working on community relations, of a parent who chairs the parents-teachers association or of a journalist who follows closely the career of a rising political star. Suspicions within the home group about the loyalties or the judgment of the boundary-spanner easily arise, valuable information brought back by the spanner may be rejected because it is not what those in the home group want to hear and the spanner may lose touch with what the home group knows or feels. In *On*

Learning to Plan – and Planning to Learn Donald Michael tells us that "personal matters will be ensnarled" in the boundary-spanner's work. Boundary spanners, being human, will make mistakes and there will be a tendency to exaggerate these because it will then be easier to ignore the spanner's messages. "Boundary spanners will often be distrusted and resented by all parties they span between." The person whose task it is to facilitate communication between groups must have some sympathy for each and cannot be totally committed only to one of them. The translator is often perceived as a traitor and, it must be said, occasionally becomes one.

What happens when the boundary to be spanned is between two creative compartments? Should we expect things in this case to be different from those cases where the groups are less coherent and less skilled in communication? A critically important feature of the creative compartment is its intense internal communication. Any boundary-spanner must miss some of this because he or she is physically absent or is giving more attention to external than to internal communication. Being away from the flow of ideas and moods within the home compartment may be hard for the spanner, hard personally and hard in doing the spanning job.

Process Skills

What can be done to help relieve the problems posed by boundary spanning – problems which at first sight may be made more difficult when the spanner's home base is a creative compartment ? Firstly, the well defined purposes of the creative compartment are of great value. If the compartment knows what it wants to achieve, then the boundary-spanner's task can become a clear one. The certainty of aim shared by a compartment's members, means that spanner based in such a compartment should be in no doubt what he or she is trying to achieve. Nor should there be a problem in explaining what he or she is doing, to others in the compartment.

Secondly, the problems caused by the spanner's physical or psychological absence from the compartment should be amply compensated by the communicative competence of the creative compartment. People skilled in inter-personal process will readily understand the dilemmas which the spanner faces and will be able to help in reducing them. 'Joining' is an example of process skill which might be particularly useful in re-integrating a boundary-spanner who had partly lost touch with fellow members of a compartment.

(Joining is one of the process skills which the Coverdale Organisation is adept at teaching.) If someone comes in at the middle of a discussion, or has missed a previous interchange shared by all the others, then that person needs to be 'joined' by being given a summary of what has happened in his or her absence.

A group with good joining skills will, without any fuss, make a pause soon after someone arrives to allow one of its members to explain what has been going on. Imagine that, during a party of some kind, Louise approaches a pair of people in conversation. One of the pair might say "Hello, Louise. Jack here has been telling me all about his holiday in Spain". On hearing this, Louise might realise that it was, after all, not the conversation she should have chosen to join, but the small courtesy at least included her in it straightaway. This is a simple example; a more elaborate one might be a welcome-home party for someone who has been away for a few months at which the traveller tells tales and the home group gets a laugh by recounting the troubles they've had while he's been away. This is straight-forward stuff, but effective. In the story I told about Pomegranate, the community, although idealistic and sincere, possibly lacked the skills needed to communicate with a member who, unlike the rest, was not present all the time.

The self-awareness and self-confidence of the creative compartment will help in making the boundary-spanner's work easier. An adaptable group, which provides mutual support among its members, will be ready to accept unpalatable news (and also palatable news, should some effort be needed to appreciate its effect). In a group of this kind the boundary-spanner's messages are less likely to be "ignored, repressed, rejected or distorted", as Michael puts it. The respect for individuals and the checks on the abuse of power in the creative compartment will help the boundary-spanner as well; it will not contain any emperors ready to kill the messenger who brings bad news.

With the benefit of this kind of support, the boundary-spanner should be free to develop spanning skills. An essential skill is being able to clarify the aims and purposes of each party in the interaction, in order to avoid misunderstanding and to reveal as many opportunities as possible for mutual advantage from collaboration. This is not as easy as it sounds; there may be a hidden agenda on either side or both, people often seek collaboration only because of a vague feeling that it could turn out to be useful and things may change as an interaction progresses.

There is nothing wrong with lack of definition at the start, as hunches are a good basis for exploring the possibilities for a reciprocal interchange. Nor is there anything wrong with an evolving relationship; if it is one with real value it will certainly make a difference to both partners and therefore change both of them and their mutual relationship.

Hidden agendas are another matter, since they imply distrust or dishonesty, and this is where the boundary spanner's interpersonal process skills will particularly be tested. The caution natural at the start of an interaction has to be distinguished from deceit. The interests of two parties will never be identical, there may be short-term advantages from cheating and it is possible to cooperate in one field while competing in another, all of which can give rise to suspicion or apprehension. Diplomacy, tact, dispassionate analysis, passionate sincerity, scrupulous honesty; the boundary spanner needs an impossible string of virtues. This is why the skills and structure of the compartment are so helpful to those human beings who have the spanning task.

Talking with Other Tribes

Even the best boundary-spanner, even when acting on behalf of an ideally creative and supportive compartment, will face problems of mutual incomprehension. An anthropologist who tries to under-stand the life of a tribe, or a scholar who tries to understand an ancient text, might try to put aside, partially and temporarily, her modern outlook on the world so as to work towards the viewpoint of what may be a very different culture. When she thinks she has gained a reasonable understanding of the tribe or the text, she will want to convey that understanding to a modern audience by building a bridge between the two cultures.

But her modern outlook cannot really be suppressed, she can never identify fully with the old or the alien culture in its own terms, and in any case that is not the point, for as a scholar or an anthropologist her job is to make available for the rest of us whatever understanding she has acquired, not to effect her own escape from the modern world. She should be a translator but the translation will inevitably be distorted to some extent, because what makes sense in one culture does so only in its particular context and in another culture the context will be different, often very different.

Consider what might have to be done to market British crafts in Japan. Japan's powerful tradition of design, which has influenced

European design and has been influenced by it but which obviously remains distinct, means that potential customers there will only partially share a stock of visual reference-points with craft workers in the North of England. Of course, the attraction of British goods in Japan will be that they are something new but if they are too far from Japanese taste the market for them will be very small.

References to red buses, helmeted policemen, the changing of the guard or the Beatles might be clear, but those to topiary or Victorian samplers might not; just as references to furnishings in the bathhouses of traditional Japanese inns or to the ornate style of the Edo period would not be picked up by many in the West. It might be argued that good design should appeal even without any of the references on which I have been dwelling, or that with luck there might be some unintended resonances across the cultural divide, but if so these would be unpredictable, making marketing a hard task (which it is anyway, because of differences in business practices).

Two Examples

Two instances from my own experience may add to this picture of boundary spanning. In the mid-1960s I went to work in New York City. The kind of work I was doing was similar to that which I had had during the past few years in Europe, so I got the chance to compare these two business environments rather directly. The biggest contrast was between the heterogeneity of Europe and the homogeneity of the US.

In Europe at that time, national differences were much more pronounced than they now are. French, German and British businessmen had quite varied expectations of life. On top of these, were differences within national groups; due to training, for example between engineers and commercial people (who in Europe had often spent a lot of time in learning languages) and accountants; differences due to social class, which were pretty prominent then; and differences due to wartime experiences.

In the USA regional differences were a lot less significant than the national differences of Europe and most business people had received an education which gave them a common array of concepts for communicating about business. This speeded up communication a great deal as the preliminaries which were necessary in Europe, just to be able to make a start on exchanging ideas, could be by-passed in the US.

In the 1990s the whole world's business culture is much more homogeneous. Boundaries are much less marked. This might be expected to make for a boring life, but I don't find that to be so. The interplay of the international business style with the remaining national differences is more interesting than the domination of the old national styles. And it is certainly more efficient.

Twenty years later, at Celltech, my colleagues and I tried really hard to communicate well with scientists in universities and research institutes, mostly in the UK. Why this was only partly successful I do not fully understand. Most of Celltech's scientists had learned their science at the very universities with which we hoped to collaborate and they had no trouble in talking about that. It was organising a mutually valuable cooperation which proved difficult. One reason for the problems might have been a lack of interest in the whole idea of boundary spanning among academic scientists, probably due to a feeling that first-class science would speak for itself and that other matters were not important. On the other hand, we at Celltech might have seemed impatient or too pleased with ourselves.

Perhaps we should have learnt more about the traditional links between academia and industry in the pharmaceutical field, which had been between chemists and pharmacologists, rather than between molecular biologists and cell biologists. What industry had usually needed from chemists and pharmacologists in academia were specific techniques, for example, a way of synthesising a certain kind of chemical compound. Getting advice on techniques was relatively simple. The industrial partner in the collaboration did not want the academic partner to change his or her research programme, only to spend a day or so transferring a particular skill.

The level of mutual understanding and mutual trust needed for skill transfer by chemists was a lot less than that needed for many of Celltech's collaborations. Often what Celltech was looking for was a deep understanding of a complex biological system, and the unravelling of such complexity was often the fundamental purpose of the academic's research. Sometimes we could give a great deal of help to the academic, for example by culturing cells on a scale which was impossible in the academic lab.

Possibly there was an assumption within a particular university that the collaboration we were seeking would be conducted along similar lines to the technique-orientated collaborations, with which scientists there were familiar. Possibly the molecular biologist to whom we were talking had spoken with a chemist colleague about the best way to work with industry, without either of them realising that Celltech was looking for something outside the chemist's experience. If this was so, we at Celltech made a mistake in failing to analyse the nature of the projected collaboration and in failing to explore the preconceptions about industrial collaboration which our prospective partner might have. In other words, we had not learned enough about the varieties of collaboration which are possible between industry and academia.

None of this says that boundary-spanning is impossible, that bridges cannot be built between differing traditions, only that it is hard work and never to be taken for granted. It helps to know that any spanner will run into social-psychological pressures and that formidable cultural barriers may be encountered anywhere. Analysis of these pressures and barriers can reduce them and as the capacity for analysis spreads so will the ease of reduction. And the creative compartment is an excellent place from which to start spanning, because of its adaptability, its commonality of purpose and its skill in interpersonal process.

Networking

In the first half of this chapter I have been discussing the practice of boundary-spanning and how the creative compartment can make this practice so much more effective and more tolerable for the individuals concerned. Now, in the second half of the chapter, I want to turn to the subject of networking. Just as with boundary-spanning, the creative compartment provides an excellent base for networking. Before looking at why this is so, I'd like to review briefly the development of the practice of networking.

One of the first to draw attention to the growth of networking was Donald Schon. His book *Beyond the Stable State* came out in 1971. Schon noted that informal networks have for long kept large organisations running, compensating for errors and inflexibilities in official channels. Centrally planned economies, like the old USSR, relied on 'fixers', operating illegally and with contacts in key positions. British military bureaucracies had the 'old boy net' through which people who had been to school together did each other favours. In Japan there were networks made up of students who studied with a particular university professor. As well as networks in elite groups of this kind, in poor black communities there were informal networks of 'nannies' who cared for the sick and the young.

In the sixties the network emerged from the shadows and started to take a leading position in, for example, the movement (or cluster of movements) across the US seeking civil rights, black power, disarmament and attention to what would today be called green issues. Schon identified this as a new phenomenon, not like a national political party or campaign which would have elected leaders, an agreed platform and policy and a bureaucratic organisation. The 'movement' had no clearly established centre, no stable message and no continuing organisation.

> "The movement must be seen as a loosely connected, shifting and evolving whole in which centres come and go and messages emerge, rise and fall. Yet the movement transforms both itself and the institutions with which it comes into contact. The movement is a learning system in which both secondary and primary messages evolve rapidly, along with the organisation itself... The learning system of the movement is survival-prone because of its fluidity and its apparent lack of structure. Its ability to transform itself allows it to continue to function with vitality as issues and situations change around it. Its scope is no longer limited by the energy or resources at the fixed centre, nor by the capacity of the 'spokes' connecting the primary centre to secondary ones."

Twenty years after this was written it all seems obvious. We have got used to the network mode and monolithic organisations are now seen as inappropriate vehicles for social change. This is so on the right as well as on the left; right wing rhetoric about the inability of government to improve social conditions exploits the widespread recognition of how clumsy bureaucracies are as social agencies.

Schon describes the roles which have to be filled if networks are to work. These include negotiator, ombudsman, fixer, project manager, consultant, connector and broker.

> "Marion Wright, at the time a young lawyer for the NAACP, made herself for several years in the Mississippi Delta virtually the sole individual trusted by the many local black groups, sympathetic elements of the white power structure, government agencies, and outsiders anxious to funnel money or help to the cause of civil rights in Mississippi...Network roles such as these vary in character and yet make common demands on their practitioners, each of whom attempts to make of himself a node connecting strands of a network which would otherwise

> exist as disconnected elements. The risks of the roles are many,
> since the broker may often be squeezed between the elements
> he is trying to connect."

The players of these roles are boundary-spanners and suffer the stresses of spanning. The best amongst them not only cope themselves but coach and counsel others towards the strengths and skills required for the roles.

By 1982 networking had, according to John Naisbitt's best-selling book *Megatrends*, become "one of the ten new directions transforming our lives". He made the point that the process of networking is more important than the structure of the network, which is fluid and only exists through use. He also emphasised the non-hierarchical, non-elitist and empowering nature of networks and that people in networks tend to nurture one another. And in 1990 you can pick out from many reports passages like this one from Harold Rheingold's *Virtual Reality*:

> "I wasn't in Japan on business, strictly speaking, but I was still
> there to consummate a transaction. I wanted information from
> them. They wanted information from me. That's what science
> and journalism are about. Although I'm neither a scientist nor a
> journalist by the strict definition of either term, by this time my
> travels had made me a courier, a carrier of ideas heard at
> conferences in Texas or Kyushu, reprints from obscure jour-
> nals, and e-mail addresses of people half a world away from each
> other who are converging on the same research goals. The
> Japanese research managers had an opportunity to transmit a
> message along with their information, and so did I. They
> certainly didn't need me to tell them about what was happening
> at UNC [University of North Carolina] or the conference at
> Santa Barbara. These people did their homework and they
> weren't afraid to travel. What they probably didn't get in their
> standard review of the research was something I was by then
> prepared to provide – strong opinions about the profundity of
> the social transformation televirtuality might trigger, and
> explicit suggestions about what we might do to anticipate such
> an upheaval".

This seems rather like a network which I know well: that between people in the UK involved in the start-up and development of biotechnology companies. This network has grown from nothing in the late 1970s to a well-developed one in the early 1990s. It includes executives and non-executive directors of biotech and venture capital firms, investment analysts and specialist fund managers in investment banks and other financial institutions, lawyers, patent experts, accountants, a few journalists, university industrial liaison officers, people involved in technology broking, academic researchers and advisers and several other kinds of people. The information they exchange is usually not confidential, it often involves advice and judgment as well as factual material, and it may be a suggestion about where in the network to go to get an answer to a question, rather than the answer itself.

The biotech network is an example of the willingness of people to cooperate as well as compete. If a venture capitalist gets to know about a really novel idea, she will probably keep it to herself until her firm has signed a deal. But after that, she will want to keep other people on the network informed about progress and may ask for advice, for example, about who to recruit for a key position in the new venture. The research director of a biotech company will not talk about its discoveries until a suitable stage in the process of getting patent protection for it, but he would not hesitate to ask his opposite number in another company to give a reference on a firm of professional advisers.

It is in everyone's interest that an effective network continues and also that the industry as a whole is successful. Clearly where someone's vital interests are involved, the network will take second place, but where this is not so, most people put real effort into cooperation within the network. They know that sooner or later they will need its help.

Networks Between Compartments

Networks connect individuals, small groups and organisations. What I want to concentrate on in this book is how they might connect compartments. Let us imagine a world in which most organisations are compartmented and most business activity consists of work done in and between these compartments. Most inter-compartmental business would be in trading or in self-organised collaborative ventures. In other words, economic activity outside the compartment would be coordinated in either a market or a clan-like mode.

The main method through which compartments would obtain those things which they could not supply for themselves would be by networking. We might expect this to be so for the exchange of goods and services, for getting information and advice, for rallying support to causes which need the resources of more than one compartment, and for other interactions aimed at producing mutual benefit. Even if such a world retained some hierarchies, hierarchies which could be political, economic or administrative, networking would be the natural style for intercommunication. Every member in a creative compartment would be used to open and unconstrained communication with other members, so even if there was a certain amount of coordination of compartments' activities by means of hierarchical structures, the tendency would be to keep this to the minimum and to rely mainly on networking.

An interesting question is how, in a world of the kind I am imagining, compartments would arrange their networking. If everyone in a compartment were to be involved in every contact in the network, that would create an intolerable volume of communicative activity and, anyhow, the effect would be to abolish the boundaries between compartments, except in those cases where a compartment only needed infrequent external contacts.

So a more normal situation would be for a few people from one compartment to make contacts with a few representatives from another. But then how could these few be sure that they may speak for the compartment as a whole? And how would a network be sustained if a compartment asks one person to make one of its external links and other people to make the other links? Might not the net unravel unless the same person formed each of its nodes?

This is where the creative compartment's continuous internal communication and skill in interpersonal process comes to the rescue. Any message received from outside is rapidly diffused throughout the compartment. If a response has to be given before this diffusion is complete, then the aims and values shared by the compartment's members should mean that it will be one which they will accept as valid, even though it may not be as richly textured as a response formulated by debate in the compartment.

The excellence of internal communication secures the adequacy, and sometimes the excellence, of external communication. It also offers a continuity which single individuals will not always be able to provide, through illness or the pressure of other work. The sharing of knowledge and aims in the compartment means that someone will be able to substitute for an absent spanner without much disturbance. The compartment can, through its own coherence, act as a proper node. It is a tightly tied knot holding the strings which bind it to the other knots in the net.

Bridges

I now want to turn from the metaphor of the network, with its strings and knots, and to look again at the compartment as a base for building bridges to other compartments and at the kind of communication best suited to bridge-building. I will take the example of distance-teaching, such as that provided in the UK by the Open University. By enrolling for a particular course, students become the recipients during an academic year of a regular mailing of texts, as well as of other material like audio tapes, schedules of radio broadcasts connected with the course, work assignments, tests of their understanding of previous texts and so on. There are also set books, which students buy from local bookshops. Tutoring is by mail and by evening sessions at local centres, although students living in more remote areas are normally unable to attend the latter. There is also a one week summer school for many courses.

The texts, tapes, broadcasts and tests are the work of a course-team of around a dozen members. These course materials are, in a sense, the embodied knowledge of the course team's members. They embody not only the knowledge of the team members on the subject of the course (the nineteenth century novel, or coordinate geometry, or whatever) but also the team's experience of how best to convey this sort of knowledge to students who may have to absorb it in a crowded family home. It will include too, what the team and their colleagues in the rest of the university know about encouraging students to persist with the difficult task of learning at a distance and about stimulating a creative engagement with the subject. So, as well as the overt transfer of subject knowledge, there is in a course text a great deal of embodied knowledge of how to teach at a distance, of which the students need not, and mostly will not, be aware.

Tutors get some feedback about the students' understanding of the course through the results of tests. The summer schools provide a vital addition of some face-to-face teaching to the regular distance teaching. The Open University has a variety of other ways for listening to its students' concerns, individually and in general. For instance, when students first enrol with the OU they have a tutor-counsellor whose job it is to help students to work through the difficulties of distance learning. And for new courses, students complete questionnaires on the course content and organisation, which give critical feedback to the course-team.

In spite of this feedback, most of the communication is from course-team to student. The course-team has to be able to embody its knowledge of the subject in a series of texts and other media. When preparing the course, the members of the course-team spend many hours in discussion in which they reach a common understanding about the key elements of the subject they are trying to teach. They argue about the relative importance of these elements and about the examples which will best explain them. Eventually a large amount of work is distilled into a fairly simple text or tape.

The segments of modern societies, such as business firms or universities, have learned how to reduce the complexity of the things they provide to other segments. If a segment has some of the features of a creative compartment, it will have good internal communication, mostly by the exchange of uncodified information, full of richness, subtlety and humanity. But in its external communication each segment has to simplify, to codify, because there would otherwise just be no time to transmit all its messages.

Some of the time the loss of richness does not matter very much. The reified information in a physical product is acceptable, as we can easily live with spoons designed for their economical use of materials and easy production. This standardisation even helps us to appreciate the different information which a hand-crafted spoon conveys. We do not object to the impersonality of an announcement at an airport that repair of a small mechanical defect will delay our plane. In fact, we are better off not knowing what the repair engineer is feeling about the problem. But that does not stop us being fascinated by a movie which gives us a vivid picture of life as an aircraft maintenance worker.

Not everything communicated throughout a society as a whole is in codified form. Poetry would not be published unless its readers shared with the poet some intricacy of language and some similarity in emotional experience. Social cohesion in Western societies would be even less complete than it presently is, had communication about values become wholly superficial. Faith in the political processes of Western states would be even less than it is now if their complexities were not to some extent understood by sizable numbers of citizens.

Nevertheless, bridge-building needs simplification and codification. The external communications of the creative compartment cannot be as complex and subtle as its internal communications. The boundary of the compartment marks the place where richness in communication, which is the cardinal virtue inside the compartment, has to give way to simplicity and clarity. The skilled boundary-spanner and the effective networker know this. They are able to change gear when they move from internal to external communication.

Things We Can Do Now

No one has to wait for the arrival of the world of creative compartments to become a skilled boundary-spanner or networker. Boundary-spanning and networking are essential in all organisations today. There is no reason to delay the improvement of our own skills. Nor is there any barrier to giving help to others in acquiring skills. We can find out for ourselves just how valuable boundary-spanning and networking can be and we can pass on to others an understanding of their value.

I think good boundary-spanning and networking need three things:

- Personal strengths, so as to be able to cope with the stresses a spanner has to face.
- Interpersonal process skills, such as the ability to listen, the ability to define your own purposes and the ability to help others define their purposes.
- Skill in managing mental models, which allows you to understand better the role of boundary spanning and of networking and to share that understanding with others. This skill will also help in developing clear models of what is on each side of the boundary being spanned, and of the interaction between the two sides.

Personal Strengths

The story I told about the tug of loyalties which Liz Maclean felt as a salesperson for Pomegranate, illustrates one of the strengths a boundary spanner needs. In the story, Liz was able to look clearly at the position she was in, to take stock of her personal priorities and those of the community and to initiate action which overcame the difficulties she was experiencing. In her case, she made the hard choice to change the work she was doing. That was good for herself but also for the community, since in her new role she could contribute much more effectively to its understanding of the export market.

Another strength is to be able to admit your mistakes. Unless mistakes are acknowledged, the lessons they can provide will not be learned. There is nothing wrong in first-time failures. Making the same mistake twice might reasonably earn some blame and if the first mistake is not admitted, a second mistake of the same kind is more likely. In spite of this, we all find it hard to deal with mistakes in a blame-free way.

Yet another strength is to be able to give credit to others. I was recently asked by a friend to help him in solving a problem. He is a clever person and I was flattered by his plea for help. I thought a lot about the problem, sent him a note analysing it and then fixed a meeting with him to talk about it. I was expecting an hour's discussion, during which my great wisdom would be displayed, and yet within a few minutes of our getting together he had come up with a simple and elegant solution, far superior to anything I had suggested. I was so upset that I failed to give him proper credit, saying instead that I was glad my analysis had proved so fruitful.

Process Skills

The best educators let the pupil be his or her own teacher. The best salespeople let the customer make the sale. The best consultants let the client think he or she has solved the problem, which often is the case anyway. Here you see interpersonal process skills being used for boundary spanning.

The skills needed are those of listening, of steering a discussion, of joining newcomers into a continuing dialogue, of bringing into the open the purposes which each participant has in the situation. Skill in defining purpose is perhaps the most critical when spanning a boundary. Asking people to say what they want to get out of an interaction with others can sound offensive. It can imply that you suspect their motives, or that you think they are concealing something. If the situation is simple, a declaration of your own purposes can be a good start. If the situation is more complicated, you may not know very clearly what your own purposes are, and in that case you can ask for help in exploring what they might be. Either of these initiatives should encourage others to discover and reveal their own purposes.

Mental Models

The very idea of boundary-spanning is a mental model, or a metaphor, if you prefer. So, too, is the idea of a network. Working with mental models (or, as they might alternatively be called, theories-in-use) involves bringing to the surface the models which you have of the activities which I have described as boundary spanning and networking. Perhaps you see them differently. Perhaps others in your organisation have further models, explicit or implicit. Comparison of the models I have suggested with the ones you and you colleagues may have in mind, should provide stimulating insights about these activities.

The model of a boundary stimulates thought about the nature of that boundary, about the different ways of looking at the world which there might be on each side of the boundary, about the different purposes on each side, about the problems of crossing from one side to the other and back again.

Bridge-building can be viewed as forming, for a while, a joined compartment from two separate ones. To build a bridge, there has to be a certain commonality of purpose, some shared language, some shared views of the world, together with open communication, at least on certain subjects. So a good bridge could be seen as creating a temporary joint compartment. This is a model which prompts plenty of questions.

The model of a network stimulates thought about the pattern of the net. Do you see yourself or your organisation at the centre of a spider's web? Or do you see yourself as just one of the nodes of a roughly uniform net? The spider's web model might discourage you from thinking about the interactions between members of your network which did not directly involve you. The uniform net model might suggest that you could assemble a vast array of answers by asking each of your network contacts not only to give you their answer to a question, but also to pass on the question to each of their contacts and to feed back the response to you.

Thinking about the model of a network suggests still more ideas. Can a network be consciously created, or does just have to evolve? Having got started, can a network be extended, or managed in a planned way? Is it worthwhile trying to map a network, or to define one?

But here is where I had better stop asking so many questions and leave the reader to figure out some answers. For, as I have said, that is the best means of learning.

Notes

Boundary Spanning, pages 134-137. See Donald N. Michael. *On Learning to Plan – and Planning to Learn*. Jossey-Bass, San Francisco, CA (1973). pp 240-1. Don Michael's work on boundary spanning has, in my view, never been surpassed. See also Donald N. Michael and Philip H. Mirvis, 'Changing, Erring and Learning' in Mirvis, P.H. and Berg, D. (eds) *Failures in Organizational Development and Change*, Wiley Interscience (1977) pp 311-334 and Donald N. Michael, 'Forecasting and Planning in an Incoherent Context', *Technological Forecasting and Social Change*, **36**, 79-87 (1989).

Networking, pages 140-143. See Donald A. Schon, *Beyond the Stable State*, Temple Smith, London (1971), especially pp 108-115 and 190-200 from which the quotations are taken. Also John Naisbitt, *Megatrends: Ten New Directions Transforming our Lives*, Warner Books, New York (1982) Chapter Eight – 'From Hierarchies to Networks'. And Howard Rheingold, *Virtual Reality*, Summit Books, New York (1991) p246.

9

The Practice of Critique

This chapter is about critique – about the concept of critique and its practice. I think effective critique is essential for creative compartments. In introducing the idea of critique I will start with an example described, with a co-author, by that perceptive thinker about organisations, Henry Mintzberg.

During the 1940s documentary films were a distinctive feature of the English-speaking world. In Britain the makers of these films shared many of the motivations of people at the BBC (then a radio broadcasting organisation) which were partly paternalistic and nationalistic, partly egalitarian and educational, partly artistic; certainly both filmmakers and broadcasters were excited by the possibilities of the new media. In wartime, 'documentaries' were inevitably government propaganda. But they were also a celebration of some of the best aspects of civilian life and for this they were appreciated as an escape from the insanities of war.

In Canada in 1939 the federal government set up an agency, the National Film Board (NFB), to make and distribute films about Canadian life to be shown at home and abroad. Henry Mintzberg and Alexandra McHugh tell us how this agency decided its strategy and objectives over the following four decades. The first head of the NFB was John Grierson, who came to Canada from Britain, where he had been making documentary films for some time. This is how Mintzberg and McHugh describe the wartime years of the NFB:

> "[Grierson] hired creative and energetic but inexperienced Canadians and began to train them under a trio of trusted colleagues he brought over from England. Organic in the extreme – in its on-the-spot hiring practices, rapid job shifts, and deliberate and gleeful flaunting of civil service procedures – the organization was dominated by a sense of excitement and mission. By the end of the war, the NFB contained over 700 people.

Under Grierson's dictum, "bang 'em out and no misses", production rose to about 60 films per year by 1943 and stabilized there. About half the films were made under the Wartime Information Programme, with others on subjects such as Canadian agriculture, cultural activities, and industry. A fair proportion of films in 1940-1942 was sponsored by Government departments (notably the armed forces), with Grierson the master salesman.

Thanks to special wartime government allotments, important newsreel series developed for distribution in commercial theatres. This was part of a four-pronged, intended (and subsequently realized) strategy of distribution, announced in 1940: to reach urban audiences through theatres and special screenings (e.g. in factories), to make films and projectors available for private screenings, and to reach, through travelling NFB projectionists, the rural half of the Canadian population that could not get to theatres....

... the fundamental norms established in this period did not [change for decades] – a concentration on documentary-style filmmaking, a concern for the social impact of films, grass-roots distribution, and high standards of excellence and innovation. A confluence of three situational factors gave rise to [this] strategy: the newness of the organization, which allowed for organic structure and the enthusiasm of creation; the outbreak of war, which provided an unexpected but compelling sense of mission; and the naming of a highly charismatic leader, who could resist bureaucratic pressures and exploit the first two factors to impel the organization on a course of excitement and excellence."

In the early 1940s the National Film Board of Canada had, on this account, most of the things that make up a creative compartment. It probably lacked deliberate care for internal communications and no doubt on most administrative matters Grierson, as its head, took decisions without consulting widely. But its film-makers must have had great freedom where they really wanted it: in making films. Certainly the creativity of the NFB was beyond doubt and its separateness from the government machine made it a true compartment. Mintzberg and McHugh report that Grierson explicitly reserved to himself the task of keeping the bureaucrats at bay. In this he had the great advantage of the personal backing of the Canadian Prime Minister, Mackenzie King, who was impressed by Grierson's vitality and his radical approach. Grierson was the boundary spanner and boundary manager, whose efforts allowed the rest of the organisation to get on with making and distributing films.

This is an inspiring story, especially as the pattern set in these early years continued, at least until the 1970s. The organisation adapted successfully to the arrival of television, its films continued to win acclaim and awards and it deflected many pressures to bureaucratise. Because most of us might agree that the NFB was a great idea, the question of *accountability* might be forgotten. Yet here was an outfit, funded by the Canadian taxpayer, which was setting its own goals, always being flexible and innovative, scorning civil service procedures, using a lot of ingenuity to keep bureaucracy off its back and often influencing the image of the nation held by Canadian citizens and by outsiders. Can this be justified? Was there sufficient check that monies voted by Parliament were being properly spent and that the NFB's activities were those which the country's elected representatives intended?

The Idea of Critique

I will use the term *critique* for the process of testing a compartment's or an organisation's validity. Critique involves things like calling the compartment to account, assessing the quality of what it does, comparing its actual practices with the principles it claims to hold, auditing its compliance with certain rules and judging its performance in a wide variety of ways. This all may sound like heavy-handed regulation but critique should not be that, unless there is clearly something seriously wrong. It should aim for improvement rather than punishment and its influence should usually be to prevent the compartment from straying from its chosen path, not to jump on it if it does. Critique can be automatic, as competition is a form of critique. It can be informal, tacit or self-generated. Behind it may be the forces of money and power but critique will not have worked as well as it should if these forces have to be used.

What kind of critique was there in the early years of the National Film Board of Canada? And did it work effectively? One view could be that while Grierson was head of the agency he avoided critique by skillfully persuading Ottawa's civil servants, who were anyway busy with wartime problems, to ignore the agency except when the time came to renew its funding. He would have been helped in this by its small size and its uniqueness. But I think this view is wrong. The NFB was continually in the public eye and made every effort to stay there, by getting its films to all parts of the country. If the films had not appealed to Canadians there would in the end have been complaints, politicians would have taken note and they, or the civil servants, would have acted to change what the NFB was doing. In fact the films met a real need at the time and the organisation built up a store of goodwill as a result. Although far from being a commercial organisation, the NFB did get some revenue from commercial showings, giving some objective proof of its worth. The international prizes it won were further proof. And although the NFB did not follow bureaucratic rules it avoided scandal, probably because it was quite small for a government agency and had a dedicated staff. I expect that any people who might have been tempted to abuse the freedom they had at the NFB knew that its continuation depended on their avoiding abuse. So there was critique of the best kind: enlightened self-interest leading to self-restraint plus a high level of public awareness of what the organisation was doing.

Critique depends either on 'exit' or on an external 'voice'. Critique by exit is the loss of market share by businesses, the loss of members by voluntary organisations and the loss of votes by politicians. Critique by external voice is specific complaint by members of the public, perhaps in private at first but later in public, investigations by the news media and assessments by authorised bodies, including audits of companies and official investigations. In some of these situations the investigator has legal power and in others adverse publicity is the main sanction. Given free and active news media, publicity is usually the most flexible and potent weapon of critique, since damage to an organisation's reputation harms it in many ways, even if countered by public relations devices. This is why throughout the modern era a free press has been fundamental to liberty.

Although, as I have said, the critique which has its effect by inducing self-discipline is to be preferred, since the ills it aims to correct then never take place, another excellent type of critique is that which assists learning. In the UK the Health and Safety Executive is the government agency which regulates conditions in factories, offices and other workplaces. This body has the power to suspend dangerous operations or to seek other penalties for infringers but most of the time the result of an inspection is a series of recommendations for improvement. Sometimes these take the form: "improve or else...". Sometimes they are tips about training people to notice what should be obvious hazards, like a power cable crossing an office passageway. In a place where safety standards are high there will, fortunately, be few mistakes to learn from, so no one working there will have anything like the experience of a visiting safety inspector about what can go wrong. This example suggests that critique should be a means of teaching; it should be an external voice worth listening to.

Seymour Sarason, writes in his book *The Creation of Settings and the Future Societies* (a setting being any group of people who work together over time to achieve common goals):

> "By external critic I refer to someone (or a group) who, at the earliest time possible, accepts the task of understanding and responding to the purposes and values of the setting, the consistency between words and actions, and the sources of actual and potential problems. He is *not* a member of the setting. He is an outsider, independent, knowledgeable about, and sympathetic to the purposes of the setting. He makes a long-term commitment and regularly spends time in the setting in whatever ways he deems necessary to gain knowledge and understanding. His relationship to the setting is explicitly based on agreement that his task is to contrast reality as he sees it with the way those in the setting see it, that his goal is not to be loved or admired, and that his remuneration will not depend on the cheeriness of his perceptions."

This is a picture of the role of a non-executive director or other external adviser. It is not the only way to arrange critique, but in its advocacy of the need for a combination of sympathy and stringency, it expresses very well what critique should provide.

Publicity about definite shortcomings is valuable, but do reports about excellence help too? If you read a particular theatre critic regularly and have seen quite a few of the plays she has recommended in the past, you will know how to interpret a review she writes of a new play. You will be able to allow for differences between her taste and yours and for what you think are her blind spots. You will be able to rely on her critique. But if, when visiting an unfamiliar city, you see in the local entertainment guide a symbol indicating 'highly recommended' against the name of a play, that will be of very little help. You will not know who is making the recommendation, what the critic's tastes are, whether he may have been influenced by the advertising revenue the guide gets from that theatre or whether he is in love with someone in the cast.

Another example of public critique is the restaurant guide, say the Guide Michelin, which is able by symbols to pack a lot of information into a small space, information which is consistent and, no doubt, pretty reliable. Some might question whether a two-star restaurant really is inferior to a three-star one or whether an extra crossed-knife-and-fork is worth what that symbol in the guide adds to the bill, but the system of inspection, classification and presentation which the Guide Michelin has evolved over many years is a work of some artistry and professionalism.

The points I want to make with these examples are that critique is not easy. For it to be useful and reliable it has to be honest, competent, well communicated and well adapted to the needs of the people who use it. Restaurant guides and theatre critics are themselves subject to critique as people can switch to rival guides and critics if they do not get what they want. Critique is improvable by being subject to critique.

Standards for Critique

Compartments will need to interact, to trade with each other, to help each other in disaster and also in easy times, to live alongside each other. This will be so even in remote rural surroundings. The claim that small is beautiful is not a claim that complexity can be banished; rather it is a claim that there are better ways of living with complexity than we generally have now. Compartmentation, which so enhances cooperation, must be complemented by critique and critique includes competition but is not confined to it. It is a spur to continual self-improvement in each compartment.

Even if we leave on one side for the moment the problem of ensuring that critique is honest, perceptive and constructive, it is not obvious how critique ought to work in a largely compartmented world. Which of the compartment's activities should be the subject of critique? What should be the criteria for judgment?

Who is to say when an organisation is performing well? Should we take an organisation's own statements about what it is trying to achieve and judge its performance by seeing to what extent it has succeeded in its self-chosen aims? However, the example of the early years of the NFB of Canada suggests that some organisations can succeed without having clearly expressed long-term goals. In any case an organisation might have the wrong goals. Michael Keeley writes:

> " From the fact that an organizational goal exists, one cannot logically infer that it ought to exist and be attained. Perhaps organizations like the Ku Klux Klan do try to survive; it does

not follow that they should survive or be judged on their survival capacity. In fact, the attainment of all sorts of goals of all sorts of organizations is regularly subordinated to other values in our courts, press, customs, and within many organizations themselves. Theorists have been reluctant to become entangled in debate over the value of organizational goal attainment...but it is a mistake to think it is not a matter for debate, that it is a self-evident good."

In other words, it is simply not enough to judge an organisation by its own criteria, so critique must to some extent be guided by external standards. If an organisation's purpose is a fairly straightforward one, let us say collecting household garbage in a particular district, then it is possible to see how well the job has been done by measures like the frequency of collection or how satisfied the residents feel with the service. The resources used to provide the service can also be measured by their cost or through ratios of various kinds. This sort of judgment takes for granted things such as the fairness of employing people to do a dirty job like garbage collection and the desirability of collection rather than the alternative of getting people to bring their ready-sorted rubbish to a central point for recycling or composting. If critique tries to raise every possible question it will never end, but it should not be blinkered either. Can we find a limited number of principles which should always apply?

One principle might be that a compartment should act fairly towards other compartments and towards the rest of society – but how could this be judged? Some compartments will be better-off than others – is this fair? Keeley makes the suggestion that organisations should be judged by the principle that they should not cause serious harm to others. Identifying harms such as physical injury or environmental pollution and even racial discrimination or misleading advertising is clearly possible. Although practical problems remain, for instance the one of deciding when harm becomes serious, any critique which did not censure serious harms would not be worth much.

Compartmentation could result in a multitude of small units all trying, but failing, to solve a problem, which they could easily tackle if they worked together. Their problem-solving attempts could all be of sub-critical size. We should expect compartments to learn from each other, to be willing to work together on problems which need the resources of several compartments and in this way to avoid the need for larger structures for coordination of the problem-solving task. This suggests that critique should pay attention to the boundary-spanning and networking capabilities of compartments.

Stability and Change

Mancur Olson, in his book *The Rise and Decline of Nations*, gives many examples of nations whose economic performance suffered as a result of rigidities in their social organisation. He attributes this largely to collusive behaviour in which certain groups in a society get together to fix things so that their lives are more secure and more comfortable, but at the expense of the society as a whole. The practices he is talking about are those of business firms which form cartels or simply find implicit ways to control prices; they are those of trades unions which look after their own members to the detriment of other workers; and they are those of politicians who stultify economic and social change for their own electoral advantage. He summarises some of the implications of his research in this way:

> "Stable societies with unchanged boundaries tend to accumu-
> late more collusions and organizations for collective action...
> special-interest organizations and collusions reduce efficiency
> and aggregate income in the societies in which they operate and
> make political life more divisive..."

Thus cooperation within a group can be to its mutual benefit but to the disbenefit of those outside that group. The accumulation of collusions which Olson finds in stable societies may be explained by the opportunity which stability gives for the evolution of coopera-tion, a point noted by Axelrod. The effect of long-term stability in a rigid society is illustrated on a huge scale by the Soviet Union which for thirty years or more was run for the benefit of a colluding group of party *apparatchiks*. In the 1960s the USSR's boasts about overtaking the West were not incredible; by the 1990s the failure of the Soviet system had become dramatically obvious. This suggests that critique should be concerned with lack of change. Great stability might indicate collusion, resulting in harm to other compartments, or it could be a pointer to a lack of learning capacity in the compartment.

Stability, however, can also be a good thing. It promotes cooperation and that is in many situations exactly what is wanted. It promotes learning as shown by the 'experience curve'. This curve summarises numerous observations showing that operational capability improves, or cost declines, by some 20 percent every time the accumulated experience of a particular operation doubles. Hence the dilemma: stability is both good and bad. A study by Modesto Maidique and Robert Hayes on high-technology firms reached a similar conclusion:

> "When we grouped our findings into general themes of success, a significant paradox gradually emerged – which is a product of the unique challenge that high-technology firms face. Some of the behavioral patterns that these companies displayed seemed to favor promoting disorder and informality, while others would have us conclude that it was consistency, continuity, integration, and order that were the keys to success. As we grappled with this apparent paradox, we came to realise that continued success in a high-technology environment requires periodic shifts between chaos and continuity."

Maidique and Hayes suggest that the need to interweave change and continuity is unique to high-technology industry but I believe the combination is needed everywhere, although the need becomes evident more quickly in the fast-moving high-technology field, showing up in two or three years rather than two or three decades which might be the case in a traditional industry or in a stable country. An essential aim of critique should be to avoid complacency within compartments and collusion between them at the expense of others. The automatic control provided by competition is one form of critique, an injection of a degree of turmoil could be another. But too much turmoil nullifies the very basis for compartmentation.

The automatic kind of critique, such as the effects of the market or the loss of membership from an organisation, will do some of the work. This will happen only if conditions are right, if there is no collusion or coercion. And automatic pressures are easily used as excuses for unfair or evil actions. So I think that a continuing, general and constructive critique of a compartment's activity is required. This critique should respect the compartment's autonomy but encourage it in boundary-spanning and networking; it should question whether the declared aims of the compartment are being achieved but recognise that it will not always be possible to define clear aims; it should discover whether its activities are harmful to people outside the compartment or to the environment; it should judge how far the compartments's internal and external practice meets its own standards and whether those standards are seriously discordant with the standards of surrounding communities; it should look for signs of corruption and coercion, of rigidity or suppressed communication and of denial of exit or voice; and it should seek to enhance democracy, fairness in allocation of tasks and in rewards and respect for all persons within the compartment.

Critique as Quality Assurance

Most UK newspapers reported a speech by Gerald Ratner, then Chairman of a retail chain selling cheap jewellry, in which he told a gathering of businesspeople that most of his firm's products were "crap". (A year later the same papers were reporting that his firm was in financial trouble). Business leaders rarely admit, even to themselves, that their products are of low quality, but in my experience many of them feel uneasy about discussing the subject, even when their firms have good reputations. Quality assurance is not a topic which generates great excitement in a boardroom. When it is raised, directors will put on serious faces, declare that quality is of overriding importance, insist that systems must be in place to assure it, and quickly pass on to the next item on the agenda. The same can happen when safety is the topic, or financial audit or regulatory compliance. Perhaps I have been unlucky in some of my former board colleagues, but I suspect that this reaction is widespread.

At least it is a common reaction when everything seems to be fine, when the firm's products are not thought to be unreliable, when no one has been killed in an accident, when no fraud has been detected and when the US Food and Drug Administration has found no deviations from Good Manufacturing Practice in the firm's production plants. If disaster strikes, the topic presumably does become exciting in any boardroom. One of the people around the table might get fired, and in the unlikely case that the disaster happens to a Japanese firm, one of the people round the table might feel obliged to commit suicide.

All of us can imagine disaster and this, if nothing else, should make us take quality assurance seriously. This should be so in all areas of human activity, not just in business. The reason why quality assurance is a difficult subject to get excited about is that quality (or safety, or financial probity, or regulatory compliance) comes mainly from people's attitudes, not from systems. If everyone was keen to embezzle and alert to every loophole, it would be hard to run financial systems. In fact, most people are honest, which allows systems to be designed to catch the occasional rogue, and to detect the occasional honest mistake.

Unfortunately, attitudes towards quality in manufacturing are not generally so positive. There is less of a social commitment to occupational safety and health, to product quality and good practice in manufacturing. The reason for this no doubt lies in the de-skilling and reduction in personal responsibility among workers, generated by work study of the stop-watch and clip-board kind introduced by F. W. Taylor, and by assembly-line mass-production introduced by Henry Ford. Germany, which has kept more of a craft tradition than the the US or the UK, has suffered less de-skilling and has better attitudes to quality. There is more enjoyment in doing and pleasure in the final product, which leads to higher motivation and ever-increasing standards of excellence. Frantic efforts are now being made to change things in those countries and industries where wrong attitudes to quality are now recognised as a crippling disadvantage.

Although a devotion to quality among all concerned is the key, systems are needed too. These include internal systems of regular checking, systems of quality control. They also include systems for quality assurance, at a higher or meta-level, to review things like training, record-keeping, regular maintenance of plant and the setting of standards. As well as internal systems, external review is needed to avoid organisations becoming too inward-looking, complacent or even corrupt. This is where external audit of all kinds comes in, whether it is financial audit, quality audit, safety audit or audit of some other kind. The best quality assurance and audit aims as much at raising standards, and giving help in meeting them, as it does at spotting mistakes or malfeasance.

Let me give one example of external quality assurance which has worked well and which encouraged the institutions it reviewed as much as it policed them. This is the UK's Council for National Academic Awards, a body which for nearly thirty years awarded degrees to students studying in higher education institutions which did not have the power to award their own degrees, that is polytechnics, colleges and similar institutions other than universities. In its early years the CNAA used to check and recheck each course of study leading to a degree, but later it started validating colleges rather than courses and later still moved towards ensuring that colleges had in place proper quality assurance systems of their own. All this was accompanied by quality support, that is, the giving of advice and help to institutions in quality matters. The whole process was so successful that in 1992 the UK Government decided that most of the polytechnics and colleges whose degrees the CNAA had, until then, been validating should become universities, with their own degree-awarding powers. The CNAA had worked itself out of a job.

The CNAA mainly used peer review. Decisions were taken by "groups of responsible and experienced people drawn from: inside and outside the field of study, inside and outside the institution and inside and outside higher education." It was the Council's task to organise subjective judgment on a vast scale and in a way which was seen to be fair. The aim was to achieve high standards of quality while helping a rapid expansion of higher education in the UK. In 1976, Sir Michael Clapham, then Chairman of the CNAA gave this answer to the question: what is quality in higher education?

> "It is the quality of those who teach and those who plan the courses which are taught. It is the quality of those who are admitted to a course of study, and the quality of those who assess and examine them. It is the quality of the academic environment in which teachers and taught alike move and have their being: that unquantifiable, ideal blend of intellectual freedom and intellectual discipline in which ideas multiply and are cross-fertilised, learning flourishes and sciolism wilts. It is an atmosphere which encourages a broad diversity of interests combined with a profound depth of penetration."

This is a statement about quality in higher education. But its spirit applies to quality in human activities in general, and to the assurance of that quality. Its spirit equally applies to what I call critique.

Critique of a Powerful Organisation

In 1976 the Pennsylvania legislature established a Bureau of Consumer Services (BCS), within the state Public Utility Commission, partly in response to public outcry about the freezing to death of an elderly woman whose heating had been cut off when she failed to pay her bill. The new bureau was given a mild remit: to investigate and reply to complaints from consumers and to report on them to the Commission. But ten years later the BCS had, according to Richard Ritti and Jonathan Silver, become a force to be reckoned with, examining the services of utility companies, passing judgment on them in public and influencing the outcome of reviews of the prices gas, electricity, telephone and other utility companies were permitted to charge. Politicians, the press and the companies all took notice of what the BCS said. The Bureau was small, with a staff of 45 backed up by the Pennsylvania State University who were contracted by the BCS to do research.

The BCS had no way of enforcing its recommendations and if it was to push the utility companies into giving a better service to the public it needed a power base and of course it also needed continued state funding. To get and keep influence and funds it paid close attention to a number of groups. First it built up with the press an image of a friend of the consumer by presenting its reports in newsworthy fashion and reacting promptly whenever utility service became a hot issue.

The Bureau operated independently but it was part of the Public Utility Commission and relied on the Commission for its annual budget. So the BCS made sure that its reports added to the Commission's image as a well-informed agency which had con-sumers' (and voters') interests very much at heart. Similar attention was paid to the members of the state legislature and reports were presented in ways which were helpful to politicians, for example by listing consumer complaints by electoral districts. At the time of Ritti's and Silver's study consumer groups were only just getting organised and limited, but increasing, attention was paid to them.

A fifth and very important group which the BCS had to influence was that of the utility companies. Although Ritti and Silver do not name the companies, it is clear that they were some of the largest in the United States, with large resources, great experience in public relations and lobbying and considerable political influence. I imag-ine that the employees of all the utility companies taken together would add up to a significant number of Pennsylvania voters. These were dangerous adversaries for a small new government bureau with no formal power to do anything except publish reports. But unless the BCS was able to take on these companies it would achieve nothing much. In one battle the vice-president in charge of consumer affairs in a gas company hit back, accusing the BCS of producing incorrect data and causing delays in settling consumer complaints. The bureau worked hard on its files and put forward a good case at a meeting between the chairman of the Commission and the president of the gas company. As a result the vice-president was replaced and the company accepted that it had a duty to respond to consumer complaints, acknowledging that reports from the BCS would help it to do so.

Ritti's and Silver's paper claims that much of the interaction between the companies and the bureau was ceremonial. They suggest that the BCS wanted companies to admit that the bureau was a knowledgeable defender of the consumer and in return the BCS would declare that the company concerned was improving its service. The ceremony of exchange with companies and other partners in communication builds a myth about the role of the bureau, a myth which, according to the authors, enables it to function and to survive. They make it clear that:

> "Although myth carries the connotation of falsity, this is not necessarily the case for organizational myths. Indeed, myths embedded in organizational culture likely reflect a blend of truth and untruth in such a way as to dramatize origins and purposes."

Even if it is true that the BCS is an effective opponent of the big utility companies, its existence may in fact be quite convenient to them. The public may feel happier about the companies with the BCS on their side. Ritti and Silver quote Barthes: "a little 'confessed' evil saves one from acknowledging a lot of hidden evil". They are not, however, making out that those at the BCS are hypocrites.

> "...the people responsible for building the BCS believe deeply in what they are doing. They are highly committed to an ideology that casts industry in the role of the callous exploiter of consumers, especially the elderly and disadvantaged, and themselves as champions of a just society".

This much seems clear from Ritti's and Silver's account: the staff of the BCS were sincerely working for consumers' interests, they established the 'myth' that they were doing so effectively and they had at least ceremonial effects.

Lessons from the BCS Story

The kind of critique in which the BCS was engaged is very different from the critique of compartments which I am advocating. The utility companies which that bureau tried to oversee were huge organisations. A 45 person bureau concerned only with one aspect of such an organisation's activity could not possibly undertake the generalised and supportive critique which compartments need. In spite of the differences there are lessons to be taken from this story which would be of use in the critique of compartments.

Firstly, critique needs power. As individuals we tend to reject or ignore uncomfortable comments and groups are even better equipped to do this than are individuals. The BCS had to build a power base, if the utility companies were to take it seriously. Effective critique, however supportive and sympathetic, will always need a reserve of power in the background. Power derives from legal or administrative rights, from political influence or the ability to influence public opinion, from expert knowledge or strong personalities, or from a combination of these. When exercised skillfully it is self-reinforcing because its results demonstrate its existence. Just as learning often comes through doing, power often comes through influencing. Secondly, power corrupts. An over-mighty utility company or an over-mighty regulatory agency tends to behave disdainfully unless there is a countervailing power, so critique needs a reasonable balance of power. And when there is balance then another danger arises: collusion between the agent of critique and the body which is that critique's subject. The answer to this danger must be further critique, largely through public comment, which itself depends on an open society with freedom of speech, freedom of the press and other media, and freedom of access to official information. Of course the press is a fickle instrument, often as corrupt as those it investigates, concerned mainly with raking up scandals to increase sales, unsuitable for the plodding improvement which must usually be the aim of critique. But democracy relies on uncertain means. J.S.Mill said that governments must be made for human beings as they are, or as they are capable of speedily becoming. And critique on the small scale will be just the same; it will be done by fallible individuals accountable to a fallible public opinion through biased media.

Thirdly, critique will require procedures which command public respect and which are as impartial as possible. Judgment will always be necessary in order to strike a balance between diverse objectives and conflicting principles. When exploring what the world is like, explanation must stop somewhere. It is the same when examining a human situation – critique must have an ending, and if all compartments are to be the subject of critique the ending will mostly have to be quite close at hand. That arguments have to be brought to a conclusion, at least temporarily, is inevitable but where they end is a choice which has to be well justified and acceptable to all concerned. Right judgment about the place to stop is a key aspect of critique.

Design for Critique

" Among the Barotse everyone took part in the judicial process. No voice was too junior, no evidence too remote to be admitted. For the essence of every such situation was that order, that prized collective tribal possession, had been violated and the object of the exercise was to restore it to its habitual unquestioned place. The wife-stealing, the cattle-stealing, or whatever had precipitated the dispute, was probably a mere symptom. The cause might be found in a family dispute originating with the moving of a boundary stone generations before.

English lawyers had no difficulty in understanding and sympathizing with this logic, for they used it – in children's courts. Even the most sinister act if committed by a child was to be considered first as a symptom of disorder in the only area of life, family life, where the breach of order could still be treated as a mere symptom directing attention primarily to the treatment of a social disorder. Happy Barotse! Order among them still had something of the sanctity of biological order; of health as opposed to disease."

We might be inclined to discount any insights from this passage, which gets close to equating wives with cattle and an African tribe with English children, but in it Geoffrey Vickers makes two valuable points: first, instead of trying to correct a few symptoms the health of a whole activity needs to be improved and, second, this process should involve non-experts and seek unusual insights.

A very good model for the critique of compartments is the trial jury of the Anglo-Saxon legal system. Critique is not a trial and the number of jurors need not be twelve, but the principle of lay people working together to reach reasonable conclusions has been tested and proved good by juries during many centuries. Every compartment might have to account for itself once a year to a body of lay people coming from different compartments. Let us call these bodies review groups. Each review group could have a clerk or secretary who would organise meetings, advise on the group's legal rights and duties, facilitate the process of the review and help in preparing a written report.

The members of every review group should first have some training, made up mostly of dummy reviews or case studies, which would get the group working together and give them confidence in tackling their task. This training would make these groups less dependent on their secretaries, who might otherwise be able to use their professionalism to overwhelm the lay members. Including training, the review might need five or six days, probably spread out over three weeks. Part of the time would be spent visiting the compartment, receiving presentations from its representatives, talking informally with its members and consulting with people outside the compartment under review, people whose activities involved regular contact with it. Part of the time would, so to speak, be in the jury room as the review group tried to agree on a judgment about the compartment and to formulate a report.

If critique of the kind I have just sketched out were to be an established practice, then most people would, throughout their adult lives, have the experience of conducting reviews of a compartment. Most people would every year have the experience of their compartment being reviewed. Critique would have become a familiar activity and its advantages and its shortcomings would be well understood. Receiving critique and providing it to other compartments would be everyday events. Skill in giving and receiving critique would grow. Self-critique would become automatic.

Varied Designs

Review groups, like those I have just described, are a general model for the design of non-hierarchical, reciprocal critique. The work of regulatory agencies can provide plenty of models for hierarchical critique. External audit by professional accountancy firms is another model which can be followed in designing critique, a model which does not only apply to financial audit.

Another design model, described in Peter Senge's book *The Fifth Discipline*, is Hanover Insurance's use of 'internal boards', composed of three or four experienced managers from elsewhere in the organisation, who advise local management teams. In some ways these internal boards function like corporate boards of directors, but they do not control, nor do they carry the ultimate responsibility for performance. Mainly they counsel, advise and coach. But they could act as whistle-blowers if they found something seriously wrong and because of their seniority in the corporation, their whistle-blowing would definitely be heard.

A further model can be found in university governance. In the UK, most universities have a Council, with a majority of lay members, which meets four times a year and reviews major decisions before they are implemented. The decisions reviewed are both those of administrators and academic decisions reached by the university senate.

Anyone can set up a system of critique for his or her own activities, and can propose a system for any organisational unit to which they belong. You could ask two or three people with whom you network regularly to become a review group for yourself or your unit. If you do, you should choose people you can trust, but people who will speak their minds, who will not be embarrassed by having to give you a hard time, if they think you are making a mistake or doing something wrong. A certain amount of formality in the review is a good idea, so that no one doubts its seriousness, but not too much, to avoid making it hard for you or your co-workers to reveal past errors and to admit present uncertainties.

Stringent, but sympathetic, critique can help us all, so we should set about organising it for ourselves, if we don't already have it. And in a world of compartments, this kind of critique will be essential for success.

Notes

National Film Board of Canada, pages 151-153. See Henry Mintzberg and Alexandra McHugh. Strategy Formation in an Adhocracy. *Administrative Science Quarterly*. **30**, 160-197. (1985). The form of the NFB's organisation, which is what Mintzberg calls an 'adhocracy', involves ever-changing, multi-disciplinary teams and for coordination relies largely on mutual adjustment between these teams. There is more about the NFB in a biography of Grierson by Forsythe Hardy. (*John Grierson: A Documentary Biography*. Faber and Faber, London. 1979) Mackenzie King's support of Grierson is described on p 114 of this biography.

External Critics, page 155. See Seymour B. Sarason, *The Creation of Settings and the Future Societies*, Jossey-Bass, San Francisco, CA (1972) p 250.

Organisational Goals, pages 156-7. See Michael Keeley, Impartiality and Participant-Interest Theories of Organizational Effectiveness, *Administrative Science Quarterly*, **29**, 1-25 (1984).

Stability and Change, page 158. See Mancur Olson, *The Rise and Decline of Nations: Economic Growth, Stagflation, and Social Rigidities*, Yale U.P. (1982). Robert Axelrod, *The Evolution of Cooperation*, Penguin, London (1990) pp 17-18. "Collusive business practices are good for the businesses involved but not so good for the rest of society. In fact, most forms of corruption are welcome instances of cooperation for the participants but are unwelcome to everyone else." And Modesto A. Maidique and Robert H. Hayes, The Art of High-Technology Management, *Sloan Management Review*, Winter 1984, pp 17-30.

Quality in Manufacturing, page 161. See Michael J. Piore and Charles F. Sabel, *The Second Industrial Divide: Possibilities for Prosperity*, Basic Books, New York (1984) pp 142-151.

Quality in Academia, pages 161-2. *Academic Quality in Higher Education: A Guide to Good Practice in Framing Regulations*. Council for National Academic Awards, London (1992) p 5. The quotation from Clapham's speech is from Harold Silver, *A Higher Education: The Council for National Academic Awards and British Higher Education 1964-1989*. The Falmer Press, London (1990) p 263.

Critique and Power, pages 162-4. See R. Richard Ritti and Jonathan H. Silver. Early Processes of Institutionalization: The Dramaturgy of Exchange in Interorganizational Relations. *Administrative Science Quarterly*, **31**, (1986), pp 25-42. Both authors were closely connected with the Bureau of Consumer Services in its early days, Ritti at the Pennsylvania State University and Silver as an employee of the BCS. John Stuart Mill's view on human fallibility comes from *Representative Government*, Everyman edition, p253.

Among the Barotse, page 166. Geoffrey Vickers, *Human Systems are Different*, Harper and Row, London (1983) p37. Vickers' information about the Barotse comes from H.M. Gluckman, *The Judicial Process Among the Barotse of Northern Rhodesia*, Manchester U.P. Manchester, (1955).

Part III

To achieve the full potential promised by the two virtuous circles – openness and trust, empowerment and commitment – we need to adopt compartmentation as the key principle in organisation design. The uncodified communication, broadcast communication, communicative competence, shared purposes and democratic style of the creative compartment have the power to lift human capability to a wholly new level. But how can organisations move, from where they now are, to this most desirable future state?

In Part III of this book I discuss how this move can be made, starting in Chapter Ten with the redesign of large organisations. I follow this by showing how small organisations can gain strength through varied associations. In Chapter Twelve, I go beyond design to implementation, examining how organisations can achieve substantial and durable change.

10

Redesigning Large Organisations

Let me start with a story of the redesign of an organisation – not a particularly large one, but one whose products are very well-known: Rolls-Royce Motors.

Rolls-Royces – hand-crafted luxury, heads of state gliding through the waving crowds, the bejewelled rich disembarking for a film premiere – these cars are symbols of tradition and status. If any business could be excused from change, Rolls-Royce Motors might be it. Nevertheless, in 1990 the company decided that, in order to survive, it had totally to redesign the way it made cars. It decided to make the same number of cars with less than half the number of people, to improve quality by getting things right first time, to reduce inventories manyfold and to quadruple the range of models made in its main plant.

Impossible for a company whose chief business advantage is tradition? Apparently not. In two years all the objectives of Rolls-Royce's manufacturing organisation redesign seem to have been achieved. Even more importantly for the future, the new organisation is far more flexible than the old, which means that adapting to changing market needs will be a lot easier in future.

The plant now has 16 zones, each with around a hundred people grouped into teams of six to ten. Each zone acts as a small business, with full responsibility for its own costs, for purchasing materials from outside suppliers, for quality and for delivery. The teams are multi-skilled. They combine people who formerly worked only within a single craft and those formerly labelled as engineers or managers. Income differences within teams are large, some earning three times as much as others. This does not seem to matter, since team members recognise that the more highly paid bring capabilities which are needed to get the work done. Task definition and task execution are no longer the provinces of separate people.

My guess is that, once the new style of working becomes well established, the size of the zones could increase without much difficulty, simply by adding more teams within a zone. This would allow the whole plant to grow without any increase in the complexity of its present simple structure of zones and teams. Another guess is the rest of the firm – design and development, sales and marketing, finance and administration – will be changed by the example of what has happened in the manufacturing plant. Then the company will be ready for the twenty-first century.

Rolls-Royce Motors, now with less than 2,500 people, is not a large business, although it is part of Vickers, one of the UK's bigger engineering groups. But what Rolls-Royce has done is a model for large-scale organisational redesign. Their change was driven by competitive pressures and by the example of those Japanese manufacturers who showed that luxury cars could be made better and much more cheaply than traditional makers had ever thought possible. They are not the only firm facing fierce competition.

We can find examples of organisation redesign from many other industries, where traditional wisdom about organisation has been ditched, mental barriers to change have been overcome and results achieved which, with old thinking, appeared ridiculously infeasible. This sometimes stems from new technology, but more often comes simply through organisational change.

In exploring for oil and gas, and after finding it, getting it out of the ground, the oil industry has traditionally organised itself into specialist disciplines:

- exploration disciplines, like seismology – charting geological structures with sound waves, and exploratory drilling – learning about these structures by down-the-hole measurement and by bringing up samples of rock.
- petroleum engineering – once an oil field has been discovered, devising ways to get out the maximum amount of oil, which is often thick and sticky, from underground strata of rocks and sands.
- production engineering – designing the complex array of drill-holes, pipelines, equipment for separating oil, gas and associated water and so on, so as to extract oil and gas safely, economically and without harm to the environment.
- drilling and construction – putting the production engineers' plans into effect.
- operations – producing oil to meet market demand.

Traditionally, the different disciplines were deployed sequentially, in a series of stages, with the petroleum engineers waiting to get involved until the field was discovered, the production engineers waiting until the best way of getting out the oil had been decided and the operators waiting to do their job once the facilities had been built. Such a separation of tasks allowed top management to oversee the moves from stage to stage.

But today things have changed. Increasingly, there is a multi-disciplinary approach from the start of exploration right through to the end of an oilfield's productive life. Shell companies, for instance, have set up integrated working groups, with considerable auto-nomy, for lifetime management of fields. Specialist departments remain, but as consultants, not decision-takers. Top management approves overall plans and budgets and then supports the integrated teams.

Another example comes from brewing. One of the largest breweries in the UK is the Whitbread company's plant in Wales. It is organised into four areas – brewing, processing, kegging and canning – each with around a hundred people. Because many of the operations in a brewery go on day and night, the areas each have shift teams, which run the area for eight hours and then hand on to the next team. The brewery as a whole is operated as a business and so are the four areas, each of which have the skills to handle all tasks without control by specialist departments. Organisation redesign at this plant was stimulated by increased decentralisation within the whole Whitbread company, which gave the plant management more strategic responsibility. This encouraged the plant mangers to hand over operational management to the areas, leading, in turn, to self-management by the shift teams. Here again we see the end of the distinction between task definition and task execution. The teams both define tasks and carry them out, which is the essence of empowerment.

Richard Florida calls this 'the new shop floor'.

> "The new shop floor involves both the reintegration of intellec-tual and manual labour and a blurring of the imposed distinc-tions between innovation and production. There are three related dimensions to this process:
>
> - the harnessing of shop-floor workers' intelligence in production;
> - the increasing importance of continuous improvement inno-vation as a source of value; and

- the blurring of the lines between the R&D lab and the factory."

Florida quotes Akio Morita, the former Chairman of Sony:

"A company will get nowhere if all the thinking is left to management. Everybody in the company must contribute, and for the lower level employees their contribution must be more than just manual labour. We insist that all of our employees contribute their minds."

Humbling the Dinosaurs

In the 1990s we have seen the humbling of several dinosaurs. Some proud corporations, whose names had formerly symbolised corporate might, have been forced to accept that they cannot continue as they were, that radical redesign is necessary for survival. Other, less arrogant, companies have made sweeping changes. So have some government organisations. Downsizing, delayering, hollowing out has been one kind of reaction to hard times. Getting back to basics, sticking to the knitting, cutting out the frills has been another. Total quality management, empowerment and learning from the management practices of the Far East has been a third. The blankets of hierarchy are being given up.

I believe that compartmentation will be the next leap forward in organisation redesign. The flexibility and adaptability of an organisation made up of creative compartments should solve problems and create opportunities on an extraordinary scale. Compartmented companies and economies may be able to out-perform uncompartmented ones in the same way that capitalist economies outperformed communist ones in the decades of the nineteen sixties, seventies and eighties.

But is this really possible? Have there not been, for a century or more, economic factors, the so-called economies of scale, which have favoured large-scale organisation? Surely the "universal idolatry of giantism" which E.F.Schumacher criticised did not happen by accident. Aren't there things which can only be done by big organisations?

It is true that there are many situations in which large firms are the only ones with the resources to introduce expensive new technologies and complex systems. But this does not mean that they have to introduce them with the old hierarchical organisation style. In difficult conditions like the North Sea, exploration and production of oil and gas needs investment on a scale that only huge firms can undertake. However, the example of Shell's integrated oilfield teams shows that these huge firms are starting to give the management of such tasks to compartment-sized work groups.

Another striking example of the coordination of complex activities through self-organisation comes from CERN, the European centre for particle physics research in Geneva. Numerous measuring systems, of highly intricate design, are required to detect the results of millions of collisions between high-energy particles. The detailed design and construction of these systems was carried out by teams in universities and research institutes throughout Europe and elsewhere in the world. There was a general layout into which the various detectors had to fit, but each detector was built separately and taken to Geneva to be assembled. The teams had to have enough contact with each other to ensure that their instrument would be compatible with the others in the detector system. Quite a gamble you might think. But the teams were all made up of very intelligent people, all driven by the desire to advance knowledge of physics and to impress their peers. This self-organisation apparently worked with great accuracy. It had to, because no single designer could have tackled the task of fitting all this complexity together.

System complexity always means that compartments will have to work extensively with each other. Compartmentation certainly does not do away with the need to coordinate the activities of compart-ments. But much of the coordination can be achieved by networking between compartments, even when they are all part of a large organisation. Clan-like coordination, or market coordination, or a combination of both can work as well, or better, within a large firm than it can between separate small firms. Empowerment involves not only the combination of task-definition and task-execution, but adds the job of coordinating the task with the tasks done by others.

Where activities are closely interlinked, the old style of organisa-tion design used to put them under a manager who supervised and coordinated them. The new, compartmented style looks for self-supervision and self-coordination. The new style of management defines purposes rather than tasks and leaves compartments to use their creativity to achieve the defined purposes. It also leaves compartments free to use their boundary-spanning skills to achieve coordination between themselves.

Technology and Productivity

Might it not be possible that technological change will, in future, inexorably determine the shape of organisations? Could the very idea of organisation redesign, as a matter of choice, be made out-of-date by the pressure of technological change? To try to answer this question, I'd now like to look at the nature of technological change, so as to discover what might be its effects on organisation design in general and on compartmentation in particular.

Commentators have been talking for years about the coming of the 'information age' and about the 'post-industrial society'. In spite of the huge influence which information technology has had on business, warfare, science, travel and entertainment and of dramatic growth in the use of personal computers, it it is not yet clear that these changes add up to anything as profound as a post-industrial age. Carlotta Perez has put forward a theory which proposes that really fundamental technological change depends on a cluster of mutually supporting innovations, not only technical innovations but also social innovations which complement the technical ones. She believes that a range of organisational innovations in industry plus developments in areas like taxation and employment law are needed before a new cluster of technologies can reach an all-pervading level of influence.

After World War II, an all-pervading technological cluster developed around automobiles, oil and synthetic materials, a cluster which worked superbly well until the mid-1970s. Those who know the film *the Graduate* will remember the advice given to Ben, the character played by Dustin Hoffman, which was "Get into plastics!" Ben decided to do other things, but plenty of people joined the plastics business, or joined other large firms which produced the organisational innovations needed for the expansion of the auto-mobile, oil and chemicals industries. Huge multinationals had the financial control systems, the production know-how, the marketing techniques, the planning methods and the overall management skill to spread these technologies around the world. Large organisations were demonstrably successful, and no doubt this is one of the reasons why the idolatry of giantism took hold.

In the 1990s these technologies are no longer the innovative ones and the matching social structures are out of date too. Perhaps we are waiting for the right social innovations to match those of information and communications technology.

I think compartmentation will fit very well with them. Consider first the producer aspects. The manufacture of electronic hardware and the writing of software are activities much more suitable for decentralisation than production in the previous cluster with its large oil refineries and automobile assembly lines.

A company in the computer software business, called F International, draws on the services of some 1,000 people of whom 250 are employees and the rest associates with regular sub-contract work. Nearly all of them work from home, communicating with each other by normal mail, telephone, electronic mail and fax. Most of the workforce are women and many have children of school age. Some are disabled or looking after a disabled person at home. Many work *from* rather than *at* home; sales and customer service people are with customers a lot of the time and there are frequent training sessions and group meetings for all. In fact F International is obsessive about training.

Steve Shirley, who founded and built the company, says that she thinks of training as the equivalent of research and development. F International seems to be an organisation which really knows how to learn. It is also an organisation which communicates intensively and which is democratic. It is a creative compartment, an unusual one because it is distributed geographically but, in the way it works, not particularly unusual for the information technology field.

Now let us look at the consumer side. In North America shopping and travel to shops together occupy an average of well over one hour a day for every adult in the population and the average in Europe is rapidly approaching the same level. Information technology might substantially reduce this, according to Jonathan Gershuny.

> "....I'm not talking about science fiction, in the sense of a speculation about some future technical possibility. The technology necessary for a very effective home-based system for purchase of the great majority of consumer goods and services, already exists. With current technology computer terminals in our homes we could make orders from remote warehouses, which could be collected into batches using automatic warehousing techniques, and delivered within a few hours to our doors. The same systems could have, in addition to the basic retail services, additional sophisticated ancillary services, advising consumers on prices and quality and the location of 'best buys'. These sorts of services are now *possible* in the sense that all the basic technological components of such a system exist, at affordable prices."

The examples of home-working and home-shopping show what is possible technologically. Obviously, home-working and home-shopping will not necessarily be central to any novel pattern of technology. But these examples illustrate Perez' theory that social innovation is at least as critical as technological innovation to the emergence of a novel cluster of social and economic activity. Today the large majority of businesses do not, unlike F International, know how to manage a distributed organisation; they think they need centralised offices and workshops in order to function.

Better information need not lead to tighter central control. There is a great difference between having a lot of information and being able to put it to valuable use. Advances in information technology can support networking even better than they can support central control. Fortunately, things don't work very well if Big Brother is watching you. They work a lot better if millions of brothers and sisters have the information they need to work together in an ever-changing pattern of networking, trading and cooperation.

Whether or not we move to a post-industrial economy, many old style industrial plants will presumably remain. The success of the pattern of matching technology and organisation, which worked so well in the nineteen fifties, sixties and early seventies, has left a feeling that these physically large plants, and the financially large companies which own them, have to be organisationally large, too. But this view is out of date. Due to improved process design, greater understanding of process control and widespread computerisation, productivity has progressed to the stage that large plants do not mean lots of people. Surprisingly small numbers of highly skilled people can operate large, expensive plants. Beyond a certain point, adding more operators makes these plants less efficient and less safe.

In summary, then, we need expect few barriers to compartmentation from scale-economy or technological necessity. Self-supervision, self-coordination and high productivity allow compartments to function with any technology. Compartmentation may well be the only way to get full value from information technology.

An Example of Redesign

In the following sections of this chapter, I am going to use an extended example – longer than the others in this book – to describe how the move towards compartmentation can take place.

Redesign of an organisation need not be accomplished in one big bang. Instead, it is possible to move steadily towards an organisation made up of creative compartments in a number of stages, varying the number and even the order of the stages, and the time between them, to suit the situation. To illustrate this, I have invented a story, which can be imagined as taking place during the decade of the 1990s.

A Supermarket Chain

My story is about a British supermarket chain – let's call it Superway – which is part of a larger group of retail stores. During the 1980s the group was put together by merger of three previously independent retail companies, all of whom felt they were too small to compete with the two or three highly successful major supermarket chains in the UK. They had been persuaded by a merchant bank that by getting together they would have enough economy of scale and financial muscle to compete with the majors. But after the merger, they found that the group's larger size did little to help and that the group's stores were a bit of a ragbag collection – in a wide variety of sizes and types of location, with some good and some bad buildings and having a varied reputation with shoppers.

A new management team, recruited from major retailers, took over and set about getting some order into the group. They decided to create three reasonably homogeneous chains out of the collection of stores they had inherited. These were, first, a chain of hyper-markets sited near motorways and able to attract shoppers from miles around, second, a chain of Do-It-Yourself supply stores and third, Superway, a chain with stores in smaller towns and in suburbs away from major roads.

Seeking to distinguish Superway from its major competitors, the new management decided to take advantage of the smaller catch-ment areas its stores mostly had. The product lines, trading hours and marketing styles of each Superway store would be finely adapted to the particular town or neighbourhood it served. In all its activities, including staff recruitment and the local purchase of goods and services, each store would try to fit into the locality as closely and helpfully as possible. The aim was to live up to the slogan: 'Superway – The store that understands YOUR town.'

Empowered People

Jim Turner was the manager of Superway's Western Region. He was convinced that the only genuine way to adapt to local conditions was to devolve responsibility to the managers of the stores. Otherwise the idea of local adaptation would be little more than a public relations gimmick. The other regions had offices and assistant managers. Jim decided that he would work from his home, helped only by a part-time secretary, and that he would spend over half his time visiting the twenty five stores in his region. He also kept close contact with people in the Superway head office, particularly with the heads of planning and of personnel. Jim was very open with these two. They valued the insight into the everyday problems of a region which he gave them, while he was able to bounce ideas off them and to get their help on specific tasks.

Although the Western Region had the lowest budget for regional management costs, it had the highest budget for training. Jim was determined that every member of his stores' management teams would be comprehensively trained when they started and that their training would go on and on, however experienced they became. They would also learn how to train properly every staff member in their stores. Jim was a trainer, too. Once in two weeks, he was in every store in his region and much of his visit was spent in coaching the store's staff.

Equal to training in the Western Region's priorities was networking. Store managers were encouraged to help each other all the time – by a 'phone call for advice on a security problem, by a quick visit to look at a new layout for the goods reception area, or by recommending a printing firm who could produce attractive posters for a locally-organised promotion. Head Office was a networking resource, as well. One of the advantages of so much training was that it kept store staff in touch with various specialists working in, or as consultants to, Head Office.

Superway's excellent information systems provided the regional mangers with a weekly trading report for all stores. Once a year, Jim Turner held a regional meeting to which all his store managers came to exchange experience and to make plans for the coming year. Apart from these, there was no formality in the Western Region's management. The staff in every store were well trained and constantly coached, they knew where to ask when they needed help and they were empowered to get on with their job of running a high quality store, responsive to local needs.

Standards and Critique

Superway's store in Barchester was managed by Kath Harding. She was a self-confident person and liked the responsibility given her by Jim Turner's style of empowerment. She was an enthusiast for training, for open communication and for the empowerment of staff in her store. In this she was responding to Jim's lead, but two other initiatives were her own.

The first initiative was an advisory group. Kath had found that she did not always want to discuss her more ambitious ideas for the store with her boss, until she'd tested them out on someone else. In any case Jim was a very busy man. So Kath got Jim's agreement to her setting up a three-person advisory group, which met quarterly. She persuaded two local people to join it, plus the head of Superway's distribution organisation. The two locals were a member of the faculty at the Barchester Business School and the regional business development manager of a major bank, whose office happened to be in Barchester. All three were willing to join the group for token reward, because they found it gave them various insights which were professionally useful.

The advisory group didn't always give Kath an easy time. They pulled her half-formed ideas to pieces – and then helped her to put them together again. They embarrassed her when they uncovered potential problems she hadn't thought of. But she knew the group had a lot of respect for her and that their advice enabled her to do her job better.

Her second initiative was designed to make the store, as trader, as employer and in its community service role, more responsive to local needs. Kath organised an annual audit of the store's operations, carried out during a single day by half a dozen local citizens, who were nominated by various local organisations. The way the store welcomed the elderly, the disabled and children was discussed, as were opening hours, car parking arrangements and waste recycling. The audits produced some requests which were impossible to fulfil, but also revealed several ways to improve service at little or no extra cost. And the fact the Kath and her staff were willing to listen was much appreciated. After a couple of years, both the other supermarkets in the town felt obliged to do something similar.

Five years after Kath had become its manager, the Barchester store was delivering a very good trading result and had twice been in the top three in Superway's 'Store of the Year' competition.

New Opportunities

Kath now began to think about her own future. For family reasons, she did not want to leave Barchester, but she felt ready for greater responsibility. So when Jim Turner asked whether she'd be willing to run the store with even more autonomy, she responded positively. Jim wanted to experiment with the idea of making each store a legally separate business, which would require a degree of formality in defining the relationship between the store and Superway, the parent company.

He thought that if two stores in his region were keen to try the idea, it would have a reasonable trial, without serious risk should things go wrong. By choosing two of the best managed stores the risk would be further reduced and the practices developed during the trial would most probably be sound, so that they could be spread to other stores, if it were later decided to extend the idea of greater autonomy to the whole of the region's stores.

Kath's husband was a chartered accountant, a partner in a local accountancy firm. He liked any idea which would give Kath scope to use her business talents and agreed to join the venture. They formed a company, Barchester Trading Limited, with Jim Turner chairing its board of directors, Kath as Managing Director and her husband plus the three members of the advisory group as non-executive directors. Initially only 5% of the shares were owned by Kath, the rest being retained by Superway, but the deal was that over five years Kath and others working in the store could earn bonuses which would allow them to acquire up to 40% of the shares. The size of the bonuses would be decided by a formula based on the trading results of the store.

Barchester Trading entered into a legal agreement with Superway under which the store was leased to it, and would be operated by it as a Superway store, following certain rules. As the arrangement was a trial, Superway had the option to wind up the deal at the end of the third year, on terms which were fair to Kath and her colleagues. The operating rules laid down standards for staff training, the appearance of the store, health and safety and so on, although on past form, Kath and her team should be well capable of meeting these standards. Jim made it clear that the legal contract was really a safety net and that, if all went well, the relationship between Barchester Trading and Superway would continue to be mutually supportive, not legalistic.

The advantages of the new arrangement were a formal recognition of the autonomy and empowerment of Kath and her team and a greater financial benefit for them, if they achieved remarkable results in the store. The staff of the store were offered employment with Barchester Trading, with a guarantee that if the deal was reversed after three years, they would be reemployed by Superway. The legal documents were signed and the trial started. At first, there was not much difference in the daily life of the store, but as Kath and the staff gained confidence, their perspective on the business started to change. Kath still identified strongly with Superway, but her loyalty was now more and more to the local team. The new arrangement led to a deeper understanding of the interplay between the corporate goals of Superway and those of Barchester Trading, its directors and staff. This greater understanding led, in turn, to different, and better, business decisions.

The Experiment Succeeds

Both at Barchester and the other location, the trial was clearly successful. By now Jim Turner had been promoted to the post of Chief Operating Officer in Superway, and he started spreading the policy of legal autonomy to most of Superway's stores. New stores were still started up within the Superway company and after a couple of years of successful operation, they were then leased to a separate company partly owned by the staff of the store, as had been done at Barchester.

Now a conflict developed. At one of the 'autonomous' stores, the Managing Director became seriously ill and had to leave the job. Jim Turner assumed that the new boss would be appointed by himself and the regional manager and that it would be a good idea to move in someone who had been successful in another store. But the staff at the store had different views. They thought that the person who had been standing in during the former boss's illness would do the job well and persuaded the local members of the company's board to back them.

Jim felt this might be a 'cozy' outcome, leading to a popular but not particularly talented person getting the job. Superway, with a majority shareholding in the company, had the power to enforce its choice and Jim certainly wanted to retain that right. However, he agreed that the company's board, together with Superway's head of personnel, should formally interview the two candidates and forward their recommendations to him for the final decision. A difficult situation was avoided, largely by good luck, as the unanimous recommendation was that the local candidate was first class. It was agreed that, in future, Managing Director appointments in autonomous stores would be a joint decision of the local board and the Superway management, to be taken after full consultation with the store's staff and after full and fair consideration of all candidates.

Further Steps

Some years later, the close links which the Barchester store had with the local community led to a new proposal. The success of the store meant that it was now too small and its local supporters lobbied the local authority to make available a larger site. The board of Barchester Trading thought that they would be able to raise the finance needed to buy the new site and made an offer to Superway to do this, provided the franchise was transferred. Sale of the old site was no problem, since it was ideal for house-building.

There were opponents of this proposal in Superway. They felt that if Superway no longer owned its stores, it would start to break apart, even though it would retain a majority shareholding in the companies which owned and operated the stores. Others argued that they already had a mixture of stores, all owned by Superway, but some operated by Superway itself and others operated by autonomous companies. To add a new ingredient to the mix, of stores which were both owned and operated autonomously, was no great change. In any case, an experiment along these lines would do no harm, especially as deals of this kind would help Superway's cash flow.

So the deal went ahead. Kath's initiatives did not stop there. She'd always wanted to sell local produce in the store, so together with four or five other Superway stores in the region, she organised a quality control scheme for vegetables and fruit grown locally and for dairy products from local farms. Although most of the goods sold in the store still came from Superway's central merchandising operation, the local flavour appealed to shoppers. The networking between stores which led to this development spread into other activities. Central management still felt a little threatened by the independence which its stores were now displaying so strongly, but the moves were always ones which could be reversed if they went wrong, so there was no justification for opposing them.

Sometimes one of the autonomous stores got into a fight with the Superway management, which took a lot of time to sort out and encouraged the old guard at the centre in their pessimistic attitude towards these Barchester-type developments. But at Barchester itself there was no fighting. Kath Harding realised how lucky she was to have been associated with a far-sighted outfit. She also knew that fighting wasn't the best way to get her ideas accepted. In her experience, persuasion had worked extraordinarily well. But then, she was a pretty persuasive person.

Jim Turner was grateful for the Barchester store's inventiveness and for Kath's persuasiveness, although his view was that these were not the most valuable of the Barchester qualities. He valued most of all the consistently good communication and trust between all staff at Barchester. Without expert communication and solid trust, Kath's initiatives might have been threatening and confusing, resulting in a badly operated store. He had seen other stores whose bright ideas had distracted staff from the main task of giving high quality service to shoppers. If he had not, in the early days, been able to start the virtuous circles of openness and trust, empowerment and commitment, Barchester would not now be a famous name throughout the Superway company.

The Stages in Redesign

The Superway story can be generalised. In the rest of the chapter, I set out some design principles which should be applicable to any large organisation, which is moving in the direction of compartmentation.

Any organisation which sets out to redesign itself using the principles of compartmentation, networking and critique, will have to do this in a series of steps. What these steps are will depend on the starting point, that is, on the current organisation design, and on the organisation's particular type of activity. For instance, in a supermarket chain, each individual store is obviously a potential compartment. In other kinds of organisation, the starting point for compartmentation may not be so clear.

It is possible to outline the stages through which the redesign of most large organisations will have to move, even if sometimes the

stages can come in a different order. In one organisation a particular
step will prove to be critical, in another it will be a different step.
Outside events, such as changes in the economic climate, may
disrupt any idea of even progress from one stage to the next.
Nevertheless, the process of redesign will generally look something
like this:

Stage One – Skill Development

Skill in interpersonal process, in communication and in defining the
aims of an organisational unit is an essential starting point. Without
a reasonably widespread base in these skills, empowerment will be
uncertain. For many people, the only way they know for organising
things is hierarchy. They may not particularly like that way, but it is
a familiar way and to move away from it can be stressful. Without
the strength provided by a solid base of interpersonal process skills,
redesign may falter halfway through.

Training and experience in expressing ideas, in listening, in
joining newcomers into a change process and in defining purposes
are therefore an essential first step in redesign.

Stage Two – Compartmentation of Tasks

Identification of the compartments into which a larger organisation
can be divided is the next step. Size is important, since compartmentation works best on a scale of a few hundred people. But natural
boundaries are equally important. In the case of a supermarket
chain, it would be foolish to ignore the natural boundary between
individual stores.

Superb communication, with full openness, should be developed
within the chosen compartments. It is critical that communication
within the compartment's boundary is felt by everyone to be of a
special kind. There may well be good communication outside, but it
is much less personal, continuous and creative than inside the
compartment.

At this stage, hierarchy will clearly remain in ultimate control.
The compartment will have a boss, appointed hierarchically, and
removable. Compartmentation can, in Stage Two, be experimental,
because it will be possible to reverse it if things go wrong. But no
experiment should be half-hearted and it must be on a scale
sufficiently large for the results to be convincing.

Training remains vital during this stage of redesign. For example,
in the reorganisation of the Whitbread brewery, which I mentioned

earlier in this chapter, a full time coordinator was appointed whose job was to organise a series of workshops for everyone working in the plant. These workshops kept the awareness of interpersonal process skills at a high level, and provided a forum at which doubts and fears could be dispelled.

Stage Three – Networking and Critique

In this stage, networking between compartments within an organisation should start to be the main method of coordination between them. Sometimes this can be complemented by internal markets, involving trading between compartments, but often the informal exchange of information, advice and help is all that is needed. The hierarchy remains, but is only used for coordination when other methods do not seem to be working.

Critique is also established during Stage Three. This is partly done by a modification of the old hierarchical methods of account-ability – budgets, targets, performance standards, and the encour-agement of continuous improvement. It should also be through a critical appraisal by other stakeholder groups or through an annual review by a peer group drawn from other, similar compartments.

Again training will be important in this stage. Networking skills can be learned. So can the skills needed for effective, supportive critique.

Stage Four – Change in Legal Status

This is the stage at which compartments can become legally separate from the parent organisation, although a controlling interest can be retained by the parent. The change in legal status means that the relationship between compartment and parent organisation has to become even more clearly defined. But the link is still strong – the contract is a 'relational' one, it is not at arms length. Relational contracting can apply horizontally, between compartments, as well as vertically.

Perhaps this stage is the most difficult for the old hierarchy, since change now becomes hard to reverse. But if the earlier stages have been thorough, this stage may actually turn out to be a natural and safe evolution.

At this stage, the ability to live with ambiguity and the ability to think in systems terms become key factors. This is because the organisational boundaries now start being blurred. In earlier stages it was possible to think of compartments within a larger organisation, but that is not really valid in and after Stage Four. Perhaps the best description for Stage Four is a cluster of compartments around a strong central core.

Training needs at this stage include a wider range of business skills than may have been necessary before.

Stage Five – Final Steps

The final steps in organisation redesign include the ownership of assets by the compartment and the choice of the compartment's leadership by its members, or at least jointly by compartment members and the parent organisation. Not all organisations will want to make these final moves.

If these moves are made, the result gets close to the Japanese *keiretsu*, a group of sub-contractors and allies around a core company. This may be the way to get the benefits of 'dual logic', the combination in an economy of large, often multi-national, corporations with small entrepreneurial firms, which Clem Sunter identifies as one of the preconditions for a 'winning' economy.

> "You need big business with high technology and financial resources to undertake the big projects in a country and compete with the other giants in the world. But underpinning big business you need a thriving small business and informal sector, because that's where most of the jobs are going to be created and that is the birthplace of the future stars of big business."

If redesign is taken right through to the end of Stage Five, the core company may become small in numbers of people, but can remain powerful financially, secure in its reputation and able to undertake ambitious projects.

Notes

Rolls-Royce, pages 173-4. *Financial Times*, March 10th, 1993, p 17.

Shell's Integrated Teams, pages 174-5. See Michael J. Pink *Exploration and Appraisal Technology – Maximising Rewards by Integration.* Shell International Petroleum Company, London, 1993.

Whitbread's Brewery, page 175. See 'Refreshing the Parts Other Breweries Cannot Reach.' *Coverdale Review*, January 1993.

The New Shopfloor, pages 175-6. See Richard Florida, 'The New Industrial Revolution' *Futures*, **23**, 6, 559-576. And Akio Morita, with Edwin Reingold and Mitsuko Shimomura, *Made in Japan*, Penguin, New York, 1986, p 165.

Fundamental Technological Change, page 178. Carlotta Perez, 'Structural change and assimilation of new technologies in the economic and social systems', *Futures*, October 1983, 357-375; See also G. H.Fairtlough, 'Can we plan for new technology?' *Long Range Planning*, **17**, 3, 14-23, 1984.

F International, page 179. Shirley, S. The Distributed Office. *Royal Society of Arts J.* **cxxxv**, 5371, 503-514. June 1987. Mrs. Shirley's paper is one of a series of three appearing together in the same issue of this journal under the general title 'Reinventing the Place of Work'. The others are by Jonathan Gershuny – 'Lifestyle, Innovation and the Future of Work' (pp 492-502) and Charles Handy – 'The Future of Work – The New Agenda' (pp 515-525).

Home Shopping, page 179. Gershuny's paper is the one mentioned above.

Dual Logic, page 190. See Clem Sunter, *The New Century: Quest for the High Road*. Human and Rousseau, Cape Town, 1992, p 106.

11

Families of Compartments

Becoming a Creative Compartment

In the last chapter I described how large organisations can redesign themselves so as to become a loosely-connected group of compartments. The reader will recall that the first stage in the process of redesign was the strengthening of the interpersonal process skills of everyone involved. This is a vital step, since it underpins the communicative competence of the creative compartment. Without this, the compartment's creativity, its problem-solving capability, generated by intense internal communication, will not develop and the greatest benefits of compartmentation will be lost.

Communicative competence allows the compartment's members to work together on factual and ethical matters and to share their feelings constructively. This competence facilitates the democratic definition of a compartment's purposes and a dispersed pattern of leadership.

Stage three in the redesign process for large organisations, described in the last chapter, was the the development of networking skills and the setting-up of a process of critique.

If small firms and other small organisations are to become creative compartments, they will have to go through the same stages of redesign, bringing in process skills, communicative competence, democratic goal-setting, and the practices of networking and critique.

When a small organisation has achieved all this it will have the strength of a true creative compartment. However, it will often be valuable for creative compartments to form family associations of various kinds. This chapter suggests how this might be done.

A Guide to the Rest of This Chapter

When we look around the world, we can see several examples of associations of small organisations, usually business firms, which provide valuable mutual support for these organisations. These associations or families of organisations are not, at present, normally made up of true creative compartments, but these examples show how smaller organisations can work together to achieve complex results, using different blends of market, clan-like and hierarchical coordination. They suggest several starting points from which families of compartments might assemble themselves.

Starting Point A is the one which I described in the last chapter: the redesign for large companies which led, in its final stage, to a family of compartments attached to a parent company. I suggested that it might be possible for the parent to be left as quite a small organisation, as far as numbers of people go, although it could well be a powerful one, financially and in public repute.

Starting Point B is a grouping of subcontractors around a primary manufacturer, for example round a large automobile maker. Starting Point C is the regional cluster, seen in traditional fields of industry, and particularly strong in Italy and other parts of continental Europe. Starting Point D is a new technology. This often produces a family of firms cooperating, and also competing, in making the new technology a commercial reality. The final Starting Point is an association of companies around a bank. This is a well established model in the Far East.

In the sections on the five starting points for families of compartments, I describe the coordination methods which would be used within the various families.

Starting-point A – Redesign of Large Companies

Coordination Methods

Market coordination: Internal markets are used, by compartments trading between themselves. If the compartments are all controlled by the centre, the internal market can be regulated differently from markets in general – more simply and cheaply, or with more sharing of information than is usual in external markets.

Clan-like coordination: Their common parentage will mean that compartments within this kind of family will retain a common language for describing business situations and a common stock of mental models. This ought to make communication between them much more effective. Likewise, there will be many purposes shared between these compartments, making coordinated action easier to achieve.

Hierarchical coordination: The centre will retain power to allocate capital for investment, to set performance standards, to encourage the transfer of staff between compartments and to resolve disputes between them.

Examples: There are opportunities for the redesign of large organisations in virtually every sector of business – publishing, financial services, retailing, food industries and many others.

Starting-point B – Subcontractors around a Primary Manufacturer.

Team Entrepreneurship

In his book entitled *Team Entrepreneurship*, Alex Stewart describes life in a humble, low-technology factory; an automobile parts factory, "utterly dependent on the automakers: one of the toughest markets in the world."

The factory is in Canada and is a division of a larger corporation; Stewart gives it the name MIDA. It is a successful business; when he wrote the book in 1988 it had a profit of $5 million on sales of $20 million a year and a record of growth in profits of 20% a year over several years. It is quite a small business; it employs 200 people all at one site. About five per cent of people at MIDA have higher education, some others are specialist toolmakers or electricians, most have a "general mechanical orientation" when they join the firm and are then trained on the job. There are two main groups of employees. One is made up chiefly of people of East European origin, some of whom have been in Canada for a long time. The other is composed of recent immigrants from Indochina. "As a result the language used on the shop floor is Chinese – Mandarin Chinese. Most Chinese-speaking establishments in North America operate in Cantonese, not Mandarin. MIDA surely offers one of the few workplaces with reasonably high take-home pay for jobs in which Mandarin is the workaday tongue." There are ethnic tensions, centred on language, but lessons in English are given at the plant and this appears to be reducing the tensions. It remains an open question whether or not promotion would be just a matter of competence, including competence in English, or whether Indochinese workers would stay stuck on the shopfloor. MIDA had no unions.

Stewart's picture of MIDA was taken over a few months while he was working in the firm, but he returned two and a half years later and found that the way the firm was working was much as before. 'World class' manufacturing requires ever-increasing levels of skill for everyone in the business. For continuous learning, barriers between the shop floor and higher employees need to be broken, there has to be a real team, there has to be what Stewart calls a 'Hot' approach.

"Running Hot is the pursuit of competitive advantage, with limited resources, through a collective learning process. Teams of employees work hard – even passionately – for the sake of non-employees' goals." (By "non-employee's goals", Stewart means principally the goals of MIDA's customers.) A Hot firm provides security of job tenure, promotion from within and continuous training, coaching and nurturing. Teams from the lower ranks are asked to do things on their own initiative, to make things happen, to learn more than they need on the current job, to be entrepreneurs. They help each other on the job and with problems of all kinds. They know enough of each other's work to cover if someone is busy or absent.

At MIDA the rewards are good and all employees participate in share ownership and profit-sharing schemes. But everyone works hard and in ways which are sometimes personally inconvenient – long hours at times of peak demand, for example. Exit is of course possible, but may be more difficult than in conventional firms, as the ways of working and the flexible skills learnt at MIDA are not particularly marketable. However this is reciprocal; MIDA can't hire in people who know how to Run Hot, they have to be trained. Voice is an option which is certainly available; on Stewart's account voice is loud and forceful at times.

How is it all controlled? How are MIDA's huge, very demanding customers consistently given the quality of product and service which keeps them loyal? This appears to happen through the detailed know-how of a handful of people at the top, who have shown, time after time, that they can deliver. "In consequence, the personal authority of the leaders is clearly recognised and meritocratic. Their organisation is like a hospital emergency ward: there is clear and centralised authority at the top, egalitarian pragmatism below....Hot firms are *meritocratic autocracies*. Their autocrats' merit is rooted in their know-how, and in their history of building their teams and sustaining the Running. (This often means actions to broaden the ranks of the players, as more and more players are needed, and more become ready, to be empowered.)"

To what extent is MIDA a democracy? Stewart found that most employees considered the firm to be democratic, mainly in the sense that superiors listen to subordinates' views. Yet there is little participation by most people in the firm's strategic decisions. MIDA is an autocracy, so why does the place *feel* democratic? Stewart believes this is because everyone knows that MIDA is vitally dependent on a few customers. The firm's leaders have shown that they understand what these customers want and can translate their wants into MIDA's operational goals. Employees sense that it would be dangerous to meddle with this process.

Stewart suggests a further reason: many of the firm's workers come from communist countries where 'democracy' was a charade. Some of them have taken great risks to escape from a situation in which the workers pretend to work and their bosses pretend to pay them. They think that having honest, competent bosses is proper democracy.

> "The rules for Running Hot at MIDA are simple: A team of people take actions to manufacture products for a set of customers....Because "'people'' (not technocrats or robots) are responsible, they invent any method they can get away with. The people at MIDA have experience in specific tasks and networks and thus adopt a corollary rule: no time to agonize, trust your intuition....The rules of this game can only be followed with faith in its players' capacities for learning. A threat to that faith is a threat to the game....Running Hot is a willingness to act above one's head; it cannot be captured with words like *commitment*. If you wish to Run Hot, you play with *passion*. Without the heat, without the passion, without the customer focus, MIDA would be just a little factory banging out auto parts, consuming a good deal of human time and effort in the process."

MIDA is unusual for North America. And it is vulnerable; vulnerable to policy decisions taken in Detroit by people who have never heard of the firm, vulnerable to technological change, vulnerable to the progress of Japanese automakers who have made 'running hot' the norm for their operations everywhere. MIDA is not quite a creative compartment as I have described it; nevertheless it is a wonderfully inspiring example of compartmentation and learning.

Subcontracting in Japan

MIDA is a small firm, which survives in the harsh North American business climate, through having virtuous circles of openness and trust, empowerment and commitment. Without these circles it is hard to see how MIDA could survive. In Japan, neither the virtuous circles nor the survival of a small auto parts company would be remarkable.

Around each major Japanese automobile maker is a family of smaller firms, with subcontractors to subcontractors, with several layers of independent firms below the principal manufacturer. Subcontractors are carefully selected, and are encouraged, for instance by the principal giving a bank guarantee, to buy state-of-the-art production equipment. They are also helped with training and management advice. Subcontractors are seldom dropped, and then only after a long period of consultation and the tapering-off of orders.

Networks between small and medium-sized firms mean that 'family' links are not only vertical. While relationships are supportive, they are grounded in high standards of quality and service and in competitive prices over the long term. Principals hold annual meetings with core suppliers, bilaterally and in groups, to disclose, in confidence, their business plans and their forecasts for future levels of orders. Subcontractors are expected to respond by using their initiative to help the principal, by being flexible and by making quality and service improvements without always getting an immediate reward. Without *shinrai*, trust based on mutual goodwill, these close, flexible relationships would not be possible.

The familiar business contract of the West tries to foresee all the outcomes which the future may bring. In many cases this is not really feasible, especially if the contract is to last for some years. In Japanese business culture there is little attempt to write contracts of this kind, since trust is thought more important than formal contracting. John Kay compares the difference between the classical, Western contract and the relational, Japanese contract to the difference between a contract to install a phone in your house and a marriage contract. "The relational contract will have a legal form (as the marriage contract does), but (as with the marriage contract) it does not incorporate the essential elements of the relationship.

These elements are implicit, and are enforced, not by any legal process, but by the need of the parties to go on doing business together."

The Logic of Subcontracting

In the West it is generally believed that large firms are the only ones with the resources to introduce expensive new technologies and complex systems. But once these technologies and systems become established, it is now much easier in the West for a number of small firms to provide what previously only the large firm could manage. The spread of reliable public telecommunications systems and of low-cost computer-based information systems has made it easier for small units to do things that before were the preserve of the giants. Eric Clemons points out that this change is well under way:

> "[In the late 19th century] the meat packer Swift owned the first refrigerated rail cars. Brewers like Pabst and Anheuser-Busch owned not only their own cooperage, but the forests necessary for manufacturing the kegs. Singer Sewing Machine owned not only the resources needed for manufacturing the iron and wooden components of their machines; they owned companies that trained would-be buyers on the use of the machines and provided financing."

A hundred years later these webs of ownership have largely vanished. Close to 70% of the value of a Chrysler car is made up of parts supplied from outside firms. In banking and in payroll and other accounting services there is the same tendency to rely on third party providers for parts of the service. Many organisations use outside services to handle their payrolls and lots of banks provide credit cards to their customers, while leaving the mechanics of the credit card business to one of a few specialist firms. Clemons says that for arrangements like these to work properly "... it is essential that the service also be readily detachable, that its complexity be within bounds that can be mastered by an outside contract servicer, and that it be safe for a company to rely upon a contractor for delivery of these services." Mutual trust is generally a good deal lower in the West than in Japan.

Clemons uses the example of a travel management company, Rosenbluth Travel, to illustrate these points. Over the past twenty years or so business has become more international and travel has become cheaper and easier. These two interacting trends have led business executives to travel more often, so controlling the cost of travel has become both important and complex for most firms. Computer systems can provide worldwide information on the services and prices of airlines, hotels, car rental companies and so on and can therefore save companies a lot of money. The Rosenbluth company saw that the right computer systems could allow them to give even large corporations a better service than these corporations' in-house travel departments.

Large firms like Du Pont and Scott Paper were willing to hand over travel management to this specialist service and Rosenbluth has now become a large business itself, although it has not forgotten the advantages of smallness. To provide an international service to their corporate accounts the firm has set up a cooperative network of independent firms rather than trying to run a world-wide organisation. So this is no second-rate outfit trying to catch up with the big ones; in fact what Rosenbluth has to watch out for is equally innovative small competitors.

As the 'hollowing out' of large firms continues we may expect them to become coordinators rather than operators, concerned with big activities but doing only some of them in-house. The Italian fashion house Benetton is an example. It has several thousand retail franchises, which contract to sell only Benetton products but remain separate firms. Much of the manufacturing of Benetton's clothes is done by subcontractors, over 200 of them, mainly in Northern Italy. The subcontractors are of various kinds – firms controlled by Benetton, firms set up by former Benetton managers, some independent firms and even homeworkers.

Design and marketing are centralised and the retail outlets, the head office and the subcontractors are all connected by electronic information systems. Indeed, the interrelation of such a large family of firms would probably not be possible without the sophistication of these electronic links. Perhaps another precondition is the tradition of interlinked firms which has persisted in the Emilia-Romagna region of Italy. Benetton did not have to invent the idea of a family of loosely-connected firms, although it certainly developed the idea well beyond the traditional form.

Benetton is a particularly well developed example, but it is not unique. The Italian textile industry is the world's second largest textile exporter, measured by value. Its competitiveness comes, not by low wages, but from substantial investment in machinery, imaginative design, alertness to fashion, marketing flair and rapid adjustment to market trends. Much of this is achieved by sub-contract networks, often supported by actual family ties.

Italy's political structure has helped the growth of the small firm sector. In the 1970s mass production factories became heavily influenced by left-wing trades unions. Many large employers reacted by decentralising production to small, non-unionised firms. Middle managers and skilled craft workers left the large firms, often with the encouragement of senior management, to set up or to join these subcontractors, in textiles, in mechanical engineering and in ceramics, for example.

Coordination Methods

Market coordination: In the Japanese system, subcontractors must in the long run be competitive to retain their place in the family. In the Western system, competitive pressures have shorter term effects.

Clan-like coordination: Goodwill, trust and relational contracting are clan-like features of existing families centred around primary manufacturers. With compartmentation, these would no doubt increase.

Hierarchical coordination: The primary manufacturer can establish a sort of hierarchical coordination in areas such as technical and service standards and through targets for reducing costs within the family.

Examples: Automotive, domestic appliance and consumer electronics industries.

Starting-point C – Regional Clusters in Traditional Industrial Fields

Starting point B is that of a family of firms centred around a principal manufacturer, or in extreme cases, around a design and marketing organisation which subcontracts the large bulk of its actual manufacture. This concept shades into Starting Point C, which is a regional cluster of similar firms, which compete between themselves, but which also subcontract to each other. In this model, when a firm achieves a marketing success it has no hesitation in using its rivals' production capacity to meet demand. Next year its designs may be less popular, and it may have to become a subcontractor for others.

In continental Europe, the clustering of similar firms, mostly dependent on a good deal of craft skill, is frequently backed up by local government, which regulates commercial practices, provides training, supports professional development of skilled workers and managers, and facilitates the flexible interaction of the firms in a competing/cooperating network. Some of this is a continuation of earlier craft traditions which were never extinguished by the mass-production techniques of Fordism.

One example of clusters of industrially-related firms given by Michael Porter is the German printing machinery industry. Germany dominated the world market for printing machinery in the 1970s and 80s, building on a tradition going back for over 150 years. Over this time, new firms were formed by break-away groups from old ones, old firms merged to form bigger ones, firms competed, firms cooperated in training and in research. The cluster extended into allied industries like printing inks and paper-making machinery.

Another example is the ceramic tile industry in the Sassulo area of Italy. Producers of tiles interact with machinery makers, consultants and designers in the area. Local government gives help in international marketing and in technological research. The industry's trade association gives a lead in raw material purchasing, labour relations and legal matters. Porter says that the complex interactions between Sassulo-area firms, taking place in the world's largest tile cluster, gives these firms unique advantages over their foreign competitors.

Coordination Methods

Market coordination: Fierce competition between family members in end-consumer markets. A changing pattern of subcontracting between family members as their fortunes in end-consumer markets rise and fall.

Clan-like coordination: Intense networking between family members, which compartmentation would enhance. Relational contracting is the norm.

Hierarchical coordination: Local government can set the rules for training, craft and professional development and commercial practices.

Examples: Textiles and clothing, paper goods and printing, furniture and ceramics.

Starting-point D – Worldwide Associations around New Technologies

High Technology Start-up Companies

Let me now turn to some absolutely new businesses, those which to start with are no more than a gleam in someone's eye. Every year huge numbers of new businesses are started all over the world, but the new businesses I want to consider are those in areas of high technology, where there are few precedents to guide the design of the new venture. And because this is where I have most experience, I will concentrate on start-up companies in the area of biotechnology.

First, two US examples. Genentech's origin was a telephone call from Robert Swanson, who at that time was working at the venture capital firm Kleiner Perkins, to Herbert Boyer, a renowned scientist at the University of California at San Francisco. The call was prompted by an article in the *San Francisco Chronicle* about Boyer's part in the discovery of the recombinant-DNA technique, an article which included the suggestion that the pharmaceutical industry would be transformed by the discovery. Swanson persuaded Boyer to meet him to discuss the potential business opportunities for the new technology and by the end of an evening they had agreed to try to found a research company which would work very closely with academic scientists in seeking rec-DNA applications. Swanson also persuaded Tom Perkins, chairman of Kleiner Perkins, to support the new venture and to become its chairman. Swanson became its chief executive and Boyer a part-time vice-president, while remaining at the university. Although Swanson had the idea that a new business could be grown out of this technology, it would probably have come to nothing unless Boyer, with his knowledge of the science and his ability to attract top-class scientists to work for the planned new firm, had not given his active support. The role of an experienced venture capital firm was obviously critical too.

Two years after the formation of Genentech, the firm of Kleiner Perkins again played a key part in getting a biotechnology company going. This time the technology was monoclonal antibodies, the firm was Hybritech and the enterprise was a conscious attempt to copy Genentech's success in recombinant-DNA, in a different but related area of science. And again it succeeded.

In the case of Celltech, the idea came from two people then working in my division at the National Enterprise Board, Peter Lane and Roger Hay. They talked about it to me, and the three of us worked out the plan for the company. It would never have succeeded without the support of the NEB Chairman, of an influential committee and of John Ashworth, the scientific advisor to the British cabinet. Particularly important was the help of the UK's Medical Research Council, who felt that it was very much in its interest to have a new biotechnology company around to counter the lethargy which the major UK pharmaceutical companies were then displaying towards the new technology.

Two other UK biotechnology companies were in some degree inspired by Celltech. The first of these, Xenova, was was founded by Louis Nisbet, following discussions with me at Celltech, which led in turn to his getting the invaluable help of a seed capital company, Korda and Co. Cantab Pharmaceuticals was the result of a sabbatical spent at Celltech by Alan Munro, then Reader in Immunology at Cambridge University. He found the atmosphere of a biotech firm very stimulating and, soon after leaving us, got together with the venture capital company Abingworth and agreed to work with them to start a biotech business.

This is how Nisbet describes his interactions with Celltech:

> "I talked with Gerard Fairtlough at Celltech initially. They really pioneered the biotech industry in this country, and I had two simple questions for him. One, do you think [the idea I have for a new company] makes sense? I talked with some of his top molecular biologists about how we bring molecular biology into this somewhat traditional field of microbial screening. He said that, yes, everyone here seems to think it makes sense. Of course the other question was, do you think that there is money available in Europe to get a business going? He said yes, that he believed so. More than that, he said, just to show how much we believe this, we will put up £45,000 to at least allow you to set up an office and work with a proper consultancy group in London."

Xenova located alongside Celltech in Slough and was able to take over a smaller building which Celltech moved out of when it constructed a new, larger one.

Helper Organisations

These examples suggest that the genesis of high technology firms is likely to be the result of a collaboration between several people. In my experience, a single entrepreneur cannot start a complex business on his or her own, because no one person will have the original scientific idea, and have knowledge of the market in which the resulting product will be sold, plus the ability to raise the initial finance, plus the ability to recruit a first-class management team, all of which are necessary for the venture to succeed.

This is why a *helper organisation* is so useful. The typical seed capital firm will not only provide equity capital (say, £250,000 for this stage of a high tech start-up) but also a lot of advice and support, particularly in raising money for the second stage of development and in recruitment of the other members of the team who will join the founder to take the fledgling firm through that second stage.

As well as seed capital firms, helper organisations include the particular investing firm which agrees to take the lead at the second stage of the high technology firm's growth and sometimes a consultancy firm. What helper organisations must have is the ability to help without interfering in detailed matters, without trying to 'micro-manage', and without weakening the authority of the chief executive of the start-up company.

People who take on the risky and exhausting job of starting a new business usually believe strongly in their own ideas and want independence in turning these ideas into reality. The good helper organisation recognises this and accepts that the drive and imagination of the start-up company's team is vital for success. At the same time, the helper firm must be able to criticise constructively, to insist that progress is maintained and to make its voice heard on issues where its experience is greater than the experience of anyone in the company's team. When its critique is supportive and persuasive, an experienced helper organisation is of huge value.

The helper organisation therefore empowers the founder of a start-up company and the management team which it has helped to recruit. At times it provides a stringent critique, at other times it coaches the team, at all times it is ready to advise the team and to seek help for them, if asked. While doing all this it builds its own experience and therefore its ability to speak with authority about the problems of small new companies.

Newly-formed companies have the advantage that they are not constrained by their own organisational histories, but the people recruited to them bring their own histories with them and new companies lack traditions which help recruits to adapt. Like an established organisation, a new one will need communication skills, interpersonal process skills, the ability to define its purposes and priorities, the ability to manage internal change and to anticipate external change. The new outfit will have to learn all this while struggling to find its feet and this is hard. But it will be made easier if there is an experienced helper organisation around, an organisation able to support an innovating group of people without taking away their autonomy.

The principle which helper, or 'meta-innovating', organisations should follow is supportive critique, which empowers those getting support. This kind of critique is based on the setting of very high standards, but also on the recognition that a new company will not find it easy to meet them. Because high technology start-up companies are doing something new and often unique, their managements will necessarily be working in unfamiliar territory. The investors will be expecting miracles, and the management will being trying to deliver them. No wonder they need a helper organisation to support them. This support must blend encouragement and criticism, it must advocate both boldness and realism, it must be forceful without removing the management's autonomy. The helper is like a sports coach or even like a parent, and being a good coach or a good parent is not easy. Particularly needed are skills in interpersonal process. These skills can be developed by training and experience.

Not all venture capital firms can really be called helper organisations. There are a few that do not recognise the need to help the companies in which they invest. There are others that recognise the need but make no claim to have the expertise required and leave the job to one of their co-investors, usually the one acting as lead investor. There are others who try to help but do not succeed, often because they get too heavily involved in the management of the start-up firm. Obviously some venture capitalists are better than others in the helping role.

My views about helper organisations started to develop when I was at the National Enterprise Board. The NEB had a number of roles, one of which was fostering high technology start-up companies, both as an investor and as a helper organisation. The helper role was made more difficult by the fact that the NEB was a government agency, which led people to think that it would not be business-like and that it would be politically-influenced, when what it was actually trying to be was a well-informed and far-sighted investor. Learning to be a good helper organisation is a hard task in any conditions, and these misperceptions made it worse. As a result the NEB never became a consistently good helper. This was unfortunate for Celltech, since the other investors in the company were not skilled helpers either, because in the early 1980s UK venture capital firms had not built-up the expertise in helping which several of them now have. So Celltech largely did without a helper organisation.

Research Collaborations

In biotechnology and pharmaceuticals, collaborations abound. I have already mentioned those between start-up companies and helper organisations, and those within a network of smaller companies. A further set of collaborations are those centred on major pharmaceutical companies. Here is how SmithKline Beecham, one of the world's largest pharmaceutical companies, describes its R&D links:

> "The environment for drug discovery has never been more complex and R&D organisations in today's scientific climate can no longer remain self-sufficient. The ability to invest internally in the ever broader range of specialised skills and techniques required for modern drug discovery is beyond the financial capacity of even the largest companies. The explosion of scientific knowledge means that SB must establish external alliances to gain access to new technologies, skills, products and patents....these trends demand constant examination of R&D priorities and a careful balance in allocation of investment between internal and external activities.
>
> SB entered into a range of collaborations in 1992. Among these are: with Yale university to develop a vaccine against Lyme disease; with Genelabs Technologies Inc. for hepatitis E and C; with Pasteur Merieux and the Michigan Department of Public Health to develop combination vaccines for children; with IDEC Pharmaceuticals for monoclonal antibodies for the therapy of rheumatoid arthritis; and with British Biotechnology to develop compounds for the treatment of arthritis and cancer."

SmithKilne Beecham's collaborations are typical of those in which major firms in this industry are now engaged. Up to half a company's research budget may be spent in collaborations. The major firm often buys shares in the smaller companies it collaborates with, not to reduce the smaller firm's independence, because the major usually wants that preserved, but because the major will gain real benefit if the smaller firm does spectacularly well.

In some ways, the group of smaller firms and university departments around a pharmaceutical major is like the subcontractors around a Japanese auto-maker. But the relationship is usually a non-exclusive one. For example, Celltech has collaborations with the US pharmaceutical majors Lederle and Merck, and with the German major Bayer. Each of these relates to a different area of human disease, which makes it possible to work with several of the majors at the same time.

Coordination Methods

Market coordination: Competition between start-up companies for access to venture capital, for corporate deals with industry majors and for links with university research groups.

Clan-like coordination: Strong industry networking, driven by everyone's need to keep abreast of a rapidly developing technology. Relational contracting between industry majors and smaller companies. Helper organisations in venture capital sector.

Hierarchical coordination: National governments often encourage new technology companies, promoting industrial links with academia and setting technical standards.

Examples: Pharmaceuticals and biotechnology, information technology and telecommunications, new materials and nanotechnology, aerospace.

Starting-point E – Association of Companies around Banks and Trading Companies

The Zaibatsu of Japan

Following Japan's amazing national transformation in 1868, known as the Meiji restoration, the late nineteenth century saw the rise in Japan of about a dozen large conglomerates. These federated firms, called *zaibatsu*, were grouped around a holding company, and included a bank, an insurance company and an international trading company as well as manufacturing enterprises. The names of several are well known today – Mitsubishi, Mitsui and Sumitomo, for example.

The companies in these federations had small shareholdings in other family companies, gave preference in trading relations to family members and loosely coordinated their activities. But the member companies in these families had considerable operating independence. They were rather unlike the conglomerate companies we have in the West today, where financial control is usually very tight and where the head office clearly has the power to do what it likes in running the group. Some commentators think that the concept of loose coordination which today extends throughout the Japanese economy, with the Ministry of International Trade and industry (MITI) at its centre, is derived from the *zaibatsu* model.

After World War II, the US occupation forces made moves to break up the *zaibatsu*, but not very determined ones, so that by ten years after the war the groups had reassembled, albeit in an even looser form than before. The looser arrangement was probably an advantage, since it gave a lot of flexibility to the whole system and plenty of independence to the member companies. Historically, the most important features of the *zaibatsu* have been financial and commercial. As each group had a bank at its centre, there was an obvious source of long-term, well-informed finance for all member companies. Also there was a trading company with offices all around the world and great experience in foreign markets, which made it relatively easy for Japanese companies to tackle world markets.

Today the *zaibatsu* system has become rather similar to the *keiretsu* system in which firms are grouped round a large manufacturer, rather than round a bank and a trading company and the term 'horizontal *keiretsu*' is often now preferred. In the two systems there is something of the same cooperative ethos, although the size of the firms in the family are generally much smaller in the vertical *keiretsu* case. It should be noted that the *zaibatsu* are certainly not associations of compartments – all the companies are big ones. But their type of association is nevertheless a potential starting point for the evolution of families of compartments.

Coordination Methods

Market coordination: To remain in the family, companies have to be competitive in their own end-consumer markets, over the long term.

Clan-like coordination: Family loyalty often strong, and sometimes based on actual family ties.

Hierarchical coordination: Some national government support for large associations of this kind.

Examples: Particularly strong in the Far East – the *zaibatsu* system of very large groups in Japan, the *chaebol* system in Korea, family groups in Taiwan. In continental Europe, relations between banks and industrial or commercial businesses have some of these features. Much of this is on a scale far beyond that of the compartment, but there seems no reason why relationships of this kind should not work well within families of compartments.

Conclusion

Many-layered hierarchies in government or corporate bureaucracies, Henry Ford's assembly lines ruling the workers serving them, huge multinational corporations able to mould consumers into using their products and to force nations into accepting their trading methods – these are images of organisation which most people carry with them. We have absorbed, directly or indirectly, Chaplin's vision of mechanised production in his film *Modern Times*, John Kenneth Galbraith's picture of the manipulative corporation in his book *The New Industrial State* and Max Weber's metaphor of the iron cage of bureaucracy. The apparent inevitability of such monolithic images has, for over a century, fed the idolatry of giantism.

My main purpose in this chapter has been to sketch an alternative image – the image of the organisation as a family. I have tried to show that a wide variety of family-type, flexible associations do work well. I have described how these associations carry out complex tasks, using different combinations of market, clan-like and hierarchical coordination methods.

I believe that we should discard monolithic images of organisation and replace them by family, or systemic, images. We should throw off the blankets of hierarchy and stop worshipping giants. Stewart Clegg suggests that we abandon our "fixation on concrete organisations as objects of analysis" and the "framing assumption of the iron cage". We would then have the freedom to discover new ways of getting things done. We would be able to think about *organising* rather than about *organisations*.

I also believe that the idea of the compartment must be coupled with that of the family. The compartment provides a solid base from which flexible, family-type associations can be formed and reformed. Without this base, many people might find it hard to live in a world of such great flexibility – they might want to climb back into the iron cage. The creative compartment's clearly defined and shared purposes, and its well understood and shared language, provide a strong foundation. To this foundation are added the skills of boundary-spanning and networking and the ability to profit from external critique. This is the base for confident dealing in a flexibly organised world.

The starting-points for families of compartments, which I described above, are indeed just starting-points, and do not prescribe how these families will develop. The creativity of individual compartments, and the interactions between them, will determine what families of compartments will come to look like.

And an existing large firm, a region or a shared new technology are probably not the only starting-points. A group of compartments who happen to share electronic networking facilities, like e-mail and electronic conferencing, might find this to be a starting-point. Another might be a shared value system – religious, ecological, feminist, aesthetic – or a shared life-style – a generational one, for instance. A third could be shared ethnic background, shared educational experience or a common natural language, especially if any of these is in a minority.

Whatever the starting-point, the association will gain a momentum of its own, certainly if the association proves successful. Successful associations are likely to be copied. They will become models for the families of the future.

Notes

Team Entrepreneurship at MIDA, pages 194-7. Alex Stewart. *Team Entrepreneurship,* Sage, Newbury Park, CA (1989). I will not give page references, since anyone who wants to know more about MIDA and Running Hot should get hold of *Team Entrepreneurship* and read the whole of this short and fascinating book.

Subcontracting in Japan, pages 197-8. See John Thorburn and Makoto Takashima, *Industrial Subcontracting in the United Kingdom and Japan*, Avebury, Aldershot, 1992, and Mari Sako, 'The Role of "Trust" in Japanese Buyer-Seller Relationships' *Ricerche Economiche,* **XLV**, 2-3, 375-399, 1991, and John Kay, *Foundations of Corporate Success*, Oxford, 1993.

The Logic of Subcontracting, pages 198-200. See Eric K. Clemons, *Information Technology and the Boundary of the Firm: Who Wins, Who Loses, Who Has to Change,* Proceedings of Colloquium on Global Competition and Telecommunications, Harvard Business School, May 1991. On Benetton, see Stewart R. Clegg, *Modern Organizations: Organization Studies in the Postmodern World*, Sage, London, (1990) pp 120-5. On Italian industry see Michael J. Piore and Charles F. Sabel, *The New Industrial Divide: Possibilities for Prosperity*, Basic Books, New York (1984) pp 151-6.

Regional Clusters, pages 200-1. See Piore and Sable, *op cit*, p 221 and Michael E. Porter, *The Competitive Advantage of Nations*, Macmillan, London (1990) pp 179-225.

High Technology Start-up Companies, pages 202-3. The genesis of Celltech is described in my paper: 'Exploitation of Biotechnology in a Smaller Company.' *Phil. Trans. R. Soc. Lond. B* **324**, 589-597 (1989). The NEB chairman was Sir Arthur Knight and the influential committee was the one chaired by Dr. Alf Spinks. See also G.H.Fairtlough. Innovation and Biotechnology. *Roy.Soc. Arts J.* **cxxx**, 5313, 565-576 (1982) and the profile of Louis J. Nisbet in *Pharmaceutical Executive*, **11**, 10 (1991).

Helper Organisations, pages 203-5. For further information about the founding of new biotechnology companies, see my article 'Three Misconceptions about Innovation' in *Technology Analysis & Strategic Management* **4**, 1, 77-82 (1992).

Research Collaborations, page 206. See SmithKline Beecham plc Annual Report 1992 pp 17-19.

Zaibatsu and *chaebol* Systems, pages 207-8. See Clegg, *op cit*, pp 125-132. Piore and Sabel, *op cit*, pp 156-162. Lester Thurow, *Head to Head: The Coming Economic Battle between Japan Europe and America*, Brealey, London (1993) pp 113-151. Cristopher Freeman, 'Japan: a New National System of Innovation ?" in G. Dosi *et al*, Eds. *Technical Change and Economic Theory*, Pinter, London (1988) pp 330-348.

Images of Organisations, pages 209-210. See J.K.Galbraith, Hamish Hamilton, London (1967), Gareth Morgan, *Images of Organisation*, Sage, Newbury Park (1986) and Clegg, *op cit*, p 125.

12

Widespread Change

Let us revisit some of the inter-linked ideas developed in this book. The first, and central, idea is that of the creative compartment, which has to be adaptable and creative in order to be useful to its members and to society, and which has to be democratic in order to be adaptable and creative. The second idea is that of coordination through a combination of market and clan-like methods, using boundary-spanning and networking skills to get things done on a scale beyond that of a single compartment. Third is the idea of critique, which includes both cybernetic and clan-like critique; that is, both signals provided to a compartment by market and market-like pressures and the informed and constructive evaluation of a compartment's activities by a kind of peer review.

I hope these three ideas will help in providing a new paradigm for organisation design and a deeper meaning for the concept of smallness. But such ideas are of little value unless there is a serious possibility of their being widely used, unless there is a chance that they lead to real change. In this final chapter I will look at how this might happen, at what the obstacles to change are and at what a world largely made up of compartments might be like.

I will start with some personal experience of organisational change, including examples both of change initiated from the top and of bottom-up change, (that is, change stemming from the spread of successful practices across an organisation). I will compare top-down and bottom-up change in organisations and try to learn some lessons from these contrasting modes of change.

I will follow this with a section drawing on the work of Donald Michael. His picture of change depends on the spread of skills in communication and interpersonal process and on the telling of stories or scenarios about possible futures for the society in question.

Scenario planning, invented at Shell, aims to prepare people to cope with an uncertain future by expanding their stock of mental models. New mental models are also the way to prepare for fundamental organisational change.

Changing Our Mental Models

In the early 1950s Western European economies, which up to then had been struggling to recover from the war, moved into a phase of growth like that already under way in North America. I started work in industry in 1953 and for twenty years my experience was of mainly steady growth. During those twenty years, much industrial success came from having better access to natural resources and raw materials and from being able to build bigger and better plants than competitors, gaining the economies of scale more quickly than they could. This certainly applied to the oil, gas and chemicals industries where I worked.

Everyone builds his or her own pictures of the workings of the various parts of the surrounding world. As far as the industrial world was concerned, the picture which my colleagues and I had at that time was centred on growth. If you built too large a pipeline, tanker or refinery, it might be difficult to use its full capacity for a couple of years but growth would soon put that right. Our pictures of the world, our mind-sets, our mental models, were naturally rather more complicated than that and no doubt varied in complexity and clarity from person to person, but most of us shared the gut feeling that growth would be unending. It had been going on for many years, so our day-to-day decisions, whether we were technologists, marketeers or planners, were shaped by mental models which had growth at their core.

For some people mental models function as security blankets, and for everyone it is hard to dump one model without having another to take its place. But dump them we must, if they are no longer useful in coping with the puzzles our lives present us with. When, as chief executive of Shell Chemicals, I found a new model for the tasks of a top team, I was able to drop my old model of the tasks of the chief executive, which did not fit the situation the company was in at that time, and I think I did a better job as a result. My change of models was a useful piece of learning, of learning about management and of learning how to learn.

I was not the only person at that time who needed to learn how to learn. After two decades in which a mental model of industrial economics based on growth had been pretty successful, something happened in 1973 which now made it dangerous. That something was the 'oil shock' caused by a four-fold increase in the world price of crude oil. The price increase happened because of a change in models in the minds of the leaders of the oil-exporting nations, led by Saudi Arabia. The old mental models of the Saudi and other leaders, which told them that increased revenue came by exporting more and more oil, were replaced by models which told them to get more revenue by making huge increases in the price, since oil importing countries had little alternative but to pay. And the new model worked, in the short term at any rate.

A big change in the world's economies would probably have happened anyway, but the way it occurred in 1973 was particularly dramatic. Within a year it was clear that a great many people's mental models would have to change in an equally dramatic way and that making this change was going to be difficult. Few people in the industry had had much experience in replacing their mental models of the world economy; few had yet learnt how to learn within the now rapidly changing scene of world economics and politics. However, in the Shell group a start had already been made on learning how to learn; in Don Michael's phrase, Shell was already planning to learn.

In the 1960s Shell, like most other large organisations, had a sophisticated planning system, designed to make sure that the various parts of the group expanded in parallel, so that there would be enough crude oil to fill the tankers, enough refining capacity to process this oil and the right number of retail outlets and other product demand to absorb the output of the refineries. All this was computerised, involving huge numbers of figures, and all depended on a particular forecast of world economic growth. So a lot of effort went into forecasting what the growth rate would be, into getting right the magic number of the world's economic growth rate. Towards the end of that decade some astute people in Shell realised that economic growth might not, after all, be unending and set about thinking of a better way of planning for the future. A key figure in this was Pierre Wack, who first in Shell Française and then in Shell's Group Planning division, stimulated the development of the technique of scenario planning.

Wack's approach was not to try and make more and more accurate forecasts but rather to accept uncertainty, to understand it, to make it part of the process of thinking. Wack saw uncertainty not as "an

occasional, temporary deviation from a reasonable predictability"
but as "a basic structural feature of the business environment."
Learning how a large organisation could actually live in practice with
economic and political uncertainty was a great achievement by Wack
and his colleagues.

Living with Uncertainty

Uncertainty was something which managers in Shell were, in fact,
already able to live with. For example, in exploring for oil it is
uncertain what you will find when you start to drill and in research it
is uncertain which of innumerable possible combinations of chemicals will give you a good catalyst. But in oil exploration or catalyst
research people are trained to reduce uncertainty, first by studying
an area's geology or by reading the scientific literature, and then by
designing a programme of drilling or of laboratory experiments
which provides answers to various questions. The questions are
formulated and the answers are interpreted by means of mental
models, models of the shapes of potentially oil-bearing rock-strata
under the earth or models of the molecular configuration of a
potential catalyst. Wack wanted to train Shell's managers to spot
clues to an uncertain economic and political future in a similar way,
by helping them to build appropriate new mental models around
which to organise their perceptions of what was happening in the
world and of good ways of reacting to what they saw. As Wack put it:

> "....we wanted to change our managers' view of reality. The
> first step was to question and destroy their existing view of the
> world in which oil demand expanded in orderly and predictable
> fashion... [But] reconstructing a new model is the most
> important job and is the responsibility of the managers them-
> selves....We listen carefully to their needs and give them the
> highest quality materials to use in making decisions....If the
> planners design the package well, managers will use scenarios to
> construct a new model of reality by selecting from them those
> elements they believe relevant to their business world."

This new approach by Shell's planners started a couple of years
before the 1973 oil shock, so changing the then prevalent view that
growth would go on for ever was not easy. Shell's managers badly
wanted growth to continue and found it hard to accept arguments to
the contrary. But the arguments were powerful. The biggest Middle
Eastern oil producers, Saudi Arabia and Kuwait, could not use the

income they were getting from oil exports and sooner or later they would realise that it was better to keep their oil in the ground than to keep money in Western banks. Once they realised that, these countries would cut back production, which would put the oil price up and they would then have their oil *and their money*. Put this way, the logic was hard to deny, but the argument was: when would this happen? When would a change take place in the mental models of the leaders of the oil exporting countries?

Wack and the other planners said that this was an uncertainty which Shell (and others) would just have to live with. To help the group's managers live with the uncertainty in a constructive manner, the planners produced a series of scenarios describing the future of the oil industry, each with a different assumption about the time at which the oil producing countries would cut production. If managers were able to keep these different possibilities in mind while making decisions about investments in new plants or about the levels of stocks to keep, then there was a chance of working out policies which would be suitable whatever happened.

In other words, scenario planning ought to lead to decisions which were less sensitive to a drastic change in the policies of oil-producing countries in the Middle East than decisions based on the assumption of continuing growth. Also, by thinking in advance about the consequences of each scenario, managers ought to be better pre-pared to react to changes, whenever they came. Thus Shell's planning was moving towards the process of changing manager's mental models and away from the process of trying to predict for these managers what the future would be.

I remember well the first time that I went to a presentation of this new approach to planning. My first feelings were of outrage at what seemed like an abdication of responsibility by the people in the Shell group whose job is was to tell us in the operating companies what the future would bring. How could we put forward our business plans to the group's central office unless we had something firm to work with? And why did there have to be this expensive planning set-up in the centre, if it wasn't going to help me, if the planners were going to take away my security blanket?

But that evening I found myself thinking around the implications of what the planners had said. It was certainly fascinating stuff and I began to see that it might actually be more useful to my part of the Shell group than official forecasts of growth rates, forecasts which I knew in my heart would probably turn out to be wrong. I began to see that this new approach was not, in fact, one of abdication, but rather one which treated Shell's managers as adults. I decided that I was grown-up and I could do without my security blanket.

The first round of the new-style planning was in 1972. Partly because Pierre Wack and his colleagues had not yet refined their technique and partly because it took time for people to understand the new approach, its impact in the first year was limited. The next time around it was different. In Wack's words:

> "We hit planning pay dirt with the 1973 scenarios because they met the deepest concerns of managers. If any managers were not fully convinced, the events of October [the oil shock] soon made them believers....Only when the oil embargo began could we appreciate the power of scenarios – power that becomes apparent when the world overturns, power that has immense and immediate value in a large, decentralised organisation....When the world changes, managers need to share some common view of the new world. Otherwise, decentralised strategic decisions will result in management anarchy. Scenarios express and communicate this common view, a shared understanding of the new realities to all parts of the organisation.
>
> Decentralized management in world-wide operating companies can adapt and use that view for strategic decisions appropriate to its varied circumstances. Its initiative is not limited by instructions from the center but facilitated and freed by a broad framework; all will speak the same language in adapting their operations to a new business environment."

The New Planning Process

Shell's new planning process was thus a process of empowerment. Managers throughout the world were given greater responsibility and scope for autonomous action. At the same time, they were given tools which helped them to act effectively and to communicate readily with others in the group about their actions. The planners had enabled the managers to develop their own new mental models and, because the new models were stimulated by the same scenarios, they were reasonably similar, which made it easy for managers to talk to each other about their conclusions.

A couple of years later I was fortunate in being able to work occasionally with Pierre Wack and others in Group Planning as they developed their techniques still further. One of the factors which we identified at that time was the importance of education as the basis for economic success, at least in the economies of the 'advanced' countries. We felt that it would be possible to gauge the future economic strength of a country by its current policies for education, an idea which is commonplace now, but was more novel in the 1970s. And after leaving Shell I have been able to make use of the scenario approach in a variety of organisations, large and small.

Shell has continued to benefit from scenario planning and in its planning remains one of the most sophisticated organisations in the world. In the competition between the major oil companies, Shell has been notably successful during the past fifteen years and I am sure that its decentralised structure, coordinated through its remarkable planning system, is the main reason for this success. As a final example of what its planning has been able to do, let me quote Peter Schwartz, who was Wack's successor in Group Planning:

> "In 1983, we presented the Royal Dutch/ Shell managing directors with two scenarios: one called Incrementalism, and the other called the Greening of Russia. By that time, we knew enough about the Soviet Government to say that if a virtually unknown man named Gorbachev came to power, you'd see massive economic and political restructuring....and major shifts in international relationships. It was not that Gorbachev, as an individual, would cause the changes. Rather, his arrival in power would be a symptom of the same underlying causes.
>
> Shell has a habit of presenting its global scenarios to government agencies, in part to glean their reactions. Every Soviet expert but one told us we were crazy....The CIA said, "You really don't have the facts." In retrospect people have credited our research, but the CIA certainly had access to all the data we did. Our insight came solely from asking the right questions. From having to consider more than one scenario. If we had to pick only one, we might have been just as wrong as the CIA."

These are some of the things I learnt from Shell's scenario planning: First, that large organisations can benefit hugely by helping their managers to develop useful new mental models.

Second, that this can happen if its planners are skilled in analysis and equally skilled in communicating their results throughout the organisation. Third, that this kind of empowerment of people throughout a large organisation allows great decentralisation without loss of coherence, due to the coordinating effect of shared scenarios and of partially-shared mental models.

Fourth, that organisations can learn, and can plan to continue this learning, and that this can enable them to live with a highly uncertain world. Finally, that we can all escape from the constraints which our pasts impose on us, from the "mind-forged manacles" which bind us all, from the "traps" set for us by our ways of thinking, and that the most valuable way of doing this is the escape from out-of-date mind-sets and the acquisition of new mental models adapted to possible future worlds.

Change in Organisations

It might seem that if any change should take place from the top down, it should be that affecting every part of an organisation. Comprehensive electronic data-processing systems certainly affect every part of an organisation and several times I have seen their installation in a top-down manner. Each time it was a frustrating and debilitating experience. On a couple of occasions, at least, the project started with the best of intentions about consultation, involving comprehensive surveys of what people throughout the organisation wanted from the planned new system. There were good briefings on the aims of the project. Excitement was generated about the advantages of once-only keyboard entry of data, rapid processing of customer orders, real-time updating of stock data and automatic input into production planning of the effects of customer's offtake of products. Regular consultation with everybody, during the whole project, was promised, no doubt sincerely.

But it never happened like that. The good intentions about consultation were swamped by the sheer effort of getting the new system to work at all, let alone getting it to work in a way which satisfied the users. Perhaps there was over-optimism or over-selling when the projects started. Perhaps the task of analysing the needs of an organisation will always be an impossible one, given that people have a lot of tacit knowledge about how their work is done, which they cannot put into words but which is vital for effective working. They can only say what they want (and what they don't want) from a new system when they have used it for a few months.

In one case, the systems designers tried to adapt for an industrial company a system for handling retail sales and stock control. The applications were superficially similar but the differences turned out to be fundamental. This made the project horribly difficult. In the end it was pushed through, regardless of its faults. It was operated for two years, and then had to be replaced.

In top-down decisions like these, some senior group of people must have said: "We need a large new system for management information and operational control, so we'll hire the best systems house to give it to us, we'll set a reasonable budget and time-schedule, and we'll get what we want." No doubt this way of doing things can work but more often it does not.

In my view the best systems are built incrementally, for instance when a small firm grows and its system grows with it. Or an extensive pilot scheme can first be run, which gets the bugs out on a smaller scale and without disrupting operations, although the problem with a pilot scheme is finding an area, reasonably typical of the organisation as a whole, in which to run the pilot. If neither incremental development nor a pilot scheme is practicable, then the best thing to do is to allow far more time for the development of the system than you really think should be necessary and to ensure than the new system can be run in parallel with the old for several months.

What this example of the introduction of a large new data-processing system shows is that top-down changes of any complexity are fraught with problems. The solutions which I have mentioned – incremental growth, pilot schemes, parallel operation – are really ways of making the change more like a bottom-up one. I have learnt that, however appealing top-down change is to the egos of those at the top, it is better to avoid it as much as possible. The best change comes as a result of leadership rather than by issuing instructions. Leadership stimulates bottom-up change, guides it in the right direction and makes sure that those initiating change from below take account of the needs of the whole system, not just their own needs.

Here are some examples of bottom-up change, change which was influenced by senior people but not imposed by them. I have already described Celltech's project management system. It was a system which both encouraged creativity and introduced discipline. Although Norman Carey, the Director of R & D, and I thought we knew what kind of system there ought to be, we did not try to impose one. Instead we spent time talking informally with a lot of people in the firm about the need for a system and what it might look like.

As the firm grew, the need for a system of project management became more and more apparent and some scientists began to ask for one. The response from Carey was: "Tell me what you want and help me find a way of providing it." The response was a range of suggestions from people in various parts of the company. Some of these probably reflected the seeding of ideas by Carey and myself, some were novel and together they formed a good basis for building the system. The widespread sense of 'ownership' of the system continued during its design, in trials and in subsequent use.

Another example of bottom-up change at Celltech is career development. In the early days, I regularly counselled people throughout the firm on their careers, taking into account their own interests as well as those of the firm. There was a risk in this, since in some cases I opened a person's eyes to career opportunities outside Celltech. It was a risk worth taking, because my counselling often led to much greater self-awareness and self-confidence and hence to a more assured and capable person. In due course, the practice of counselling spread, as did the practice of self-appraisal and self-development. The average age of staff in the firm was around twenty nine, but the spread of these practices made for a pretty mature understanding of what personal development is about.

Things are simpler in smaller organisations, but in a small organisation or a large one, I believe that effective change depends on everyone's active participation. It must draw on the creativity of a wide number of people. It needs the empowerment of all.

Learning to Change

After the 1973 oil shock, when growth stopped being reliable, the principal virtues in business were no longer boldness and energy but adaptability, prudence, endurance and the ability to face unpleasant things in a constructive way. The business culture in Shell, and in many other firms, had to switch from one of faith in unlimited expansion to one of opportunism. Until then, there had been little problem in sharing assumptions about the future, as everyone expected growth to go on. When this no longer applied, people had to communicate in a much more complicated way about their views of the future.

As mistakes were now easier to make, there was a real danger that people would always be blaming each other and would start to avoid responsibility when, inevitably, something went wrong. Since it was now hard to communicate and as mutual trust was now really being tested, it became painfully clear that only by close cooperation between people in the business would good results be achieved.

As a manager in this situation, I had to learn fast. I had to learn interpersonal process skills, such as listening properly to others. I had to change my old habit of taking-in only ten percent of what someone was saying to me and instead had to wait to think about what I was going to say in reply until the speaker had finished. I had to learn how hard it was for me, and others, to admit to mistakes but how useful it was to do so. I had to learn how to recognise others' successes and to ask for their help in improving my own practice. I had to learn the value of communication, of cooperation to mutual benefit, of holistic thinking, of methodologies for problem-solving and of thinking styles which allowed for uncertainty. I had to learn how to learn and how to help others to learn. I had to learn the importance of self-knowledge, of honesty and of humility.

The mid-1970s showed me that individuals and organisations could change quite rapidly and confidently if they wanted to and if they had the right help. In my case, help in learning to change, learning to plan and learning to learn came from people skilled in interpersonal process, notably from those trained by Ralph Coverdale; from those skilled in systems thinking; from people who had discovered how to steer very large organisations in conditions of great uncertainty, particularly Pierre Wack; and from Donald Michael, whose work seemed, and still seems, to me the best for showing how to connect personal practice to society-wide and global concerns.

The experience of that time convinced me that interpersonal process skills, skills in systematic problem-solving and skills in conceptualisation could all be learned. And learned not only by individuals but also by groups, so that they became shared skills, skills that are mutually reinforcing.

The Process of Change

Skills and Strengths.

I believe that change in individual practice, in the behaviour of groups, in organisational culture and, on a longer time-scale, in society as a whole, depends on a widespread understanding of the process of change. The work of Donald Michael, in his book *On Learning to Plan – and Planning to Learn* and later papers, is the best place I know to get this understanding.

Change brings pain as well as joy, and fear of change can bring even greater pain than change itself. That means we must start with an understanding of the social psychology of change, of its psycho-dynamics, of the burdens it places on us and of the ways those burdens are affected by the people around us. One of the burdens is living with uncertainty. This makes it hard to decide what is the best thing to do, because the possibility of making the wrong decision is great. It can also attack our self-esteem, especially for those of us who are, or claim to be, experts or leaders of some type.

> "Acknowledging that "I don't know" is dangerous enough, but acknowledging that "*we* don't know" would, in our present scheme of things, apparently leave little to keep one's world together, little for one to count on. What is more, expressing the intuitions and feelings that could well up in a "we don't know" situation runs counter to all canons of rational behaviour set by and for professionals operating in formal organizations...."

Next, there is the burden of embracing error, of admitting mistakes and of being ready to accept that we may well have to suffer for them. This burden is lightened by the realisation that we may suffer from our errors regardless of whether or not we admit them, by the relief of confession and by the opportunity which embracing them gives for avoiding the same mistakes in the future.

Then there is the burden of ambiguous roles. If I do not know it all and I admit that I don't, where do I stand as an expert, (or even as a voter)? If I embrace my errors, how in future can I be trusted as a leader, (or even as a parent)? If uncertainty and error abound, how can I express my own feelings and cope with the expression of feelings by others? If the truth is that we are all uncertain and all likely to be wrong, will we be able to bear the burdens of greater self-awareness? Michael says that in a society which knows how to learn, politics will be about learning and leaders will be educators. Leaders will be judged as learners, not as knowers.

> "Planning is usually expected to be subject to political consid-erations; in the last analysis to be subservient to them. What I am proposing does not reverse the relationship, as some have recommended. Instead, my proposal is intended to change both political and planning activities into complementary contribu-tions to a learning mode."

If change is a process of learning, and if learning requires the strength to live with uncertainty and ambiguity and to embrace error, then there will be many hard patches along the way as individuals struggle within their own psyches. Michael does not assert that psychodynamic processes are the only obstacles to change. "But in times when leaders and deciders are threatened by circumstances to a degree that questions their very self-image of competence and capability, these psychodynamic processes can very well play a major part...." Threats may be denied. The danger, whether of business collapse or of global warming, may be minimised, or characterised as solvable in some simplistic way. Or threats may be projected onto an enemy. With an enemy to blame, we need not admit that it is our own doubt or confusion which is making life so difficult.

Michael describes how unfamiliar situations can provoke denial or projection and how pressures to change our ways of doing things can provoke resistance. In spite of these reactions, we can learn to cope. Coping comes partly from self-knowledge, from admitting to ourselves, and then to others, that we are not in control of everything, that our confident air is a sham, that we and the institutions to which we belong are vulnerable. Learning how to cope is risky but necessary, threatening but exhilarating. "Very importantly, learning also highlights and legitimates an essential human quality, too often lost: compassion toward self as well as toward others."

An understandable reaction to the pressures of learning, coping and changing is to place the burden on a strong leader, to hand over responsibility to the boss, to *der Führer* or, increasingly, to 'the system'. Michael shows that 'strong leaders' are prey to the same fears and doubts as everyone else; it is just that they are better at covering up or projecting these doubts and fears. So instead of hierarchy (leadership from the top), or of anarchy (no leadership), he advocates heterarchy (leadership of a mixed or distributed kind) in which responsibility and authority are shared by everybody.

An example is 'matrix management' in organisations, a way of running things through a team that is formed for a particular task and dispersed when the task is finished. Someone will be a task group leader at one time and a member at another. The people involved belong to skill-pools as well as to task-groups. The skill-pools are their permanent, professional homes and they are responsible both to the pool leaders as well as to the task leaders. Leadership is therefore shared. And it is shared within the task teams as well; depending on the problem, one person after another will steer the team, with the titular leader taking a back seat, unless the problem is overall coordination. For teams and organisations like this to succeed, they will have to have skill in interpersonal process and some knowledge of group dynamics.

So, in short, Michael's view of change is that it is a learning process. It needs skill in communication and in interpersonal process. It needs strength in facing uncertainty and in admitting error, in avoiding the denial or projection of problems. It needs ways of sharing leadership and of supporting the leadership of others.

Symbols and Stories

If change requires heterarchy, if it requires dispersed leadership and clan-like coordination rather than hierarchy, then how can change ever be coherent? What is it that gives pattern to the initiatives of numerous groups and causes society to move in a definable direction? The slogan: "think globally, act locally" is due to Rene Dubos. How is it that many local actions can realistically add up to a global effect? Donald Michael has an answer for this quandary: coordination comes through storytelling. Change comes about through the telling of stories which are convincing enough to stick in people's minds. The contribution of the leader, the expert or the planner in a heterarchy is as "a storyteller and a teller of stories about stories".

> "The planner must tell the alternative stories in as rich detail as possible – making use of all the technical information available about what might be and what we don't know with regard to the outcomes. The political task then becomes one of choosing which risks to take, in full light of what risks are inherent in the options...."

The planner is therefore a social artist, if art is "the means by which we initially formulate or structure our perceptions of reality." The social artist produces or adopts symbols, metaphors, slogans, myths and stories. Symbols like flags or seals of office are powerful in influencing social behaviour. The metaphor of the invisible hand contributed enormously to the acceptance of Adam Smith's theories. The building of Jerusalem in England's green and pleasant land is another metaphor which has inspired lots of social action. Slogans like: "We shall overcome" have similarly great effects.

By *stories* Michael means something more extensive, but no less influential, than metaphors or myths. In fact, stories, in this sense, often contain striking metaphors and memorable myths. Michael says that there are many pasts; we can construct innumerable stories linking past events and their interpretations to our present concerns, and these stories make up our reality. "We construct (not necessarily consciously) our reality, and then construct our response to that construction – and so on into the future. This is an aesthetic enterprise more than a logical one, even though some techniques used to further the aesthetic endeavour use logic...." It is an aesthetic enterprise because, in its language, it needs the creativity of metaphor. A metaphor is, as Richard Rorty says, something one can either savor or spit out, not something you can prove to be right or wrong. But once a metaphor comes into general use, once it enters our language, then it becomes part of our shared construction of reality and can be argued for or against, like other parts of that construction. Language and our reality-constructions therefore emerge through use.

Stories in World History

A paper by Donald Michael and Walter Anderson lists examples of stories which have captured the attention of huge numbers of people, over many centuries. The first of these is the story of progress, which asks us to believe in economic prosperity, personal freedom and general happiness. Either the capitalist or the Marxist version of this story was almost universally believed in the modernised countries of the world during the two hundred years up to the middle of this century. Marxism depended even more on a story of progress than capitalism did. It is only in recent decades that suspicion of science and technology and challenge to the idea of continual growth has had more than a marginal influence, but now there is an obvious rival to the progress story: the green story of "environmental values, with the mystique of solar energy and organic farming, with the animal rights movement....[and with] adherents among idealistic young people, intellectuals and some feminists."

Another story which is sometimes opposed to, sometimes uneasily allied with, the progress story is religious fundamentalism, in its Christian and Islamic versions. These are the oldest stories, or, rather, new versions of the oldest stories, because like all stories they are evolving. For instance, the rise of Islamic fundamentalism is partly a reaction against modernisation and partly an expression of nationalism. Last in their list is what Michael and Anderson call the 'new paradigm' story; this is "super-progress: a sudden leap forward to an entirely new way of being and a new way of understanding the world." This is a super-optimistic story, distinguishing it from the green story, which tends to be pessimistic.

The point of listing these stories is not to claim that they are the only ones (for instance, the set of stories about nation-states constructed during the nineteenth century could be added) or that this is necessarily the most interesting list, but to illustrate what is meant by 'stories' and, through these illustrations, to suggest how they work to change the world. The article from which I have taken the list ends in this way:

> "We venture no prediction about the future of the stories we have identified here. Each is a partial view of reality, and none is adequate to serve as the cultural structure for a global society. But each is a human creation, and perhaps the human imagination will rise to the level of comprehending that they are things of its own making and – like other kinds of information – most useful when we know their limitations....Our hope is rather that, in the pressured and precarious milieu of the global information society, people may begin to tell one another, however uncertainly at first, a story about stories."

The stories which make a difference in human affairs are, on this account, works of art. Like medieval cathedrals, they may have been constructed over hundreds of years, they may be the work of many hands, they may incorporate several styles, they may have various spiritual and secular uses and they may mean quite different things to different people. A few of them now badly need repair. Some of these stories have shaped the lives, and caused the deaths, of millions of people. They are, in the language of philosophical pragmatism, the means which various human communities use to try to get what they want. In fact, they often determine what human communities do want. They are often the means by which human beings make sense of their condition and give purpose to their lives. Politicians, educators and prophets use them to change our views of the world, because new stories are the driving force for changes in society.

A Picture of Change

I can now summarise Michael's picture of change.

- Firstly, change depends on numerous local initiatives by individuals and groups of all sorts. These local changes, if they are to be positive ones, require individuals and groups to have, and to go on developing, considerable interpersonal process skills and psychological strengths. Leaders and planners must also have these strengths and skills if they are to attempt changes with more widespread effects. Unless such strengths and skills are widely present, constructive, evolutionary change will not be possible.

- Secondly, symbols and stories, metaphors and myths, are necessary to inspire and connect local changes. They give people ideas for change and the courage to strive for it. They are what leads to coherent change, sometimes in a particular part of an organisation, sometimes throughout the whole.

Symbols and stories are works of art, human constructs which make sense of the world and which help men and women to discover what they want in life and to try to get it. We need to understand our stories and symbols, not in order to debunk them, but to make them more useful and to reduce the conflicts which they can provoke between the supporters of rival stories.

Symbols, Stories and Mental Models at Work

The connection between symbols and stories, on one hand, and mental models, on the other, is now clear. Both are vital factors in achieving organisational change. Both determine how we see the world, how we make sense of what is going on around us. We can become passionate about both, because both can become central to the sense of our identity and enmeshed in our deeply-held values.

Mental models, symbols and stories can move us to action. They determine much of what we decide to do and the energy with which we do it. Our understanding of all three is both conscious and unconscious. Often we act on a mental model which we don't know we have. Symbols move our emotions more than they do our rational thoughts. Stories have an implicit as well as an explicit side.

Peter Senge writes that:

> "...systems thinking without the discipline of mental models loses much of its power. This is why much of our current research at MIT focuses on helping managers to integrate mental modelling and systems thinking skills. The two disciplines go naturally together because one focuses on exposing hidden assumptions and the other focuses on how to restructure assumptions to reveal causes of significant problems."

Change comes through understanding our existing mental models and from finding different ones. Change also comes through understanding the symbols and stories which influence our lives and from finding different ones. In both cases, change results from our gaining an understanding of our partly unconscious, often deeply held, beliefs. Change though mental models and through stories and symbols therefore depends on similar psychological processes.

The connection between these two approaches is not only their similar psychology, since there is a historical connection as well. Donald Michael was an important influence on the thinking of Pierre Wack and the others at Shell when they were working out the scenario planning approach. Later, Wack and his successors at Shell, notably Arie de Geus, worked closely with MIT on mental modelling.

Story telling, mental modelling, symbol creation and scenario planning are intertwined. All depend on the personal strengths and interpersonal process skills of individuals and groups. Together, these make up the most powerful force for change in the world today.

The Story of Compartments

Gregory Bateson had a beautiful metaphor for the way that human beings influence, and are influenced by, their social environment: a river shapes its banks, and the banks contain the river. My message is that we shape our stories, and our stories make our lives. The stories we tell, and the mental models we use, guide our decisions and our actions. These actions then shape our institutional structures and processes, which, eventually, affect the mental models we use and the stories we tell.

The story in this book has been that of the creative compartment. It has been a story of the compartment's internal communication, which is open and broadcast, largely uncodified and undistorted by power. It has been a story of the democratic choice of the compartment's purposes, the coordination of its purposes with those of other compartments and of the testing of those purposes through generous critique. It has been a story of the radical kind of organisation redesign made possible by the concept of the creative compartment.

Once we have creative compartments, people within them will be able to imagine many new stories of their own. Their close-knit, uncodified internal communication will make story-telling a rewarding art. Meanwhile, to move towards compartmentation needs shared stories about compartmentation, stories which are meaningful and influential across whole organisations and societies. The move to compartments needs mental models which make clear the difference between the total openness and informality which rules inside the compartment, and the necessarily less open and more codified communication outside. The move needs mental models which distinguish between the almost totally clan-like coordination inside the compartment and the blend of market, clan-like and hierarchical coordination outside it.

In this book, I have suggested a number of practices which follow from the stories I have told and the mental models I have described. I hope the practices will be useful as guides. But it's the stories and the mental models which are really important. With their aid we can work out *our own practices* to suit our particular situations.

I hope stories about compartments will become part of our general wisdom, part of what moves us and helps us to choose good paths for action. If they do, there could be really effective, ethical and beautiful organisation design in the twenty-first century.

Notes

Living with Uncertainty, pages 214-7. See Pierre Wack. 'Scenarios: Uncharted Waters Ahead', *Harvard Business Review*, Sept-Oct 1985 pp 73-89, and 'Scenarios: Shooting the Rapids', *Harvard Business Review*, Nov/Dec 1985 pp 139-149. The quotations from Wack are all from these two articles.

The New Planning Process, pages 217-8. See Peter Schwartz. *The Art of the Long View: Planning for the Future in an Uncertain World*. Doubleday, New York (1991) p58.

The Process of Change – Skills and Strengths, pages 222-5. Donald N. Michael. *On Learning to Plan – and Planning to Learn: The Social Psychology of Changing Toward Future-Responsive Societal Learning*. Jossey-Bass, San Francisco, CA (1973), referred to below as *LTP*.

"Acknowledging that "I don't know"...." is from *LTP* pp 127-8.

"Planning is usually expected...." is from 'Neither Hierarchy nor Anarchy: Notes on Norms for Governance In a Systemic World' in *Rethinking Liberalism*. Ed. Walter T. Anderson. Avon, New York (1983) p 266.

"....when leaders and deciders are threatened..." is from 'Reason's Shadow: Notes on the Psychodynamics of Obstruction' in *Technological Forecasting and Social Change*, **26**, 151 (1984).

"....compassion toward self as well as toward others." is from 'Governing by Learning in an Information Society', a paper given as part of the "Governing in an Information Society" project of Canada's Institute for Research on Public Policy (1991).

The concept of heterarchy is James Ogilvy's. See his *Many Dimensional Man*. Oxford U.P., New York (1977) and his foreword to this book.

The Process of Change – Symbols and Stories, pages 225-6. Donald N. Michael. "Neither Hierarchy nor Anarchy" *op cit.* p 265.

"....the means by which we initially formulate...." is from *Technology Assessment in an Emerging World*. Address at the Second International Congress on Technology Assessment (1976)

"We construct our reality...." is from 'With Both Feet Planted Firmly in Mid-Air; Reflections on thinking about the future'. *Futures*, **17**, 2, 96 (1985).

Richard Rorty's comment on metaphors is from *Contingency, Irony and Solidarity*. Cambridge U.P., Cambridge (1989) p 18.

Stories in World History, pages 226-7. Donald N. Michael and Walter Truett Anderson. *Norms in Conflict and Confusion: Six Stories in Search of an Author*. (1986).

Mental Models at Work, pages 228-9. See Peter M. Senge, *The Fifth Discipline:The Art and Practice of the Learning Organisation*, Doubleday, London (1992) p 203.

Bibliography and Further Reading

The books which have had the biggest influence on *Creative Compartments* are Jürgen Habermas' *The Theory of Communicative Action*, Albert Hirschman's *Exit, Voice and Loyalty*, Donald Michael's *On Learning to Plan – and Planning to Learn* and two of Roberto Unger's works: *Knowledge and Politics* and *False Necessity*. These and other key sources are listed below.

Although all the works listed are, in my view, interesting and important, some are easier to read, and closer to the subject matter of *Creative Compartments*, than others. So, for further reading, I suggest that readers might like to look first at Robert Axelrod's *The Evolution of Cooperation*, Charles Hampden-Turner's *Corporate Culture*, Peter Schwartz's *The Art of the Long View*, Peter Senge's *The Fifth Discipline* and Alex Stewart's *Team Entrepreneurship*.

Axelrod, Robert. *The Evolution of Cooperation*, Penguin, London (1990).

Bellah, Robert *et al. Habits of the Heart: Individualism and Commitment in American Life.* Harper and Row, New York (1985).

Checkland, Peter. *Systems Thinking, Systems Practice.* Wiley, Chichester (1981).

Churchman, C West. *The Design of Inquiring Systems*, Basic Books, New York (1971).

Clegg, Stewart R. *Modern Organizations: Organization Studies in the Postmodern World*, Sage, London (1990).

Clegg, Stewart and David Dunkerley. *Organization, Class and Control.* Routledge and Kegan Paul, London (1980).

Giddens, Anthony. *The Constitution of Society: Outline of the Theory of Structuration*, Polity Press, Cambridge (1984).

Habermas, Jürgen. *Knowledge and Human Interests*, trans. Jeremy Shapiro, Heinemann, London (1972).

Habermas, Jürgen. *The Theory of Communicative Action*, two volumes, trans. Thomas McCarthy, Polity Press, Cambridge (1987).

Habermas, Jürgen. *The Philosophical Discourse of Modernity*, trans. Frederick Lawrence, Polity Press, Cambridge (1987).

Hampden-Turner, Charles. *Corporate Culture: From Vicious to Virtuous Circles*, Economist, London (1990).

Handy, Charles. *The Age of Unreason*, Century, London (1989).

Hassard, John and Denis Pym. *The Theory and Philosophy of Organizations: Critical Issues and New Perspectives*, Routledge, London (1990).

Hirschman, Albert O. *Exit, Voice and Loyalty: Responses to Decline in Firms, Organizations, and States*. Harvard, Cambridge (1970).

Jacobs, Jane. *Systems of Survival: A Dialogue on the Moral Foundations of Commerce and Politics*, Random House, New York (1992).

Luhmann, Nicklas. *The Differentiation of Society*, Trans. Holmes and Larmore, Colombia, New York (1982).

MacIntyre, Alasdair. *After Virtue: A Study in Moral Theory*, Duckworth, London (1981).

MacIntyre, Alasdair. *Three Rival Versions of Moral Enquiry: Encyclopaedia, Genealogy, and Tradition*, Duckworth, London (1990).

McCarthy, Thomas. *The Critical Theory of Jürgen Habermas*, MIT Press, Cambridge MA (1988).

Michael, Donald N. *On Learning to Plan – and Planning to Learn*, Jossey-Bass, San Francisco, (1973).

Morgan, Gareth. *Images of Organization*, Sage, Newbury Park (1986).

Olson, Mançur. *The Rise and Decline of Nations: Economic Growth, Stagflation and Social Rigidities*, Yale, New Haven (1982).

Piore, Michael J. and Charles F. Sabel. *The Second Industrial Divide: Prospects for Prosperity*, Basic Book, New York (1984).

Polanyi, Michael. *The Tacit Dimension*, Doubleday, Garden City NY (1966).

Schon, Donald. *Beyond the Stable State: Public and Private Learning in a Changing Society*, Temple Smith, London (1971).

Schwartz, Peter. *The Art of the Long View: Planning for the Future in an Uncertain World*, Doubleday, New York (1990).

Senge, Peter. *The Fifth Discipline: The Art and Practice of the Learning Organization*, Doubleday, New York (1990).

Stewart, Alex. *Team Entrepreneurship*, Sage, Newbury Park (1989).

Unger, Roberto Mangaberia. *Knowledge and Politics*, The Free Press, New York (1975).

Unger, Roberto Mangaberia. *Politics: A Work in Constructive Social Theory*, Cambridge UP, Cambridge (1987). Three volumes:
Social Theory: Its Situation and Task

False Necessity: Anti-Necessitarian Social Theory in the Service of Social Democracy

Plasticity into Power: Comparative-Historical Studies on the Institutional Conditions of Economic and Military Success.

Vickers, Geoffrey. *The Art of Judgment: A Study of Policy Making*, Chapman and Hall, London (1965).

Vickers, Geoffrey. *Freedom in a Rocking Boat: Changing Values in an Unstable Society*, Allen Lane, Harmondsworth (1970).

Index